The Asbury Theological Seminary Series in Christian Revitalization Studies

This volume is published in collaboration with the Center for the Study of World Christian Revitalization Movements, a cooperative initiative of Asbury Theological Seminary faculty. Building on the work of the previous Wesleyan/Holiness Studies Center at the Seminary, the Center provides a focus for research in the Wesleyan Holiness and other related Christian renewal movements, including Pietism and Pentecostal movements, which have had a world impact. The research seeks to develop analytical models of these movements, including their biblical and theological assessment. Using an interdisciplinary approach, the Center bridges relevant discourses in several areas in order to gain insights for effective Christian mission globally. It recognizes the need for conducting research that combines insights from the history of evangelical renewal and revival movements with anthropological and religious studies literature on revitalization movements. It also networks with similar or related research and study centers around the world, in addition to sponsoring its own research projects.

This title presents the definitive research of Michael Winstead on the history of African American congregations within a major international holiness denomination, the Church of the Nazarene, in the middle years of the twentieth century. Developing a narrative engaging social and racial issues, from the analysis of a wide range of primary sources, Winstead presents the impact of black participation in the leadership of this denomination, in North America and overseas. His narrative corrects simplistic stereotypes that have misrepresented the important contributions of black Nazarenes to the larger holiness movement, and so demonstrates their vital contributions to our study of movements of revitalization within contemporary world Christianity.

J. Steven O'Malley
Editor, Pietist and Wesleyan Studies Series and
The Asbury Theological Seminary Series in
World Christian Revitalization Studies

There All Along

Black Participation in the Church of the Nazarene, 1914–1969

Brandon Winstead

The Asbury Theological Seminary Series in
World Christian Revitalization Movements in Pietist/Wesleyan Studies. No. 15

EMETH PRESS
www.emethpress.com

*There All Along: Black Participation in the
Church of the Nazarene, 1914-1969*

Copyright © 2013 Brandon Winstead
Printed in the United States of America on acid-free paper

All rights reserved. No part of this book may be reproduced, or stored in a retrieval system or transmitted in any form or by any means, electronic, mechanical, photocopying, recording, scanning or otherwise, except as permitted by the 1976 United States Copyright Act, or with the prior written permission of Emeth Press. Requests for permission should be addressed to: Emeth Press, P. O. Box 23961, Lexington, KY 40523-3961.

http://www.emethpress.com.

Library of Congress Cataloging-in-Publication Data

Winstead, Brandon.
  There all along : Black participation in the Church of the Nazarene, 1914-1969 / Brandon Winstead.
     pages cm -- (Asbury theological seminary series in world Christian revitalization movements in Pietist/Wesleyan studies ; no. 15)
  Includes bibliographical references.
  ISBN 978-1-60947-055-5 (alk. paper)
  1. Nazarenes (Church of the Nazarene)--United States. 2. Church of the Nazarene--United States. 3. Church membership--United States. 4. Church attendance--United States. 5. Blacks--Religion. 6. Blacks--United States. I. Title.
  BX8699.N35W56 2013
  287.9'908996--dc23
                    2013015364

Contents

Acknowledgments /ix

Introduction / xi

Chapter 1. The Pioneer Era: The Beginnings of Black Nazarenet Participation, 1908-1933 / 1

Chapter 2. From the Midwest to the Northweast: African American and West Indian Ministry in Kansas and New York, 1934-1946 / 29

Chapter 3. Ecclesiastical Segregation and Black Participation, 1947-1958 / 53

Chapter 4. African American Nazarenes, Social Conservatism, and Evangelistic Growth from 1958-1969 / 85

Chapter 5. The Participation Continues: West Indian and Cape Verdean Contributions to Denominational Evangelism, 1958-1969 / 121

Conclusion / 153

Epilogue / 159

Appendix I / 163

Appendix II / 167

Appendis III /168

Appendix IV / 169

Appendix V / 170

Bibliography / 171

To all the Black Pioneers of the Church of the Nazarene, This Work is Dedicated to You.

ACKNOWLEDGMENTS

I am extremely grateful to many colleagues, friends, and family members for helping bring this work to fruition. I would like to first thank my doctoral advisor Dr. Larry Murphy, for his willingness to instill in me a vision and passion for learning about the past stories of real people who struggled to make sense of their faith amidst the vicissitudes of everyday life. It was in my first class under Murphy's direction, that I learned this importance and began to develop a deep appreciation for how social and cultural history shapes our comprehension of the religious past of Americans in general and African Americans in particular.

I wish to thank Dr. Rosemary Gooden and Dr. Barry Bryant for their thought provoking questions regarding my research and their constant concern for my academic development. Without Gooden's willingness to challenge me to think about how black women shaped the course of African American religious history, my knowledge of the history of black religion in the United States would be severely shortsighted. At the same time, Bryant has always encouraged me to think about how my work contributes to understanding the multifaceted tradition of those who claim John Wesley as their theological and ethical progenitor.

In addition, I am overwhelmingly thankful to Dr. David Daniels III for his steady guidance in helping me reconstruct how the Church of the Nazarene has been shaped by the actions and contributions of its various black devotees. If it wasn't for his painstaking work, patience, and passion for this project over the past four years, it never would have been completed. I deeply appreciate his advice and friendship.

I am also indebted to my friends and peers Walter Augustine, Rusty Brian, Carmichael Crutchfield, Jason Gill, Ryan Hansen, Douglas Powè, and Andrew Wood for their interest in my work and for their tremendous support of this work. This book could not have been possible without their encouragement and their willingness to open their minds and homes as I sought to write this story.

Various staff, ministers, and lay members at the Brooklyn Historical Society, the Church of the Nazarene Archives, the Lauderdale County Public Library, the United Library, the Schomburg Center for Research in Black Culture, and Community Worship Center Church of the Nazarene, helped make the research process very rewarding. In particular, I shall never forget the kindness and hospitality shown by Ludwick Jones, a long-time member and lay historian of Community Worship Center Church of the Nazarene, as he escorted me around various locations in Brooklyn and Harlem.

Lastly, this history would merely be a thought if it wasn't for the love, wisdom, and support of the Quincy, IL Salvation Army, the youth and staff at Country Club Christian Church, Christ United Methodist Church, my parents, Ray and Donna Guthrie, grandparents, Lucille and Joe Morgan, and wife, Marlo. The specific care and devotion of my spouse and our two very energetic beagles sustained me as I researched, read, typed, edited, traveled, and wrote this dissertation. I am eternally grateful for her patience and unending support.

Introduction

Currently, there are 14,306 black members of the Church of the Nazarene (hereafter referred to as CN) in the United States. They worship in over 100 congregations in states like Alabama, Florida, Mississippi, South Carolina, Oklahoma, Missouri, Virginia, West Virginia, Texas, Georgia, Tennessee, Ohio, Michigan, Pennsylvania, Illinois, New York, and in other places around the country. Of these churches, 23 have an average worship attendance of 100 and Brooklyn Beulah CN, in New York City, has 1,000 who regularly worship on Sunday mornings—a rather large number for a denomination whose average membership is 130.[1] Moreover, within some of these bodies, not all are African American. In fact, in places like south Florida, Haitian members actively contribute to the life and ministry of seven black congregations in and around Miami. Likewise, of the 21 predominantly black Nazarene congregations in Brooklyn and metropolitan New York, many have members from different Caribbean islands like Barbados, Jamaica, and Haiti.[2]

---

[1] Official Website of Mission Support USA/Canada of the Church of the Nazarene, "Predominantly Black Churches." http://www.missionstrategy.org/missionstrategy/portals/0/pdf/bmpdf/blackchurches.pdf. (accessed 03 February 2011); Official Website of the Mission Support USA/Canada of the Church of the Nazarene, "Predominantly Black Churches, Over 100 in Average A.M. Attendance (2009)." http://www.missionstrategy.org/missionstrategy/Ministries/BlackMinistries/stats/tabid/169/Default.aspx. (accessed 03 September 2011); Official Website of Mission Support USA/Canada of the Church of the Nazarene, "Black Churches of the Nazarene: Canada and USA, (1999-2009)." http://www.missionstrategy.org/missionstrategy/Portals/0/pdf/mmpdf/Black.pdf. (accessed 03 February 2011).

[2] Official Website of Mission Support USA/Canada of the Church of the Nazarene, "Black Churches and Pastors Directory." http://www.missionstrategy.org/missionstrategy/ChurchesandPastorsDirectory/tabid/118/Default.aspx. (accessed 04

Of course, this is just a current snapshot of the ethnic reality of black congregational life in the CN in the 21st century and much more could be said about how this diversity shapes current black Nazarene life in the United States. However, this work does not seek to fulfill such a task. Instead, the goal of this book is to provide the first comprehensive look into how various "black"[3] groups participated and contributed to the CN (a predominantly white holiness body formed in 1908) before the 21st century and specifically between the years of 1914 through 1969. As such, it will help historians and scholars understand that black groups have participated in the CN since its founding years and not just since the latter decades of the 20th century.

Although it is a rather large historical timeframe, the years under investigation represent the incorporated date of the first West Indian congregation in Brooklyn, New York, until the disbanding of the Gulf Central District, which was the CN's segregated jurisdiction that governed African American churches in the South during the middle decades of the 20th century. During this time and under different jurisdictional patterns of governance, African Americans, Afro-Caribbeans, and Cape Verdeans—a black immigrant group from the West-African island of Cape Verde[4]—actively helped to expand the mission and message of the Church of the Nazarene as it grew from 10,090 members in 1908 to 378,070 members in 1969.[5]

These groups remained committed to the mission and goal of the CN and it was precisely because of their commitment to the holiness experience and message of the denomination that persons of African descent—despite

---

February 2011) and Dr. Elmer L. Gillett of Brooklyn, New York, personal interview by author, 16 September 2009, Brooklyn, New York. Brandon Winstead's Private Collection, Kansas City, KS.

[3]The word "black" is used to signify those from the African Diaspora who formed and started churches within the continental United States. Thus, it describes the African American, Caribbean, and Cape Verdean churches that were formed anywhere between 1914 and 1969.

[4]According to two different websites, there was a Cape Verdean church established in Harwich, MA in 1909 by Joseph DeGrace (five years before the first West Indian congregation established in the United States), the brother of the well-known religious leader "Daddy" Grace. However, the difficulty of finding its inclusion in New England Nazarene district journals along with any other details about the longevity and life of the congregation thus placed it outside the purview of this dissertation. For further reference see, Ray Almeida, "The Church and the People of Cape Verde," http://www1.umassd.edu/SpecialPrograms/caboverde/cvchurch.html. (accessed 01 March 2011) and Massachusetts Historical Commission, "MHC Reconnaissance Survey Town Report, Harwich: Report Date: 1984, Associated Regional Report: Cape Cod and the Islands," http://www.sec.state.ma.us/mhc/mhcpdf/townreports/Cape/hrw.pdf. (accessed 01 March 2011).

[5]Dale E. Jones, "Average US Churches Sizes, 1908-2010," November 1, 2010. Research Services, Global Ministry Center, Lenexa, KS.

their different ethnic particularities, geographical locations, historical backgrounds, and racial experiences in the CN—participated in the ecclesiastical governance, local congregational development, and evangelistic thrust of the CN during the middle years of the 20th century. In the midst of this, black ministers and churches from various ethnic backgrounds, geographical regions, and ecclesiastical experiences sustained Nazarene ministries, contributed to denominational leadership, supported international missions, created outreach ministries, and at times, addressed social and racial issues in their communities. It is this story that this work will seek to tell and in the process, help give voice to the past experiences and racial realities that shaped black Nazarene life and congregations throughout the United States.

The Investigative Assumption

The composition of this narrative is shaped by analyzing denominational archives, personal testimonies, newspaper articles, correspondence letters between denominational leaders, interdenominational publications, theological treatises, congregational histories, and printed sermons, one can begin, for the first time, to see African American, Cape Verdean, and Afro-Caribbean Nazarenes expanding the holiness and evangelistic mission of the denomination during the early to mid-20th century. Although the amount of churches were small and spread out over vast distances throughout the 20th century (by the late 1960s, there were no more than 1,700 total black members in less than 55 predominantly black congregations throughout the United States),[6] black Nazarenes provide a case study of the various ways that certain black Americans navigated through issues of ecclesiastical racism and theological beliefs to contribute to the multifaceted makeup of black religious life in the early to mid-20th century.

As Milton Sernett states in his comprehensive work on the Great Migration, such cases (like the one presented in this work) are important because they highlight the ways in which the *internal* dimensions and theological commitments of black laity and pastors impacted the private and public dimensions of black churches, especially those groups that joined or started holiness or Pentecostal churches in the early to mid-20th century. In his estimation, ever since the protest vs. accommodation model became prevalent in African American religious studies in the 1970s,[7] black holiness and

---

[6]*Gulf Central District Church of the Nazarene, Sixteenth Annual Assembly Journal* (September 1968), 31. Church of the Nazarene Archives, Lenexa, KS.

[7]This binary interpretive model gained ground after the publication of Gayraud Wilmore's 1973 text entitled, *Black Religion and Black Radicalism: An Interpretation of the Religious History of the Afro-American People*. For further detail regarding how Wilmore's historiographical approach impacted his assessment of the history of black holiness and Pentecostal groups, see Gayraud Wilmore, *Black Religion and*

Pentecostal churches have "fared poorly in scholarly accounts structured on the paradigm." Specifically, he states that many historians still interpret holiness and Pentecostal adherents as those searching for an "otherworldly" religion, which, in turn, leaves students, readers, and scholars with a simplistic understanding of black holiness or Pentecostal churches. However, by analyzing some of the internal dynamics and religious beliefs of such groups, Sernett asserts that scholars may overcome this deficiency and see how different theological beliefs, congregational ministries, ministerial commitments, and social activity created a diversity of religious expression among black holiness and Pentecostal bodies.[8]

In many ways, this assumption undergirds the entirety of this project. By analyzing the contributions, ministerial activities, racial realities, and jurisdictional contexts of West Indian, Cape Verdean, and African American Nazarene churches at the local, district, and national levels, the research will show how the different groups created a national pattern of black contribution to the CN from the early to mid-20th century. In addition to this, by analyzing archival sources and other primary documents that detail the various ways that blacks worship and ministered in the CN, the reader will understand how theological commitments, church governance, ecclesiastical racism, historical experiences, ethnic realities, and geographical experiences intersected and shaped the religious lives of black Nazarenes from 1914 to 1969. Not only that, but the reader will see that as these bodies—despite their different geographical locations, ethnic backgrounds, social realities, historical contexts, and racial experiences in the denomination—contributed to the mission and vision of the CN, they added another dimension to the diversity of black religious experience in the United States during the early to mid-20th century.

The Structure of the Book

The outline of this narrative begins in the initial chapter entitled, "The Pioneer Era: The Beginnings of Black Nazarene Participation, 1908-1933." This section outlines the early theological and historical roots of the CN. Particular attention will be given to how the CN, in its early years, embraced a more personal pietistic understanding of holiness that would come to define the denomination in its infancy and for decades to come. In addition to this, it will be shown how the CN promoted an emphasis on evangelism during the formative years of the denomination's growth and how African American and black congregations embraced these two emphases precisely

---

Black Radicalism: An Interpretation of the Religious History of Afro-American People, 2nd ed. (Maryknoll, NY: Orbis Books, 1983), ix-xiv, 152-158.

[8]Milton Sernett, *Bound for the Promised Land: African American Religion and the Great Migration* (Durham, NC: Duke University Press, 1997), 4-6.

because they were Nazarenes. They were devoted Nazarenes because they participated and contributed—alongside white congregations and amidst scant calls for national black evangelization—to the early development of the CN in states and places like Kansas, California, and Brooklyn. Although there were only four churches during this period, their contributions and strivings, especially in Brooklyn, revises typical denominational historiography that has failed to include black congregations and ministers as active contributors to domestic missions in the Northeast, Midwest, and West. Thus, early on in the story, the reader will begin to see how blacks were agents (and not merely objects of missionary conversion) in the early development of the denomination in the United States.

After this, the work describes in the second chapter entitled, "From the Midwest to the Northeast: African American and West Indian Ministry in Kansas and New York, 1934-1946," how the Afro-Caribbean congregations in Brooklyn and African American congregations in Kansas continued to participate in Nazarene life as large numerical growth took place within the denomination and as the CN failed to call for national black evangelization. Furthermore, the chapter explores how West-Indian and African American congregations continued to embrace the evangelistic and personal holiness message of the denomination as they contributed to leadership on their local jurisdictions, evangelized blacks in their communities, and supported Nazarene missions. At the same time, the reader will see how certain West Indian ministers sought to address racial, economic, and social concerns in their communities. This is highlighted to show that while certain individuals became socially active, most black adherents continued to resemble most Nazarenes in the United States in that they primarily focused their energies on promoting the personal holiness teachings and evangelistic work of the denomination.

After this, the text examines how the beginnings of national black evangelization in the CN coincided with segregated models of governing African American congregations. This chapter, called "Ecclesiastical Segregation and Black Participation, 1947-1958," begins by analyzing how the denomination established a nationally segregated jurisdiction called the Colored District (hereafter referred to as CD). The CD was established in 1947 by the denomination as a segregated jurisdiction to govern African American congregations throughout the United States. Under the CD, a handful of black churches were started throughout the country, but pastors and laity within those congregations held little ultimate decision making power over their district. Despite this, African Americans participated in leadership roles on the CD and contributed to denominational evangelism by maintaining local Nazarene ministries, supporting and improving the educational development of African American pastors, and by supporting international evangelism.

Then, the chapter outlines how the denomination, in 1953, dismantled the national judicatory in favor of a racially segregated jurisdiction based geographically in the South. The name of the judicatory was called the Gulf Central District (hereafter referred to as GCD) and in the beginning, white leaders and pastors held the highest ranks of decision-making power on the district. Despite this reality, however, this section details how African American men and women in the South continued to publicly overlook ecclesiastical racism as they remained committed to the evangelistic and personal holiness message of the denomination and as they attained positions of district leadership, sustained Nazarene ministries, started new African American congregations, trained black pastors, and created the organizational and ministerial foundation that would help to strengthen the GCD after 1958.

In order to show how these ecclesiastical practices did not impact Cape Verdean and Afro-Caribbean congregations and to show how blacks outside the South continued to carry out the personal holiness and evangelistic mission of the denomination, the chapter also details each of these groups' ministerial efforts. Specifically, the section outlines how those outside the South publicly overlooked denominational racism as they placed their energies on evangelizing, contributing to local Nazarene leadership, sustaining Nazarene ministries and missions, and supporting other outreach ministries in their communities.

The next chapter entitled, "African American Nazarenes, Social Conservatism, and Evangelistic Growth from 1958-1969," describes the ways in which African American men and women, from 1958 to 1969, acquired a greater amount of control over the affairs of the GCD and how they continued to embrace and promote the personal holiness and evangelistic theology of the denomination, recruit and educate African American pastors, strengthen their district committees, congregations, ministries, budgets, and contribute to the denomination's mission to evangelize southern blacks.

Aside from this, the chapter highlights how certain southern black ministers—under ecclesiastical freedom to do so—decided to join local civil rights movements. However, like the example of those in Brooklyn during previous decades, this section highlights the ways their actions were not the norm among most southern blacks. Instead, like the majority of Nazarenes around the country, African American men and women in the South continued to shy away from addressing societal and racial issues as they focused on supporting the denomination's overarching concerns during the late 1950s and 1960s—personal holiness and evangelism.

In addition to this, the section outlines how African American men and women outside the South embraced a similar social ethic and denominational posture. Like their counterparts in the South, African American Nazarenes in states like California, Michigan, West Virginia, Illinois, Kansas, and Missouri remained committed to "saving" and "sanctifying" black souls. They did this by maintaining Nazarene youth, Sunday school, and missionary ministries and by hosting outreach activities, promoting domestic and foreign missions, and indoctrinating youth and families in "the experience of sanctification." With such a focus on denominational evangelism, the chapter concludes by revealing why total African American congregations remained low and why average membership was small. This helps the reader to have a better grasp of why low membership numbers were not unusual or particular to African American congregations, but reflected a general pattern amongst most Nazarene congregations in the United States.

The next chapter entitled, "The Participation Continues: West Indian and Cape Verdean Contributions to Denominational Evangelism, 1958-1969," outlines the ways West Indians and Cape Verdeans continued their evangelistic commitment to the CN and how this commitment persisted as both groups remained as fully participating members of the New York and New England Districts and not as segregated participants like African Americans in the South. Finally, it reveals how these two black immigrant bodies chose not to publicly address denominational racism or other systemic racial issues in the United States. As such, this chapter reinforces how both groups—in two different regions and locations—continued to embrace, like their African American and white counterparts throughout the country, the personal holiness message and experience of the denomination during the late 1950s and 1960s.

After this, the work highlights how theological belief shaped African American, Afro-Caribbean, and Cape Verdean participation in the CN during the period studied. In addition to this, it briefly outlines the way the research adds to the historical understanding of the diverse religious experiences of black women in the early to mid-20th century. Not only that, but it also outlines how denominational research can open up new avenues to understand the diversity of black religious life in the United States. Finally, the text concludes with an Epilogue about black participation in the CN shortly after the close of the GCD.

Situating the Study and Scholarly Contribution of the Text

As it was mentioned earlier, there currently exists no scholarly study or in-depth monograph on black Nazarene life in the early to mid-20th century, even though some literature exists on the subject in Nazarene literature. For instance, Roger Bowman wrote, over thirty years ago, a brief and popular missionary book on the denomination's evangelical mission to blacks, primarily from the 1940s to the 1970s. In his work, Bowman briefly detailed how black Nazarenes worked alongside denominational leaders to organize black churches, missions, Sunday schools, and other ministries. In addition, he stressed how pastors and leaders such as D.A. Murray (black), E.E. Hale (white), A.P. Bowes (white), D.I. Vanderpool (white), Leon Chambers (white), and Warren Rogers (black) ministered under the GCD, a jurisdiction which he felt, "was not organized as an instrument of segregation but as an instrument of evangelism . . . that would . . . hopefully provide for closer supervision and greater support."

Because Bowman primarily sought to outline for lay readers when and how African Americans churches were started under the GCD and in other places in the U.S. throughout the 1940s to the 1970s, he did not examine how other organizational, historical, racial, theological, or cultural issues shaped the relationship between blacks and the CN throughout the United States. In addition to this, because the majority of his work focused on the middle decades of the 20th century, one is left with minimal knowledge of early black contributions to denominational life.[9] Not only that, but the reader is given no indication of how patterns of governing black churches changed throughout the 20th century and how those changes intersected with African-American, Afro-Caribbean, and Cape Verdean participation in the CN.

Likewise, Mendell Taylor, in the third volume of his history on Nazarene missions, which was published in 1958, briefly described (in less than five pages) how black congregations emerged in places like Kansas, New York, New England, and in other places in both the North and the South.[10] In particular, he shows how the CN took small steps to evangelize African Americans and Afro-Caribbeans in the 1910s, 20s, 30s, and early 40s and he also outlined how the GCD was able to establish more black congregations and ministers as it gave "closer supervision and assistance to the churches."[11] Thus, although Taylor differed from Bowman because he included the Cape Verdean churches among the ranks of the early black congregations, he, like Bowman, did not thoroughly examine how blacks participated in the denomination before 1958 or analyze how ecclesiastical segregation and other organizational, theological, cultural, and racial issues shaped the experience of blacks in the CN during the early to mid-20th century.

In similar fashion, when W.T. Purkiser wrote *Called Unto Holiness: The Second Twenty-five Years, 1933-1958*, vol. 2, in 1983, he described (in three and half pages) how some black churches and ministers joined the CN after the denomination made plans to begin evangelizing African Americans in the late 1940s and after the church established the GCD in 1953. Because of this focus, Purkiser neglected to discuss or even name the churches that

---

[9]Roger Bowman, *Color Us Christian: The Story of the Church of the Nazarene Among America's Blacks* (Kansas City: Beacon Hill Press, 1975).

[10]See Mendall Taylor, *Fifty Years of Mission: World Outreach Through Home Missions*, v. 3 (Kansas City: Beacon Hill Press, 1958), 149.

[11]Ibid., 152.

were in existence in New England and Brooklyn before and during the years that the GCD existed.[12]

As such, Purkiser not only failed to analyze how issues like ecclesiastical governance, ethnic background, historical context, or geographical location intersected with the religious lives of black Nazarenes the 1940s, 50s, and 60s, but he also overlooked how certain Afro-Caribbean, Cape Verdean, and African American churches contributed to the mission of the denomination since its pioneering days. Thus, after reading Purkiser, the reader is left to wonder whether there were any congregations within the denomination before white leaders decided to evangelize African Americans in the North, West, and South during the late 1940s and early 1950s.

Furthermore, in their recent general history of the CN, Floyd Cunningham, Stan Ingersol, Harold E. Raser, and David P. Whitelaw, briefly highlight how the growing issue of race relations in the post-WWII era impacted and shaped the denomination's desire to start African American churches around the country. In addition to this, they succinctly detail how the church transitioned from the CD to the GCD and how African American pastors and leaders wrestled with the racism of white district superintendents as they ministered in various parts of the country.

In short, the driving force behind the authors' analysis is how white denominational leaders, universities, and congregations wrestled with the growing reality of African Americans in their communities and how and why black evangelization grew from the mid-1940s to the late 1960s. Therefore, specific details regarding black participation in the CN in different parts of the country during this period and how the African American and West Indian churches in Kansas and Brooklyn ministered and contributed to denominational life before "the race question" arose and before national calls for black evangelization began are not addressed.[13] Thus, as it pertains to the historical understanding and contribution of black Nazarenes, this work is not only an attempt to overcome some of these scholarly limitations but it also attempts to provide the first systematic study of black Nazarene in the United States before *and* after calls for national black evangelization.

Outside of Nazarene historiography, this work is important because it adds to the growing body of literature which has analyzed the ways in which theological, jurisdictional, and racial issues intersected with how black pastors, leaders, and laity participated in predominantly white mainline, holiness, and Pentecostal denominations in the early to mid-20th cen-

---

[12]W.T. Purkiser, *Called Unto Holiness: The Second Twenty-five Years, 1933-1958*, v. 2 (Kansas City: Beacon Hill Press, 1983), 199-200.

[13]Floyd Cunningham, Stan Ingersol, Harold E. Raser, David P. Whitelaw, ed., *Our Watchword & Song: The Centennial History of the Church of the Nazarene* (Kansas City, MO: Beacon Hill Press, 2009), 362-373.

tury. For instance, in 1992, James S. Thomas published his monograph on the history of African American participation in American Methodism. In it, he tells the story of the Central Jurisdiction of the Methodist Church [hereafter referred to as the MC] (the segregated jurisdiction that was created for African Americans after the Plan of Union in 1939, which united the Methodist Episcopal Church, South and the Methodist Protestant Church with the Methodist Episcopal Church and which agreed to segregate blacks in a national jurisdiction so that white southern Methodists would not be under the same annual conference as black congregations) and how it affected both blacks and whites within the denomination.

In a similar work, *Methodists and the Crucible of Race, 1930 – 1975*, author Peter C. Murray places the racial struggles and the issues over the existence of the Central Jurisdiction in the Methodist Church within the broader context of the history of race relations in the United States. He shows how the effort to destroy racial barriers in the denomination mirrored the work of other civil rights organizations and social groups who were trying to end segregation in both the North and the South during the 1940s to the late 1960s.

By providing such works, both authors have outlined how racism shaped jurisdictional segregation in the MC during the middle of the 20th century. At the same time, Thomas and Murray have shown how blacks impacted the decision-making processes of the MC, from the 1940s through the mid-1960s and how African Americans shaped the direction of the denomination from the late 1960s to the early 1970s.[14] As such, they have provided a glimpse into how blacks churches and leaders participated and contributed to Methodist life during the 20th century.

Aside from this, several scholars have detailed how racial and ecclesiastical issues intersected with black participation in other white holiness and Pentecostal denominations that emerged from the same late 19th century American Holiness Movement (hereafter referred to as AHM) that produced the CN.[15] For instance, Cheryl Sanders, in her monograph, *Saints in Exile*:

---

[14]For further reference see James S. Thomas, *Methodism's Racial Dilemma: The Story of the Central Jurisdiction* (Nashville: Abingdon Press, 1992) and Peter C. Murray, *Methodists and the Crucible of Race, 1930-1975* (Columbia, MO: The University of Missouri Press, 2004).

[15]These works emerged after Charles Edwin Jones published his bibliographic work in the late 1980s entitled, *Black Holiness: A Guide to the Study of Black Participation in Wesleyan Perfectionist and Glossolalic Pentecostal Movements*, which documented the majority of the works written about black participation "in Wesleyan perfectionist and glossolalic Pentecostal and healing movements in Africa, the West Indies, the United States, Canada, and the United Kingdom." For further reference, see Charles Edwin Jones, *Black Holiness: A Guide to the Study of Black Participation in Wesleyan Perfectionist and Glossolalic Pentecostal Movements* (Lanham, MD: The Scarecrow Press, 1987), xix.

xxi Introduction

The Holiness-Pentecostal Experience in African American Religion and Culture, briefly discloses why African Americans joined and participated in the Church of God (Anderson, IN) (hereafter referred to as CGA) in the early 20th century. In her estimation, blacks joined the CGA and started congregations and ecclesiastical organizations in states like Pennsylvania because they were able to draw upon the theology of biblical holiness as they built racial unity in the denomination, despite the racist social ethics that were operating within the Church of God (Anderson, IN) during the 1910's and 1920's.[16]

In similar fashion, in his social history entitled, *African Americans and the Church of God (Anderson, IN): Aspects of a Social History*, James Massey gives more detailed attention to some of the historical and social factors that shaped African American participation within the CGA during the late 19th and 20th centuries and has shed new light on why blacks chose to remain with the movement during its formative years. He argues that unlike other predominantly white holiness bodies like the CN, the CGA was able to retain more African American members because blacks were drawn to the movement's doctrinal stress on scriptural holiness and the unity of all believers.[17]

Massey maintains that this theological emphasis bolstered the work and confidence of early black leaders to minister and preach the message of sanctification alongside whites and it provided a sense of equality and unity in a period when race relations were deteriorating in the Jim Crow South and in northern urban areas. Moreover, even when this message of unity and holiness was diluted by the societal demands of racial separation, black leaders continued to join the movement. In fact, by 1915, there were over two hundred African Americans who were involved as pastors, evangelists, and gospel workers.[18] Also, he argues those who were chosen to lead the all black West Middlesex Campground and the National Association Ministerial Assembly during the late 1910's were strongly related to the larger movement's witness and life. According to Massey, these actions, coupled with the belief that racial unity could be attained within the CGA, empowered African Americans to remain in the movement.[19]

Massey also contends that the denomination's congregational polity allowed blacks to control the affairs of their congregations and pool together

---

[16]Cheryl Sanders, *Saints in Exile: The Holiness-Pentecostal Experience in African American Religion and Culture* (New York: Oxford University Press, 1996), 25-27.

[17]James Earl Massey, *African Americans and the Church of God (Anderson, IN): Aspects of a Social History* (Anderson, IN: Anderson University Press, 2005).

[18]Ibid., 267-272. Although Massey notes that there were a lot of black churches and ministers involved in the movement, he does not tell how many congregations were actually incorporated into the movement throughout the 20th century.

[19]Ibid., 87, 90.

their collective financial, pastoral, and lay resources to begin predominantly black organizations and auxiliary ministries in the denomination. In particular, he states that during their early stages of formation (i.e. the late 19th and early 20th century), independent black congregations were able to control local ecclesiastical matters and were even able to establish a ministerial alliance and a black owned campground before 1930 (despite the prevailing system of racial separateness operative within the Church of God).[20]

Aside from the CGA, Edward McKinley has outlined how ecclesiastical racism and jurisdictional issues shaped the actions and contributions of blacks in the Salvation Army in the early to mid-20th century. In short, McKinley shows that segregated worship services and the lack of black ministers (i.e. officers) were the major causes that lead to only having one black church (i.e. corps) in the South before WWII. At the same time, he shows that integrated services, the more open racial environment of northern cities, and the presence of West Indians who joined the Salvation Army lead to the founding of four black congregations in New York City and Chicago before WWII.

After the war, McKinley states that the Salvation Army dropped its designation of "colored" to described black congregations in 1949 and placed the church in the South on an integrated "division" (an ecclesiastical jurisdiction similar to a Methodist conference) in 1955. In addition to this, McKinley states that during the 1950s and 1960s, seven black corps were maintained and established in northern and mid-western cities and that many of them assisted with food and other emergency services when riots broke out in the late 1960s in cities such as Milwaukee, Pittsburgh, and Cleveland.[21]

Aside from works like this, David Michel's *Telling the Story: Black Pentecostals in the Church of God*, briefly uplifts the jurisdictional and organizational issues that intersected with black participation in the Church of God (Cleveland, TN) (hereafter referred to as CGD), a predominantly white Pentecostal denomination that emerged from the vestiges of the AHM during

---

[20]Ibid., 71, 86-87.

[21]William McKinley, *Marching to Glory: The History of the Salvation Army in the United States, 1880-1992*, 2nd ed. (Grand Rapids, MI: William B. Eerdmans Publishing Company, 1995), 131, 239-241, 259-262. Aside from McKinley, Warren L. Maye has recently written a work outlining how individuals of African descent like Pearl Hurdle, Barton McIntyre, Mildred McIntyre, Mabel Broome, Maurice Smith, Grace Smith, Norma Roberts and others help lead the few congregations and other social ministries in Washington D.C., New York, and a few other northern cities in the early 20th century. Aside from this, he outlines how blacks contributed and joined the Salvation Army from the Civil Rights Era to the beginning of the 21st century. For further reference, see Warren L. Maye, *Soldiers of Uncommon Valor: The history of Salvationists of African Descent in the United States* (West Nyack, NY: Others Press, 2008).

xxiii   Introduction

the early 20th century.22 For instance, Michel shows how, after several black churches were started in Florida in the 1910s, the General Assembly of the CGD appointed Edmond Barr to lead the black churches in that state. This segregated practice led backs to establish their own annual assembly in 1923 (apart from white congregations), which allowed black immigrants and African Americans to begin their own Sunday schools, missionary societies, and youth programs.23

Michel goes on to show how blacks helped to convince the General Assembly of the denomination to establish a national segregated judicatory in 1930. Under this system, the black churches in Florida, along with the African American congregations in New Jersey and Philadelphia, were able to hold annual assemblies and consolidate their leadership and monetary capital in the 1930s to the late 1960s to strengthen their existing churches, build a school and orphanage, start a black periodical, and construct a large auditorium in Jacksonville, FL to host the national black assembly. Thus, Michel reveals that even though blacks were not elected or placed in positions of national leadership, they, under their national segregated status, were able to achieve racial autonomy across ethnic lines and strengthen the black presence in the denomination throughout the middle decades of the 20th century.24

By situating the work inside this seam of scholarship, this work provides another study on the diversity of black religious life in the 20th century and another look into how African Americans and other black groups from the African Diaspora stayed and remained within a predominantly white Protestant body, from the days of WWI to the end of the 1960s. Moreover, as just stated, each work mentioned above outlines the ways various black groups navigated through issues of race, ecclesiastical governance, theological belief, and social realities as they participated in denominational life. In particular, each scholar shows how issues of race and ecclesiastical racism intersected with the lives of black adherents. In Methodism and the CGC for instance, blacks, whether African American or otherwise, ministered under a national segregated judicatory for much of the 1930s to the end of the 1960s, while the Salvation Army segregated black congregations from white corps in the South until the mid-1950s. During the same period, authors like Massey show how African Americans in the CGA participated under a congregational polity, while maintaining a national connection through black organizations.

22David Michel, *Telling the Story: Black Pentecostals in the Church of God* (Cleveland, TN: Pathway Press, 2000), 11, 35, 61-85.

23Ibid., 29. See also, David Edwin Harrell, Jr., *White Sects and Black Men in the Recent South* (Nashville: Vanderbilt University Press, 1971), 42.

24Michel, 143-155.

Unlike these scholars, however, no one, until now, has systematically or thoroughly analyzed how racial realities and changes in ecclesiastical governance intersected with black participation in the CN, from the founding of the first black congregation in New York to the ending of the GCD in 1969. As the proceeding narrative will show, unlike the CGA, the CN did not have a congregational polity and unlike Methodism and the GCG, it did not have a continuous national jurisdiction that governed all black churches. Moreover, the CN decided to take a regional segregated approach to governing African American churches around the same time that the Salvation Army placed all of its black congregations in integrated divisions throughout the country. Thus, by showing how the CN transitioned from an integrated approach of black congregational governance to a nationally segregated jurisdiction and then to a system of segregating African American churches in the South, the reader is able to see how black participation in the CN took shape under different ecclesiastical realities than what the above scholars have described in other predominantly white mainline, holiness, and Pentecostal bodies.

Furthermore, describing such details and how ecclesiastical governance changed or remained the same in the CN during the early to mid-20th century allows scholars and readers to see how issues like geography, ethnic background, and missionary ideals impacted African American, Cape Verdean, and Afro-Caribbean participation in the CN. For instance, African Americans went through various patterns of church governance in the 1940s and 1950s, while Cape Verdeans and Afro-Caribbeans remained a part of their local integrated jurisdictions. As such, African Americans went through several forms of ecclesiastical segregation, while black immigrants avoided any form of denominational governance along racial lines.

In addition to outlining how black Nazarenes contributed to denominational life under various forms of jurisdictional practices based on race and ethnicity during this period, this work also reveals how gender, ecclesiastical, and ethnic realities intersected in the CN to shape how black Nazarene women participated in the CN in different ways than black women in other predominantly African American denominations. For example, as scholars like Evelyn Brooks Higginbotham and Anthea Butler have shown, women in the National Baptist Convention in the 1910s and 1920s and women in the Church of God in Christ (during the middle decades of the 20th century) created "gendered" spaces in their respective denominations to fulfill their ministerial callings. In the former body, women developed the Women's Convention (hereafter referred to as WC) in 1900 and used the auxiliary to fight off gender and racial discrimination by bolstering the NAACP's struggle against lynching, establishing a training school for young African American women, supporting moral respectability in the black community (i.e. in order to change the way whites viewed them), maintaining ties with the National Association of Colored Women, and debating ecclesiastical issues. As such, Higgenbotham argues that the WC provided a discursive realm where black women could learn about the basics of self-government, fend off white racism, support black concerns, and implement nationally supported programs that were sensitive to African American male and female concerns around the country.25

Likewise, Butler maintains that in the Church of God in Christ (hereafter referred to as COGIC), women, barred from ordained ministry and an equal footing within the denomination, utilized the Women's Department (hereafter referred to as WD) throughout the early to mid-20th century to live out their "sanctified" lives and to "negotiate for and obtain power both within the denomination and outside it." Initially used to pursue a life of "holiness" that refrained from the "sins and pollutions of modern life," Butler asserts that around WWII to the early 1960s, the WD transformed the meaning of sanctification by supporting and leading a denominational school in Mississippi and by adding auxiliaries that helped them increased their engagement with broader African American social organizations like the National Council of Negro Women and the NAACP. Because of this, Butler maintains that black women in the COGIC were able to pursue and fulfill their definition of sanctification alongside the ecclesiastical structure of the denomination and a part from the administrative oversight of male ministers.26

In this work, the reader will see how black Nazarene women's faith and ministerial efforts were not confined to similar gendered spaces that were created in black Baptist circles and in the COGIC. Instead, the ecclesiastical practices of the denomination allowed women, regardless of color, educational background, or class standing, to further the evangelistic and holiness mission of the denomination by preaching, teaching, pastoring churches, joining NWMS chapters, and leading congregational ministries and by legislating on matters related to black evangelism, Christian education, ordination, and ministerial training. As a result, for the first time, this work reveals how black women in the CN were not circumscribed along gender lines like their African American counterparts in other black faith communities and thus were free to pursue their ministerial calling alongside black men in the denomination.

Moreover, this book highlights how, beginning in 1944, African American women, like black men, ministered under different levels of jurisdictional segregation, while black immigrant women continued to minister in

---

[25] Evelyn Brooks Higgenbotham, *Righteous Discontent: The Women's Movement in the Black Baptist Church, 1880-1920* (Cambridge, MA: Harvard University Press, 1993), 150-229.

[26] Anthea Butler, *Women in the Church of God in Christ: Making a Sanctified World* (Chapel Hill, NC: The University of North Carolina Press, 2007). For further reference about the role of the Women's Department in the Church of God in Christ, see Cheryl Townsend Gilkes, "Together and in Harness: Women's Traditions in the Sanctified Church," in *African American Religious Thought: An Anthology*, ed., Cornel West and Eddie S. Glaude Jr. (Louisville: Westminster John Knox Press, 2003), 629-650.

their congregations and contributed to the CN alongside whites on racially integrated districts. Due to this, African American women, beginning in the middle of the 20th century, were often situated in an official secondary racial status within the CN, while black immigrant women were not. Thus, this dynamic adds to the complexity of understanding the diversity of black women's religious experience, because it reveals that the category of ethnicity, combined with race, class, and gender, shaped the ways in which some black women lived out their religious lives in the United States during the middle of the 20th century.

In sum, despite the various levels of ecclesiastical segregation and governance, this historical work ultimately shows readers that blacks throughout the United States promoted and remained committed to the personal holiness and evangelistic mission of the denomination throughout the early to mid-20th century. Despite each groups' different historical context, ethnic background, geographical location, or racial standing in the denomination, Afro-Caribbeans, Cape-Verdeans, and African Americans chose to evangelize blacks and promote personal holiness as expressed in denominational teachings. Even as the country moved into the burgeoning Civil Rights Era after WWII and tarried through the racial changes that transpired in the 1960s, blacks throughout the United States primarily chose to teach and instruct others with the theology of personal holiness and to evangelize blacks with the same message. Therefore, the project shows that without analyzing theological belief and denominational commitment, one cannot comprehend the various ways that blacks contributed to the life and mission of predominantly white holiness bodies in general and the CN in particular throughout the early to mid-20th century.

Chapter One

The Pioneer Era: The Beginnings of Black Nazarene Participation, 1908-1933

The Theological, Organizational, and Evangelistic Roots of the Early Church of the Nazarene

In 1908 in Pilot Point, TX, the Church of the Nazarene was formed after ten holiness associations agreed to unify into one denominational body.[27] The groups who joined included the Association of Pentecostal Churches, the Church of the Nazarene—Los Angeles, the Eastern Pennsylvania Conference of the Holiness Christian Church, the New Testament Church of Christ, the Holiness Church of Christ, and the Holiness Association of Texas. They represented a variety of geographical locations across the United States. For instance, the Central Evangelical Holiness Association was comprised primarily of churches in the cities of Providence, Rhode Island and Lynn, Massachusetts, while the Church of the Nazarene—Los Angeles, represented congregations from San Diego to Washington to as far east as Chicago. Similarly, groups such as the New Testament Church of Christ and the Holiness Church of Christ had churches in the states of Tennessee, Texas, Georgia, Arkansas, and New Mexico and supported missionaries in Japan, Mexico, China, India, and Africa.[28]

---

[27]Stan Ingersol, "Merging Holiness Bodies: Documentary Sources on the History of Ten Nazarene Parent Bodies" (April 2007): 1-4. Church of the Nazarene Archives, Lenexa, KS.

Despite their various locales, these bodies were joined together by a common theological conviction—Christian holiness. The theological roots of holiness, as it became known among those who joined the CN, were found in the words and writings of John Wesley, the 18th century founder of Methodism. In short, Wesley believed that Christians who confessed and repented of their sins to Jesus Christ received "salvation" and were "justified" as righteous in the eyes of God. By justification, Wesley meant that the sinner was "saved from the guilt of sin and restored to the favor of God." However, he also contended that God's grace could fill Christian believers with "pure love to God and man."

Wesley argued that this infusion of God's love is what enabled the believer to perfectly love God and one's neighbor. He noted that at the moment of justification, holy love was given to the believer and would gradually increase over the course of one's life—if that person remained obedient to the "guidance of the Holy Spirit."[29] He stressed this point in his treatise entitled "A Plain Account of Christian Perfection." In it, he stated that those were who were in a sanctified state could "grow in grace" or fall from it. Thus, he counseled those in the Methodist fold to pray continually for God's Spirit to create within them a longing for holiness and to help them resist such temptations as pride, greed, lust, and malice. He reiterated this when he stated that,

> the Holy Spirit works the same in our hearts, not merely creating desires after holiness in general, but strongly inclining us to every particular grace, leading us to every individual part of 'whatsoever is lovely.' And this with the greatest propriety; for us 'by works faith is made perfect,' so the completing or destroying the work of faith, and enjoying the favor, or suffering the displeasure, of God, greatly depends on every single act of obedience or disobedience.[30]

Moreover, he went on to add that one should continually perform "works of mercy" if they were to "perfectly love God" and maintain their holiness:

> Lose no opportunity of doing good in any kind. Be zealous of good works; willing omit no work, either of piety or mercy. Do all the good you possibly can, to the bodies and souls of mean . . . Be active . . . God does not love men

---

[28]Ibid., 3-4 and *The Manual of the Twelfth General Assembly of the Church of the Nazarene* (1948), 15-21. Church of the Nazarene Archives, Lenexa, KS.

[29]Paul M. Bassett and William M. Greathouse, ed., *Exploring Christian Holiness: The Historical Development*, v. 2 (Kansas City, MO: Beacon Hill Press, 1985), 207-209 and Stan Ingersol and Wes Tracy, *What is a Nazarene: Understanding our Place in the Religious Community* (Kansas City, MO: Beacon Hill Press, 1998), 11-13.

[30]John Wesley, *A Plain Account of Christian Perfection* (London: Wesleyan Conference Office, 1872; reprint, Kansas City, MO: Beacon Hill Publishing Company, 1966), 101.

that are inconstant, nor good works that are intermitted. Nothing is pleasing to Him, but what has a resemblance of His own immutability . . . A constant attention to the work which God entrusts us with is a mark of solid piety.[31]

When Wesley's teaching on holiness became more popular in America during the mid-19th century and especially after the Civil War, it developed and reflected the millennial and revivalistic tendencies of American evangelicalism. For example, prominent lay, educational, and ministerial figures like Phoebe Palmer (1807-1874), Charles Finney (1792-1875), Asa Mahan (1779-1889), and Daniel Steele (1824-1904) taught that one could attain the life of practical holiness if they would faithfully consecrate themselves to Christ. For Palmer, a daughter of Methodists and a wife of a prominent New York physician, this meant that the believer had to be aware that God required holiness now and that it could be attained if one placed themselves "entirely upon God's altar" and conformed themselves to the will of God.[32] She underscored this point in 1853, in her periodical entitled, *Guide to Christian Perfection*:

> On everyone who will specifically present himself upon the altar . . . for the sole object of being ceaselessly consumed, body and soul, in the self-sacrificing service of God, he will cause the fire to descend. And . . . He will not delay to do this for every waiting soul, for He standeth waiting, and the moment the offerer presents sacrifice, the hallowing, consuming touch will be given.[33]

Likewise, Finney, the 19th century social reformer and one of the fathers of modern evangelical revivalism, argued that sin was a voluntary act and could be removed through Christian conversion. Since sin was a consequence of human volition and could be overcome through one's commitment to the Christian faith, Finney felt that holiness could be attained on earth.[34] He argued that the believer could find assurance of this at the point of their conversion when the Holy Spirit filled their hearts "with love" and removed them from the state of sinfulness. He testified to having this experience in his personal memoir, which was written in 1868:

---

[31]Ibid., 111-112.

[32]Phoebe Palmer, "The Way of Holiness, with notes by the way: being a narrative of religious experience resulting from a determination to be a Bible Christian," in *A Documentary History of Religion in America to 1877*, 3rd ed, ed., Edwin S. Gaustad and Mark A. Noll, (Grand Rapids, MI: William B. Eerdmans Publishing Company, 2003), 415-416.

[33]Phoebe Palmer, *Guide to Christian Perfection*, 23 (June 1853), 176; quoted in Bassett and Greathouse, 300.

[34]Sydney Ahlstrom, *A Religious History of the American People* (New Haven, CT: Yale University Press, 1972), 459-460.

The Holy Spirit descended upon me in a manner that seemed to go through me, body and soul. I could feel the impression, like a wave of electricity, going through and through me. Indeed it seemed to come in waves and waves of liquid love; for I could not express it in any other way. It seemed like the very breath of God ... This was just the revelation that I needed. I felt myself justified by faith: and, so far as I could see, I was in a state in which I did not sin. Instead of feeling that I was sinning all the time, my heart was so full of love that it overflowed. My cup ran over with blessing and with love; and I could not feel that I was sinning against God.[35]

Of course, Palmer's and Finney's stress on attaining entire sanctification before death represented some of American evangelicalism's pragmatism. As Melvin Dieter notes in his monograph entitled, *The Holiness Revival of the 19th Century*, figures like Palmer, Finney, and Mahan simplified the various nuances of Wesley's understanding of holiness by borrowing from the prevailing mood of revivalism that always sought "to make a reality at the moment whatever is considered at all possible in the future."[36] Dieter goes on to state that those who adhered to this belief wedded the present possibilities of holiness with American millennialism in a "popular quest" to transform American society and to spread the holiness message throughout the world.[37]

By the time the CN was formed in 1908, many of the bodies and followers mentioned previously only fit one part of Dieter's characterization—namely that God's "holy" people could live free from personal sin and perfectly love without having to reform the world. Thus, the former emphasis on social reform and living out a form of social holiness was largely abandoned even though early founders like Dr. Phineas Bresee had ministries amongst the poor in Los Angeles and although early missionaries in the 1910s and 1920s helped to improve the educational and medical standards of persons on the mission field.[38] In other words, the church was not pri-

---

[35]Charles Grandison Finney, "Memoirs" in *American Religions: A Documentary History*, R. Marie Griffith, ed. (New York: Oxford University Press, 2008), 193-195.

[36]Melvin E. Dieter, *The Holiness Revival of the Nineteenth Century* (Metuchen, NJ: The Scarecrow Press, 1980), 31.

[37]Timothy Smith, *Revivalism and Social Reform in Mid-Nineteenth Century America* (Nashville: Abingdon Press, 1957), 49, 75 and Nancy Hardesty, "Holiness Movements," in *Encyclopedia of Women and Religion in North America*, vol. 1, ed., Rosemary Skinner Keller and Rosemary Radford Reuther (Bloomington, IN: Indiana University Press, 2006), 430.

[38]For instance, W.T. Purkiser notes that by the early 1930s, the church was operating eighty-four day schools on its mission fields, with most of them located in Africa. Also, there were two hospitals (one in Africa and one in China) and fourteen dispensaries. Eight physicians and twenty-four nurses staffed these medical units and by 1933, a total of 29, 359 patients were treated at the various facilities. For further reference see, W.T. Purkiser, *Called Unto Holiness*, v. 2 (Kansas City, MO: Beacon Hill Press, 1983), 41.

5 The Pioneer Era

marily concerned about reforming the political or social landscape of the United States. Instead, the denomination and its leaders focused on communicating how individuals could live a "Christlike" life by perfectly loving God and having "victory" over various "sins" such as reading "secular papers," "trafficking intoxicating liquors," using tobacco, working on Sunday, and other personal taboos.[39]

Aside from this, the CN and its denominational leaders primarily focused on cultivating and supporting missionary work, both foreign and domestic. For instance, as early as 1897 and 1905, bodies like the Association of Pentecostal Churches and the Holiness Church of Christ supported missionaries in places like India and Japan, while the Pentecostal Mission had commissioned workers in British Honduras and Guatemala before they joined the denomination in 1915. Moreover, by 1933-34, the denomination had 26 missionaries and 153 national workers serving in Africa, 11 national pastors in Mexico, five organized churches in Argentina, 370 Nazarene members in Peru, one missionary in Syria, and a total of 7,568 international members with an additional 2,885 probationers.[40]

In the United States, denominational workers and laity also worked to evangelize and establish more congregations on districts. Districts were geographical jurisdictions that governed and oversaw Nazarene congregations in the U.S. A District Superintendent (hereafter referred to as DS) supervised each district and in the beginning decades, their primary duty was to evangelize and start churches on their districts. Aside from this, they administered and oversaw—along with district committees—church budgets and ministries, district budgets and financial contributions to international and domestic evangelism, and final decisions regarding theological debates and ecclesiastical quarrels in local churches. Not only that, but each DS made recommendations to churches looking for pastors and oversaw the annual District Assembly (hereafter referred to as DA).

On a district, churches were required to submit their church budgets, congregational, Sunday school and Nazarene Young People's Society (hereafter referred to as NYPS) membership numbers, and other relevant highlights pertinent to their congregational life to the yearly DA. As participating churches on a district, Nazarene congregations were also asked to send voting delegates to the annual DA—which usually lasted four to five days—in order to vote and legislate on how the churches on the district would use money for Sunday school ministries and missionary work. Moreover, certain representatives from churches on the district were elected to the DA to

---

[39]Floyd Cunningham, Stan Ingersol, Harold E. Raser, David P. Whitelaw, ed., *Our Watchword & Song: The Centennial History of the Church of the Nazarene* (Kansas City, MO: Beacon Hill Press, 2009), 188.

[40]Purkiser, 38-40 and Smith, 341-343.

sit on a variety of district committees that decided on how churches should properly observe the Sabbath, live a "holy" life in conjunction with denominational principles and morals, and evangelize others. In addition, district committees decided who would be ordained and licensed as ministers, who would be commissioned as evangelists, and what local Sunday schools and NYPS chapters would focus on throughout the year.[41]

At these yearly gatherings in the 1910s and 1920s, the church's internal political culture was solidified and ecclesiastical business was completed for the year. At the same time, by participating in the yearly DA, churches were able to worship together, hear evangelistic and holiness sermons, strengthen bonds between churches and pastors with leaders from the general church, garner their collective resources to carry out the evangelistic mission of the denomination, and share how the general church was growing at the local level.[42] For instance, in the summer of 1915, H.M. Chambers told his district of how the denomination was expanding its message and growing in the state of Kansas when he noted that,

> New churches have been organized at Lyons... at Liberty... at Cherryville... and at Buffalo. We also have the nucleus for an organization at Coffeyville. At all of these places the outlook truly is promising. Most of the new churches are small in numbers, but all are composed of faithful, dependable people... debts are being paid off, and properties are being improved in several places. So temporal success is accompanying spiritual achievement in a special manner. Reports from the various churches, will, I am sure, indicate a good degree of growth along all lines.[43]

Districts far removed from Kansas also reported about how leaders and laity were holding evangelistic services and starting new churches. In New York, for example, committee leaders, at times, told about how local evangelists and preachers helped to start congregations. A story retold by G. Howard Rowe, Home Field Secretary and Evangelist of the New York District in 1922, highlights how such evangelistic services and mission work helped to inaugurate new churches in New York:

> We began a home mission campaign in our new baby work at Gouverneur. It now being cold weather, we held this meeting in the church building. This building had previously been bought from the Methodists. The Lord gave us a rich meeting here...God gave us some seventy souls here in direct answer to prayer. Brother Angell came on for one night and we organized a church with about thirty members.[44]

---

[41]Cunningham, Ingersol, Raser, and Whitelaw, 161, 259, 350-351, 379.
[42]Ibid., 259-260.
[43]*Kansas District Pentecostal Church of the Nazarene, Sixth Annual Assembly Journal* (April 11-15, 1915), 27. Church of the Nazarene Archives, Lenexa, KS.
[44]*New York District Church of the Nazarene, Fifteenth Annual Assembly Journal* (April 1922), 27. Church of the Nazarene Archives, Lenexa, KS.

During this same year, Howe and his constituents continued to hold evangelistic services and start churches in towns like Clintondale, Nyack, and Canastota to push the total number of congregations on the district to 31, which was a six-fold increase from the previous year.[45] By 1928, this methodology helped to increase the total number of churches on the district to 35, with over 60 licensed and ordained pastors actively ministering on the district.[46]

Across the country, in southern California, pastors and leaders evangelized others with the same message of "scriptural holiness" and started mission stations and churches during the 1910s. Ordained and lay evangelists (who were predominantly women) such as Phebe J. Epperson, L.M. Williams, Lulu B. Rogers, C.W. Ruth, Flora C. Johnson, and Bertha M. Milson "reached" non-Nazarenes with the message of holiness and helped to bolster the membership rolls of existing congregations. In 1910, their efforts helped to increase the total membership of the district by 170, which brought the total of the governing body to 2,231.[47] Four years later, several of these evangelists were still preaching and laboring on the district and had pushed the district's membership to 3,290 with 33 missions and churches in operation from San Diego to Bakersfield.[48]

Because of these labors across the world and particularly in the United States, early church leaders, evangelists, laity, and pastors had helped to spread "scriptural holiness" across the country and start numerous churches throughout the 1910s, 20s, and early 30s. The spreading of this "scriptural holiness," as mentioned above, was primarily focused on personal holiness and evangelistic outreach. During these the early decades, the CN had created a bifurcation between the personal and social dimensions of holiness while at the same time placing their energies on evangelization and starting new churches.

This stress on personal holiness and evangelistic emphasis would come to define the life of most Nazarene congregations in the United States, whether white or black. Most white and black Nazarenes, in other words, would come to place their emphasis on personal holiness and evangelistic outreach, while avoiding political or social issues that fell outside the purview of individual morality. However, as Timothy Smith highlights, this trajectory especially during the early period of the denomination helped the CN grow and expand. Smith underscores this fact when outlining some of the data of church growth during this period:

---

[45]Ibid., 42-45.

[46]*New York District Church of the Nazarene, Twenty-First Annual Assembly Journal* (April 1928), 6-7. Church of the Nazarene Archives, Lenexa, KS.

[47]*Southern California District Pentecostal Church of the Nazarene, Fourth Annual Assembly Journal* (July 1910), 6-8. Church of the Nazarene Archives, Lenexa, KS.

[48]*Southern California District Pentecostal Church of the Nazarene, Eighth Annual Assembly* (August 1914), 6-7, 28. Church of the Nazarene Archives, Lenexa, KS.

A chart of membership gains during four-year periods after 1911 showed over 56 percent increase between 1911 and 1915, only 5 ½ percent the next quadrennium, then additions of 45 percent, 35 percent, 35 percent, and 40 percent in the four-year periods following, until 1935.[49]

The Lack of Systematic Black Evangelization and the First African American Congregations in Kansas and Southern California

During this early period of denominational growth in the U.S. and around the globe, the denomination did not take a unified approach to evangelize blacks in the South or the numerous African American migrants that moved to large northern cities during and after World War I to build a better life and to escape the harsh racial realities of the South.[50] This lack of concern to reach out to southern blacks or the thousands of African Americans that migrated to northern urban areas[51] was largely due to the fact that the congregational, financial, and decision making power of the CN during the mid-1910s to early 1930s was concentrated in the Upper South and Midwest, where most communities and towns were smaller and whiter. For instance, by 1920, districts in the upper Mississippi Valley and plain states—Ohio, Kentucky, Indiana, Illinois, Michigan, Missouri, Iowa, Nebraska, Kansas, and

---

[49]Smith, 348.

[50]Milton Sernett, *Bound For the Promised Land: African American Religion and the Great Migration* (Durham, NC: Duke University Press, 1997), 3-8; Wallace D. Best, *Passionately Human, No Less Divine: Religion and Culture in Black Chicago, 1915-1952* (Princeton, NJ: Princeton University Press, 2005), 128 and Hans A. Baer and Merrill Singer, "Religious Diversification during the Era of Advance Industrial Capitalism," in *African American Religions Thought: An Anthology*, ed., Cornel West and Eddie S. Glaude Jr. (Louisville: Westminster John Knox Press, 2003), 514-515.

[51]For a look into how some African American churches sought to creatively address some of the social needs of black migrants in places like New York City, Chicago, and Detroit, see Abyssinian Church Holds Services in New Community Edifice," *New York Amsterdam News*, 28 February 1923; "What to Do With Delinquent Girls Discussed at Federation Meeting," *New York Amsterdam News*, 09 May 1928; "Mt. Olivet Baptist Church," *New York Amsterdam News*, 31 October 1928 and "Unity in Business Urged Upon Harlem," *New York Amsterdam News*, 11 December 1929; "New Bethel Church Dedicated in Detroit," *New Amsterdam News*, 10 June 1925; "Metropolitan Community Center," *Chicago Defender*, 04 December 1920 and "Olivet in the Limelight," *Chicago Defender*, 20 November 1920; Clarence Taylor, *The Black Churches of Brooklyn* (New York: Columbia University Press, 1994), 85-89; Albert Raboteau, *Canaan Land: A Religious History of African Americans* (New York: Oxford University Press, 2001), 85 and Best, 128.

Oklahoma—possessed over 40 percent of the total Nazarene membership, half of the estimated church property, and four of the denominational colleges. Within these districts, the overwhelming amount of churches were populated by white believers and located in smaller towns. Moreover, even though there wasn't a single Nazarene church in Kansas City, MO before 1911, the denomination decided to make it the location of its denominational headquarters, signifying where the power of the CN would be located for years to come.

The lack of black outreach was not only shaped by this reality, but by the dearth of public and written calls for the denomination to begin evangelizing blacks throughout the United States. In fact, only three written pieces appeared before 1920 that were related to the subject of black and African American evangelization. B.F. Haynes, a former southern Methodist minister and editor of the denomination's publication entitled *The Herald of Holiness*, wrote the first account in 1917. According to Haynes, the few northern Nazarene churches that were located in urban areas where southern blacks were migrating should "reach out" to the "negro people" by helping them find employment and adjust to the new social environment of the North. By doing this, he felt that northern Nazarenes could exhibit an "applied Christianity" to southern migrants and evangelize them with the message of Christian holiness.[52]

The Rev. R.J. Kirkland wrote the second article in 1919. His text appeared in *The Herald of Holiness* and like Haynes, Kirkland—despite his apparent white paternalism—tried to convince his readers that the denomination needed to extend a hand of fellowship to a "few independent holiness churches, colored" so that the CN could evangelize and start black churches in the South. In it, he stated and asked,

> since leaving the northern states and coming south my heart is made to ache as I see the colored man, woman, and child running hither and tither as sheep without a shepherd. I see them as they stand at a distance at our street meetings, trying to get a crumb "from under the master's table" ... The write has been told that there are a few independent holiness churches, colored, with preachers as pastors who see the necessity of a real holiness church among their people ... Therefore, shall we at our General Assembly of 1919 invite a delegation from these churches and see if they can be organized into one great body, "The Pentecostal Church of the Nazarene, Colored" ... [53]

Likewise, at the fifth Annual General Assembly of the CN—the quadrennial gathering of denominational leaders of church laity that voted and decided on important ecclesiastical issues—Rev. C.B. Jernigan, another white de-

---

[52] B.F. Haynes, "A Problem to be Met," in *The Herald of Holiness* (September 26, 1917): 2. Church of the Nazarene Archives, Lenexa, KS.

[53] Rev. R.J. Kirkland, "The Negro Problem," in *The Herald of Holiness* (May 7, 1919): 6. Church of the Nazarene Archives, Lenexa, KS.

nominational leader, urged the General Foreign Missionary Board (hereafter referred to as GFMB) "to send missionaries to work among the Negroes of the South, and, as occasion demands, organize them into colored Churches of the Nazarene."[54]

Thus, calls to evangelize blacks in the United States were rarely raised and when they did arise, the general church failed to develop systematic efforts to evangelize and begin black churches in the United States. Moreover, after Nazarene officials met with representatives from the Church of Christ (Holiness) (an African American holiness denomination lead by Charles Price Jones)[55] in Kansas City in the fall of 1923 and again before the spring of 1925, it was decided by both parties that the Church of Christ (Holiness) would not join the CN. The reasons for the failure of the merger are largely unknown, but one could only surmise that the prevailing governmental structure, racial dynamics, and lack of concern for African American evangelization had a large impact on why the southern-based group did not join the CN.

Yet, the locus of congregational and decision making power in the Upper South and Midwest, the lack of calls for black evangelization, and the failed denominational merger with Jones' group did not preclude a few African American Nazarene congregations from forming in Kansas and southern

---

[54]For further reference see, *The Fifth Annual Assembly Journal of the Church of the Nazarene* (Oct. 1919), 118. Church of the Nazarene Archives, Lenexa, KS.

[55]In the late 19th century, Charles Price Jones was part of a group of black Baptists in Mississippi who embraced holiness teachings. During a local meeting in Mississippi, Jones met C.H. Mason, another believer in holiness and shortly after their encounter; the two men studied the scriptures together and began teaching the doctrine of sanctification in churches around Jackson, MS. Before long, Jones gathered Baptists who believed in sanctification and organized them into a believing fellowship called the Church of God in Christ (COGIC), which Mason came up with after he returned from a preaching event in Little Rock, AR. After the two men settled on the name for their newly formed church, the body began to grow in the tri-state region of Tennessee, Mississippi, and Arkansas. However, after Mason returned from a trip to the now famous Azusa Street Revival in Los Angeles in early 1907, Mason experienced "the gifts of tongues," which, in his estimation, was proof of sanctification. Jones disagreed with this notion and after months of disagreement the two men split ways. Mason was elected head of the COGIC, while Jones renamed his group the Church of Christ, Holiness and remained in charge of most of the church's ministerial and financial operations. By the time of the mid-1920s, most of Jones' denomination's membership was concentrated in the states of Mississippi, Tennessee, and Arkansas. For further reference see, Anthea Bulter, *Women in the Church of God in Christ: Making a Sanctified World* (Chapel Hill, NC: University of North Carolina Press, 2007), 26-29 and George Eaton Simpson, "Black Pentecostalism in the United States," in *Phylon* 35, no. 2 (2nd Qtr. 1976): 208.

California in the 1910s and 1920s.⁵⁶ For instance, according to the 1915 journal of the Kansas District, a "colored" church was established in Hutchinson, KS. The district report stated the following,

> We are also getting a start among the colored people, a church having been organized in East Hutchinson, due to the faith and persistence of Brother B.C. Johnson, and which promises well. This work should enlist the prayers of the whole District as truly as should our missions in Africa ... The Holy Spirit, whose tenderest name is fulfilling His ministry ... ⁵⁷

The person named in the report, Buford C. Johnson, became the church's first pastor when it was officially organized in 1916. Within a year of its inception, Johnson had pushed the congregational membership roll to nineteen and oversaw a church whose property value stood at around $1,200.00. These numbers may seem miniscule, but the membership numbers and church property value was comparable to other white churches on the district. In fact, of the forty-eight churches on the district in 1917, twenty-seven had lower membership numbers than Hutchinson, Second CN. Moreover, in the same year, there were ten churches whose property value was less or equal to the black congregation in Hutchinson.⁵⁸

---

⁵⁶James Massey also claims that blacks did not join predominantly white holiness groups like the CN in the early 20th century because they usually focused on the individual's call to live a sanctified life that honors God and the divine will, while African Americans were more concerned with other issues that pertained to racial uplift, social equality, social survival, theological anthropology, racial unity, and the betterment of American society. For further discussion, see James Earl Massey, "Race Relations and the American Holiness Movement," *The Wesleyan Theological Journal* 31, no. 1 (Spring 1996): 43-46; Charles V. Hamilton, *The Black Preacher in America* (New York: William Morrow & Company, Inc., 1972), 110-169; John Brown Childs, *The Political Black Minister: A Study in Afro-American Politics and Religion* (Boston: G.K. Hall & Co., 1980), 120-138; Donald Dayton, *Discovering an Evangelical Heritage* (USA: Hendrickson Publishers, 2000) and Charles Edwin Jones, *Perfectionist Persuasion: The Holiness Movement and American Methodism, 1867-1936* (Lanham, MD: The Scarecrow Press, Inc., 2002), 62-78; Smith, 220-223, 234-238; George M. Marsden, *Understanding Fundamentalism and Evangelicalism* (Grand Rapids, MI: William B. Eerdmans Company, 1991), 70-71 and Winthrop S. Hudson and John Corrigan, ed., *Religion in America*, 6th ed. (Upper Saddle River, NJ: Prentice Hall, 1999), 333-334.

⁵⁷*Kansas District Church of the Nazarene, Sixth Annual Assembly Journal* (Aug.1915): 27. Church of the Nazarene Archives, Lenexa, KS. Although the beginnings of the congregation started in 1915, it wasn't until the next year that the district began to record the number of members and financial expenditures of the church. See *Kansas District Church of the Nazarene, Seventh Annual Assembly Journal* (Oct. 1916): 5, 36-39. Church of the Nazarene Archives, Lenexa, KS.

⁵⁸*Kansas District Church of the Nazarene, Eighth Annual Assembly Journal* (Sep. 1917): 29, 36-37, 40-41. Church of the Nazarene Archives, Lenexa, KS.

Throughout the 1910s and 1920s, Hutchinson, Second's congregational life remained relatively steady. Even though their membership numbers dropped to seven by 1928, their property value did not significantly decrease and one of their members was commissioned as a district deaconess, which was a lay female leader that was consecrated by their pastor and the district to assist with their church's ministries and evangelistic efforts, especially amongst the poor, sick, or dying.[59]

Aside from this, during the 1920s to the early 1930s, the church often sent a voting lay delegate and a Sunday School Superintendent to the yearly DA to vote and legislate on matters related to Christian education.[60] Moreover, Hutchinson, Second contributed to local youth evangelization among African Americans by establishing and maintaining a NYPS chapter.[61] For instance, in 1920, Hutchinson, Second, reported having seven members in its local NYPS (a low number no doubt) but the church was one of only sixteen churches on a district of 51 Nazarene congregations that reported having a NYPS chapter. Six years later, the church still had NYPS members and by doing this, they continued to provide a weekly Bible study and other youth related ministries in an effort to evangelize young African Americans in Hutchinson with the personal holiness message of the denomination.[62]

By performing such actions, members from Hutchinson, Second participated in district life and carried out the evangelistic and personal holiness mission of the denomination in a time when few were calling for the evangelization of African Americans. This "faithfulness" to the CN drew the attention and praise of white district leaders. On August 9, 1922, for instance, H.M. Chambers, the district superintendent of the Kansas District, asserted,

> As a result of earnest prayer and faith through a period of years, as well as by persistent effort and sacrifice, the second Church of the Nazarene (Colored) was organized in Hutchinson, Kas., and a neat building erected . . . A feeling that this work should be brought to the attention of Nazarenes generally, so that . . . this devoted band of loyal Nazarenes might be commended

---

[59]Cunningham, Ingersol, Raser, and Whitelaw, 262.

[60]*Kansas District Church of the Nazarene, Seventeenth Annual Assembly Journal* (Sept. 1926): 6-7. Church of the Nazarene Archives, Lenexa, KS and *Kansas District Church of the Nazarene, Nineteenth Annual Assembly Journal* (Sept. 1928), 7. Church of the Nazarene Archives, Lenexa, KS and *Kansas District Church of the Nazarene, Twenty-Fourth Annual Assembly* (Sept. 1933), 13-14. Church of the Nazarene Archives, Lenexa, KS.

[61]*Kansas District Church of the Nazarene, Seventeenth Annual Assembly Journal*, 6-7 and *Kansas District Church of the Nazarene, Nineteenth Annual Assembly Journal*, 6-7, 52-53.

[62]*Kansas District Church of the Nazarene, Seventeenth Annual Assembly Journal*, statistical index.

13   The Pioneer Era

through the columns of the HERALD for their faithfulness is our reason for writing this article.[63]

By the time that Hutchinson, Second was receiving such praise, another African American congregation was operating in Plainville, KS. According to Mendell Taylor, the church was founded in 1920 and was called Plainville, Second CN. When one looks at the district assembly minutes during the 1920's, Taylor's assertion seems to be correct. The minutes reveal that from 1926 to 1930 Ray E. Poole and Mrs. E.B. Heckley pastored the congregation and helped the church maintain no less than ten church and Sunday school members. Again, like Hutchinson, Second, such numbers sound small, but in 1926 the church had eleven church members and sixteen in Sunday school, while there were ten other white churches on the district who had equal or less church members and three who had less Sunday school members.[64]

In short, African American churches in Kansas, alongside other white congregations on the Kansas District, sustained Nazarene ministries, participated in district life, and maintained the life of their congregations in the late 1910s to the early 1930s. Moreover, although their churches were small, they worked to carry out the evangelistic and personal holiness message of the CN among those the denomination had largely forgotten to evangelize on a systematic level. This stress on personal holiness and evangelistic outreach came to define Nazarene life and like white congregations, this emphasis was carried out by the African American churches in Kansas and other black churches in the United States during this time.

For example, aside from the churches in Kansas, an African American woman named M.E. Palmer formed a congregation among blacks and whites in Pasadena, CA during the early to mid-1910s. In 1909, Palmer helped the racially mixed church—called Grace Church of the Nazarene—join the denomination in 1909 because of the CN's commitment to scriptural holiness. When the congregation joined, it only had nine members and didn't report having any Sunday school members or deaconesses. Also, Palmer and the church did not report any monies given to Sunday school expenses, missionary work, or other benevolences. However, by 1913, the situation changed. At the DA, the church reported having a church deaconess, a Sunday school superintendent, seventeen church members, sixteen

---

[63]H.M. Chambers, "Our Church and the American Negro," in *The Herald of Holiness* (August 9, 1922): 9. Church of the Nazarene Archives, Lenexa, KS. See also, Charles Edwin Jones, *Black Holiness: A Guide to the Study of Black Participation in Wesleyan Perfectionist and Glossolalic Pentecostal Movements* (Metuchen, N.J.: The Scarecrow Press, 1987), 72.

[64]*Kansas District Church of the Nazarene, Seventeenth Annual Assembly Journal* (Sept. 1926): 50. Nazarene Archives, Lenexa, KS; *Kansas District Church of the Nazarene, Nineteenth Annual Assembly Journal*, 6-9 and *Kansas District Church of the Nazarene, Twenty-First Annual Assembly Journal* (Aug. 1930), 4-10, 52-54. Church of the Nazarene Archives, Lenexa, KS.

Sunday school members, and a total of seven voting members that voted and legislated on church matters at the California District Assembly. In addition, the church's property value was three thousand dollars, which was an average amount on the district, and reported a total church giving of nine hundred and twenty-four dollars for the year.[65]

Judging from this, it would seem that Palmer and her church did not face racial or gender stigma[66] from white leaders and churches on the district. Operating within this environment alongside white congregations, they sustained and participated in Nazarene ministries and carried on the holiness message of the denomination. Moreover, Grace Church contributed to the decision-making process on the district. Thus, Palmer and other church members at Grace Church of the Nazarene, alongside other white congregations, were active contributors to the CN on the California District in the early to mid-1910s and helped to spread the message among African Americans when few in the denomination were attempting such a task.

Yet, this participation by Palmer and her congregation did not last long. Sometime between 1914 and 1915, Palmer was also able to convince her congregation to leave the CN when theological disagreements arose between her and the denomination. According to an unpublished report, Palmer stated that the "flesh" was possessed by unclean spirits and that one had "to enter into a physical, mental and spiritual struggle" to rid the body and soul of such unrighteousness. She went on to note that some of her members had been "saved" from the condition after experiencing physical "contortions," which often made them into "virtually maniacs." After making these claims public, the CN made it clear that they disagreed with her

---

[65] *Southern California District Church of the Nazarene, Third Annual Assembly Journal*, (June 1909): no pagination. Church of the Nazarene Archives, Kansas City, MO and *Southern California District Church of the Nazarene, Eighth Annual Assembly Journal* (Aug. 1914): no pagination. Church of the Nazarene Archives, Lenexa, KS.

[66] In the first two decades of the denomination's existence, it was not uncommon for women to be ordained as ministers and evangelists and for them to organize and lead both domestic mission stations and congregations. In fact, Susie Stanley, in her monograph entitled, *Holy Boldness: Women Preachers' Autobiographies and the Sanctified Self*, notes that in 1920, there were 320 ordained female preachers, evangelists, and ministers who were actively participating and leading in the denomination. This number is quite staggering when one considers Stanley's assertion that in the same year, only 180 ordained women were actively ministering in ten non-Wesleyan/Holiness denominations. For further reference on the licensing and ordaining of women in the CN and other Wesleyan/Holiness bodies see Susie Stanley, *Holy Boldness: Women Preachers' Autobiographies and the Sanctified Self* (Knoxville, TN: University of Tennessee Press, 2002), 106-111.

theological pronouncements and because of this ideological rift, Palmer, along with most of her members, withdrew from the denomination.[67]

Around the same time that African American Nazarenes were evangelizing, ministering, and contributing to denominational life in Kansas and California, West Indians in New York City, one of the few places where the denomination continued to have an urban presence by the late 1920s and early 1930s. How they came into the fold of the CN and contributed to the mission and vision of the denomination addressed.

The Beginnings of Afro-Caribbean Congregations and Evangelization in Brooklyn

In 1902, a white Nazarene Canadian minister named Rev. George E. Miller established an urban storefront mission in Brooklyn that eventually became an organized church called Miller Memorial Church of the Nazarene in 1914.[68] Miller founded the mission and evangelized whites that lived in the area, but over time, it became increasingly populated by the growing number of black Barbadian immigrants that were already affiliated with other holiness bodies before migrating to the Bedford-Stuyvesant (Bed-Stuy) neighborhood of Brooklyn in the 1900s and 1910s. For instance, according to a 1977 Miller Memorial church celebration booklet, many of the Afro-Bajans (i.e. black Barbadians) that joined Miller's mission in its early years "were primarily members of a movement known as the 'Christian Mission of Barbados, West Indies'," a movement on the island that stressed the primacy of Christians to live a holy and sanctified life.[69] Aside from this, many who joined Miller's worshipping body were affiliated with the Pilgrim Holi-

---

[67]This split happened sometime around 1914-1915, because after 1914, the church no longer appeared in the Southern California District Minutes. For further details surrounding the church's withdrawal see, "Creeds Make Split in Church: Grace Nazarene Withdraws From General Body of Organization," (Undated document): 1. Church of the Nazarene Archives, Lenexa, KS and *Southern California District Church of the Nazarene, Ninth Annual Assembly Journal* (Aug. 1915): 1-10. Church of the Nazarene Archives, Lenexa, KS.

[68]Rev. G. Howard Rowe, to Dr. R.W. Hurn, 29 November 1972, transcript in the hand of Rev. G. Howard Rowe, Church of the Nazarene Archives, Lenexa, KS; Mrs. Edward Mann, to Dr. R.W. Hurn, 10 October 1972, transcript in the hand of Mrs. Edward Mann, Church of the Nazarene Archives, Lenexa, KS and Clarence Jacobs, "Miller Memorial, 1972 Black Church Information, 6 October 1972," Church of the Nazarene Archives, Lenexa, KS.

[69]Clarence Jacobs, "The Miller Memorial Church of the Nazarene: Dedication of Our Church," (1977), 2. Church of the Nazarene Archives, Lenexa, KS.

ness Church (hereafter referred to as PHC), which today is called the Wesleyan Church, after it joined the Wesleyan Methodist Church in 1968.[70]

In its infancy, the PHC was comprised of a variety of persons and ministers across the United States that were driven by a similar theological and ecclesiastical issue as Nazarenes—primarily the emphasis on personal holiness and mission work.[71] It was this concern that led representatives and leaders from the PHC to build on the work of holiness preachers that had been holding "full-salvation" services and starting mission stations on Barbados as early as 1891. For instance, in 1890, Rev. Samuel H. Hayley, "a retired Wesleyan minister from Barbados," made an appeal at the "convention of the Christian Alliance" for workers to begin holding holiness meetings in the West Indies and Barbados. Along with Bayley, several decided to heed the call such as Rev. Richmond Penny, "Sis." I.D. Haines, "Deacon" J.F. Guild, Rev. J. Harman, "Bro. S. A. Ross, and Rev. Baily. It is unclear whether or not these persons preached alongside Bayley when he began having holiness meetings in 1891 in Barbados, but what we do know is that he helped to establish the Immanuel Mission in 1892 in Bridgetown. For years, he maintained the work with the assistance of a "national minister" and over time it became an official congregation of the PHC when the congregation united with the denomination in 1923.[72]

A decade after 1892, white PHC missionaries such as "Rev. and Mrs. C.O. Moulten," Rev. James M. Taylor, and Rev. Ralph G. Finch began holding holiness meetings on the island. They preached at various locations on Barbados over the next decade and their labors eventually helped to lay the foundation for another PHC congregation in 1912. Tony Wynton, an unofficial

---

[70]J. Gilbertson Stuart, personal interview Brandon Winstead, Brooklyn, New York, September 18, 2009 and Ludwick Jones, personal interview Brandon Winstead, Brooklyn, New York, September 18, 2009. Brandon Winstead's Private Collection, Kansas City, KS.

[71]T. Rennie Warburton, "Holiness Religion: An Anomaly of Sectarian Typologies," *The Journal for the Scientific Study of Religion*, 8, no. 1 (Spring 1969): 132-137. The denomination adopted the name the Pilgrim Holiness Church in 1919. Two years earlier, most of the independent churches and associations in California, the Midwest, and Caribbean that eventually joined the PHC came together under the banner of International Apostolic Holiness Church. However, it wasn't until 1919 that the churches and leaders, primarily Seth Rees, a former Nazarene minister, officially joined together and adopted the title, Pilgrim Holiness Church. For further reference, see Smith 274-281.

[72]Webmaster, "Our Church, Our History: The History of the Christian Mission," Welches Christian Mission, http://welchescm.com/ourchurch history.html. (accessed March 13, 2011) and Annie Eubanks, *Pilgrim Missions in the Caribbean Area: Adult Missionary Society Programs and Field Studies* (Indianapolis: Pilgrim Holiness Church, 1962), 31.

historian of the PHC in the Caribbean, describes how their missionary efforts led to the founding of the congregation:

> These American pioneers carved out the foundation for our Pilgrim Holiness Church, which was organized as a permanent assembly in 1912. The first assembly room, known as 'the Outlet Hall', and located at the corner of Swan and Lucas Streets in Bridgetown in a 15' x 40' upstairs room over a rum shop was rented at one dollar a month.[73]

Wynton goes on to note that over the course of the next two decades, numerous other churches were started in and around Bridgetown and that thousands of black Barbadians joined these congregations:

> The church, within seventeen years of spiritual toil, recorded the establishment of twenty-nine congregations and mission points in nine parishes. The parishes of St. James and St. Andrew were the two exceptions. The Sunday school enrollment reached twenty-five hundred (2,500), and the church membership reached one thousand, two hundred and eighty-eight (1,288) persons. This period 1912-1929 is regarded as the best harvest season in our church history.[74]

Some of those that were a part of this growth or the Christian Mission, left the island, migrated to New York, and joined Miller's mission. One of those who did so was William Murray Greene. After Greene migrated to New York and joined Miller's mission in the early 1910s, he was asked to assist Miller with his work in Brooklyn. Greene, as a former Barbadian teacher, helped Miller to expand the ministry of the newly formed congregation by "serving" both white and West Indian members with "great zeal, love, and compassion," by assisting with many of the day-to-day operations of the church, and by helping to deal with the constant complaints of white members who were uncomfortable worshipping next to West Indians.[75]

After the congregation was incorporated as a Nazarene church, Miller and Greene continued to work together as a ministerial team that pastored white Brooklynites and black Barbadians.[76] However, after the death of Miller in 1921, Greene became the senior minister of the congregation, which had become predominantly black. At the same time, it was also one of the

---

[73] Tony Lynton, "Historical Sketch of Barbados District," The Wesleyan Holiness Church in the Caribbean: The Source Information for the Official Website, http://vikratistos.com/bdh.html. (accessed November 13, 2011); W. Burghardt Turner and Joyce Moore Turner, ed., *Richard B. Moore: Caribbean Militant in Harlem: Collected Writings, 1920-1972* (Bloomington, IN: Indiana University Press, 1992), 22-23 and Eubanks, 31.

[74] Ibid.

[75] "Miller Memorial Church Closing 30th Anniversary," *New York Amsterdam News*, 22 February 1936 and "Rev. Greene Dead; Pastored Miller Church," *New York Amsterdam News*, 29 August 1959.

[76] "Nazarene Pastors Return," *The Brooklyn Daily Eagle*, 16 May 1921.

largest and strongest churches on the New York District, both in terms of congregational membership and its commitment to local evangelism through their Sunday school and NYPS ministries. For example, according to the 1922 district minutes, the church had a congregational membership of 128, which was second only to John Wesley CN, a predominantly white congregation in Brooklyn that had 200 congregational members. In addition to this, Miller reported having the second highest Sunday school membership on the district with one hundred and forty members enrolled throughout the year. Moreover, they had the largest NYPS chapter on the district with a total membership of 48.[77]

By the next DA, Miller Memorial's numerical presence on the New York District remained one of the strongest on the district. Their congregational membership stood at 128, while they retained the highest NYPS[78] membership and the second highest total in Sunday school membership (158) on a district with twenty-nine churches.[79] This high number in Sunday school membership as opposed to congregational membership was not unique to Miller Memorial or any other Nazarene congregation in New York or around the country. According to denominational historians, Sunday school membership for all Nazarene churches during this period remained higher than church membership in large part because of the evangelistic focus of Sunday school ministries and the individual requirements for church membership. Sunday school was primarily intended to evangelize youth and adults with the message of personal holiness. If, over time, they accepted the message, then they could choose to become a member of a local congregation. However, to be a church member, one had to avoid consuming liquor and alcohol, using tobacco, working on the Sabbath, reading "secular" literature, wearing "immodest dress" such as gold and jewelry, taking the name of God in vain, and attending the circus, theatre, and ballroom.

Aside from this, church members were required to contribute to the ministry of the congregation, adhere to all the doctrines of the denomination, faithfully attend all worship services, evangelize others, and testify to

---

[77]*New York District Church of the Nazarene, Fifteenth Annual Assembly Journal* (April 1922) 42-43. Church of the Nazarene Archives, Lenexa, KS and *Brooklyn Daily Almanac: A Book of Information, General of the World, and Special of New York City and Long Island, 1921* (New York: Allied Publishers, 1921), 236.

[78]During the same year, at the General Assembly of the denomination, the denomination decided to form the General Nazarene Young's People's Society (NYPS). This decision required Nazarene churches to organize their youth ministries under a local NYPS chapter and report their membership numbers to their district NYPS every year and to the General NYPS every four years. For further reference see, Purkiser, 36-37.

[79]*New York District Church of the Nazarene, Sixteenth Annual Assembly Journal* (April 1923), 41-42. Church of the Nazarene Archives, Lenexa, KS.

having experienced the second work of grace—sanctification. If one performed all these functions, then they could join the church. Thus, these ethical standards, combined with the doctrinal requirements of the denomination, deterred many Sunday school members (whether black or white) from joining a local congregation and it probably contributed to why West Indians, like white Nazarene congregations in New York and around the country, had a larger proportion of those who attended Sunday school than church members.[80]

For instance, in 1923, large white Nazarene congregations like East Rockaway CN in East Rockaway, NY had a church membership of 53, but 163 Sunday School members. Similarly, John Wesley CN in Brooklyn, NY had 135 church members and a Sunday school membership of 158. Moreover, other average sized white congregations resembled similar patterns—Springfield CN in Springfield, NY (44 church members and 137 Sunday school members), Syracuse CN in Syracuse, NY (45 Sunday school members and 34 church members), and New Berlin CN in New Berlin, NY (68 Sunday school members as opposed to 31 church members).[81] With these numbers in mind, the West Indian churches in New York were like their white peers in that they continued to evangelize and teach numerous individuals in their Sunday schools but their work did not always translate to having an equal amount of church membership.

In the midst of this, Miller Memorial also maintained a strong presence on the district in terms of its monetary giving to missionary work. In 1923, Miller gave a total of twenty-three dollars to the Department of Home Missions and $149.34 to Foreign Missions, which was given largely to support missionary labors in Barbados.[82] Because of these evangelistic and financial contributions, the DS took a moment to publicly acknowledge the work done at Miller Memorial at the District Assembly. At the ecclesiastical gathering, H.M. Moore, the DS, noted that Miller Memorial was committed to "reaching" out to those in the local community and to supporting missionary work in Barbados, the native home of many of Miller Memorial's members.[83]

When the district minutes were reported six years later, Miller Memorial still retained its commitment to holiness evangelism as well as remaining one of the strongest churches on the district. Out of thirty-five churches on the district it was second in total church membership with a total of 75 members (congregational membership was lower because many white

---

[80]Stan Ingersol, singersol@nazarene.org. "Sunday School Attendance for the Church of the Nazarene." Private e-mail message to Brandon Winstead. 10 October 2010 and Cunningham, Ingersol, Raser, and Whitelaw, 449-450.

[81]*New York District Church of the Nazarene, Sixteenth Annual Assembly Journal*, 41-42.

[82]Ibid., 41-42.

[83]Ibid., 23.

congregational members had left to join other white Nazarene churches in the area). The church also had 129 people on its Sunday school roll, twenty-eight active members who participated in the weekly functions of the NYPS, and seventeen women who were members of the Women's Foreign Missionary Society (hereafter referred to as WFMS)—a female led missionary society that almost every Nazarene church and district possessed in the United States by the end of the 1920s.[84] Along with other members of the congregation, Miller Memorial's WFMS contributed fourteen hundred dollars to church building projects, gave money to certain district, national, and international budgets, and supported missionaries in Barbados.[85]

Throughout the 1920s, these congregations also participated and contributed (alongside other white Nazarenes) to the decision making-processes of the New York District. In fact, ever since 1914, when Miller Memorial became incorporated as a church, Greene and other members of the congregation sat on district boards and councils. Moreover, by the time the church entered the second decade of its existence, it had several ordained ministers on the district role and sent voting delegates to the DA to vote on matters related to missionary work, Sunday school education, and evangelism. For instance, before 1924, Miller Memorial had three licensed deaconesses on the district rolls, Mrs. Margarette Campbell, Miss Beatrice Robinson, and Mrs. Rhoda Gittens—women who could assist with the teaching, educational, preaching, evangelistic, and social ministries of the church.[86] At the same time, the church had a voting member on the district's NYPS and sent several lay delegates to vote at the 1923 New York District Assembly. Five years later, when the district convened again for its annual meeting, James Prescott represented the church's NYPS and Joseph Ford was mentioned as the church's Sunday school superintendent. Furthermore, William Greene sat on the Foreign Missions Committee and Gertrude Miller, Louise Crawford, and Helen Rouse were sent as lay delegates for Miller Memorial.[87]

Likewise, by 1933, the church still maintained an active leadership presence on the predominantly white New York District. They sent voting NYPS, Sunday school, and WFMS delegates to the DA to vote and help decide on issues related to youth and adult evangelization and how the district would delegate and spend money on foreign missions. In addition to this, men and

---

[84]Cunningham, Ingersol, Raser, and Whitelaw, 262-265.

[85]*New York District Church of the Nazarene, Twenty-Second Annual Assembly Journal*, (April 1929), no pagination. Church of the Nazarene Archives, Lenexa, KS.

[86]*New York District Church of the Nazarene, Sixteenth Annual Assembly Journal*, 6-7 and Smith, 318.

[87]*New York District Church of the Nazarene, Twenty-First Annual Assembly Journal* (April 1928), 6-9. Church of the Nazarene Archives, Lenexa, KS.

women from Miller Memorial like Louis and Grace Reed sat on the Missions Committee and the Campmeeting Committee, two committees designed to create and develop worship services and ministries throughout the year that would assist with local and international evangelism. Moreover, Jennie Beatty, a long-time black female member of Miller Memorial, was a voting member of the Social Welfare and Orphanage committee and was voted as the district deaconess by her white and black peers on the New York District. By accepting this position, Beatty lead the deaconesses on the district in how they would better "do the Lord's work by visiting the sick and afflicted, relieving the distressed, and encourages the discourage ones..."[88]

During this time, Greene and his congregation also took it upon themselves to begin another West Indian church in the neighborhood of Bedford-Stuyvesant. The church was originally started as an urban mission in 1917 and was housed on Rochester Avenue. Rev. Greene, along with a minister named Jonathan Foster, began the Rochester Avenue Mission as a way to spread the evangelistic mission and theological teachings of the denomination among Barbadian immigrants. Even though it remained an urban mission for a few years, it was organized as Beulah CN in 1923 with forty charter members. At the District Assembly of that year, Moore recounted how the church started and expressed his expectations about the future prosperity of the congregation:

> The Rochester Avenue Mission has moved over on Utica Avenue and purchased a building of their own. In October we organized them as Beulah Church of the Nazarene with forty charter members. The work has been looked after ... by brethren from G.E. Miller church ... They have already outgrown their building and are expecting to build an addition to accommodate the people.[89]

In some ways, his enthusiasm regarding the future of the church was garnered by the fact that Greene, Foster, and the original Barbadians immigrants who formed the nucleus of the church's membership, were committed to strengthening the life and vitality of Beulah. People and families such as Simeon Harris, "Sister" M. Atwell, "Sister" Tyrell, "Sister" Thornhill, "Sister" Prescot, the Derrel's, the Mayen's, the Thorp's, and the Brathwaite's combined their financial resources and committed their time to establishing a "holiness" church that resembled those they had attended in Barbados. In a somewhat hagiographic interpretation of how this commitment lead to

---

[88]*New York District Church of the Nazarene, Twenty-Sixth Annual Assembly Journal* (April 1933), 3-4, 38. Church of the Nazarene Archives, Lenexa, KS.

[89]*New York District Church of the Nazarene, Sixteenth Annual Assembly Journal*, 24 and E. Albert Brathwaite, "50th Anniversary Celebration Booklet: The Beulah Church of the Nazarene," (unpublished paper, 1974), 2-3. Brandpn Winstead's Private Collection, Kansas City, KS.

the founding of the church, E. Albert Brathwaite, one of the descendants of the original families, claimed the following:

> Incorporated in the year of our Lord 1924, it was earlier organized by a few migrating families mostly from the island of Barbados. Their faith in God was firmly established in their living before coming to this land. They gave sacrificially of their time and money for the progress of the Church and its work. They taught holiness in the Sunday school, preached holiness from the pulpit, appealing to all to serve the Lord with holiness of heart. And the Church grew spiritually, and numerically.[90]

Brathwaite's assertion points to the reality that members of Beulah were interested in preserving their commitment to teaching and spreading the doctrine of personal holiness, much like their counterparts at Miller Memorial. Since its inception, the church was organized and led by Afro-Bajans who wanted to make sure they taught "scriptural holiness" in their congregation and participated in the evangelistic mission of the CN. Thus, shortly after the church was incorporated, the church called Levi Franklin, a Barbadian immigrant and licensed minister at Miller Memorial CN, to lead and pastor the congregation.[91]

Franklin, like Greene, was educated and before he came to pastor Beulah CN in 1925, had pastored holiness churches in the country of Panama and in the southern and midwestern portions of the United States.[92] As a minister, his peers and members knew Franklin as a "very nice fellow" who was diligent in spreading the message of personal holiness and challenging his congregants to grow deeper in their faith. This description of Franklin was emphasized in the church's 50th Anniversary Celebration Booklet.

> Rev. Levi Franklin, Pastor, was a meticulous sheperd (sic). He was firm, often dogmatic, but always a consistent man of God, preaching the Word through illness and through hardship, watchful of his charge and obedient to God. He warned often against the "sham, shoddy, and potash" of a hypocritical religious walk, but let the people know his heart of love in his fervent prayers for them.[93]

Under Franklin's "firm" leadership, the church contributed to spreading and discipling other West Indians with the message of scriptural holiness by sustaining strong church, Sunday school, NYPS, and WFMS membership numbers. For instance, in 1928, the church had a total membership of forty-

---

[90]Brathwaite, 2.

[91]"Church Honors Levi Franklin," *New York Amsterdam News*, 11 February 1950 and Randolph Holder, "Beulah Church of the Nazarene, 1972 Black Church Information, 11 October 1972," Church of Nazarene Archives, Lenexa, KS.

[92]Brathwaite, 3 and "Church Honors Levi Franklin," *New York Amsterdam News*, 11 February 1950.

[93]J. Gilbertson Stuart, personal interview with Brandon Winstead, and Brathwaite, 5.

one, which was the fourteenth highest total on the district. They also possessed a Sunday school enrollment of one hundred and ten—only seven other churches held a higher membership. Moreover, with twenty members on the NYPS rolls, Beulah boasted a higher number of youth that participated in weekly bible studies and other youth ministries than many other churches on the district (Beulah had the fifth highest NYPS membership out of the thirty-four churches on the district).

When the DA gathered the following year, Beulah still maintained consistent membership numbers and faithfully supported educational and evangelistic ministries of the congregation. They had almost forty congregational members and even though they did not report their Sunday school numbers to the district, they did report a gain of three members to their NYPS and reported a WFMS membership of twenty-five, which was the tenth largest number on the district. Likewise, by 1933, the church still had 23 NYPS members that regularly attended NYPS gatherings and 38 WFMS members that supported local and foreign missionary work.[94]

Aside from this, Beulah, like other churches on the New York District, continued to give substantial amounts of money to church budgets and to local and international missions. For instance, in 1928, the church spent $2,342.00 on building improvements and gave $4,067.00 to support educational, missionary, and community ministries, which was the second highest on the district. They also sent care packages to missionaries overseas, sent money to help support Native American ministries, and gave over thirty dollars to support missionary work on their native island of Barbados.[95] At the following DA, Beulah reported giving money to Native American ministries and contributed five thousand six hundred and fifty-two dollars to the local, district, and general budgets, which was the sixth highest amount on district of thirty-five churches. Not only that, but they also financial supported missionary work in Barbados and other locations in the West Indies.[96]

Moreover, in the late 1920s and early 1930s Beulah voted at district assemblies and sat on district boards and committees. In 1928, Levi Franklin sat on the Home Missions Committee, which, as the title implies, was designed to make decisions on how churches would evangelize people on the

---

[94]Church of the Nazarene Research Center, "Membership Status and Attendance of Beulah Church of the Nazarene—New York District." http://app.nazarene.org/FindAChurch/viewReport.jsp?reportId=21196&sIDType=rpt&orgId=4320. (accessed 04 August 2010).

[95]*New York District Church of the Nazarene, Twenty-First Annual Assembly Journal*, statistical index.

[96]*New York District Church of the Nazarene, Twenty-Second Annual Assembly Journal*, statistical index.

New York District.⁹⁷ At the next annual gathering, Beulah sent lay delegates to vote on a variety of district matters. Also, Franklin switched his committee membership to the Publishing Interests Committee and Rhoda Gittens reported to the New York District as Beulah's WFMS representative.⁹⁸

By 1933, Beulah still contributed to district leadership. At the DA, Beulah sent a voting lay delegate and had their Sunday school Superintendent vote on matters related to Christian evangelization and education. In addition to this, the church also had their NYPS and WFMS leaders in attendance to weigh in on how their local chapters could contribute to the overall mission and goal of each ministry. Furthermore, Rev. Franklin sat on the Missions Committee, alongside others from Miller Memorial and white pastors and laity throughout the New York District.

This type of participation and contribution to the personal holiness and evangelistic mission of the denomination among West Indians in Brooklyn, however, did not end at Beulah or Memorial. It also extended to Free Gospel CN, another West Indian congregation that was started in the Bedford-Stuyvesant neighborhood of Brooklyn in 1929. When the congregation and its first pastor, David King (who was also a black Barbadian) reported to the District Assembly during its first year of existence, it reported having a small membership of twenty-eight.

Despite their small size, they were committed to fully participating as a West Indian congregation on a predominantly white Nazarene district. They sent two voting delegates, King and "Miss" Keturah Pilgram, to the DA and James Moseley was sent as the church's Sunday school representative. They also gave funds to missionary work in Barbados and the West Indies, paid their district budgets, and gave to other district benevolences.⁹⁹ Likewise, four years later, Free Gospel sent a voting delegate to the DA. They also sent a representative from their local NYPS, Sunday school, and WFMS gave reports of their ministries and were provided the opportunity, like white representatives, to legislate and discuss on matters related to each district ministry.¹⁰⁰

Contributions to these ministries transpired because Free Gospel maintained local Sunday school, NYPS, and WFMS chapters. In 1930, for example, the church had an average Sunday school attendance of 50 and a NYPS and WFMS membership of 22 and 28. Three years later, similar numbers still remained. While the church had a total membership of 31, they still had

⁹⁷*New York District Church of the Nazarene, Twenty-First Annual Assembly Journal*, 8-9.

⁹⁸*New York District Church of the Nazarene, Twenty-Second Annual Assembly Journal*, 6-9.

⁹⁹Ibid, 8-9 and J. Gilbertson Stuart, personal interview with Brandon Winstead.

¹⁰⁰*New York District Church of the Nazarene, Twenty-Sixth Annual Assembly Journal*, 3-12, 20-21.

21 WFMS members, an average Sunday school attendance of 50 and a NYPS membership of 24. By maintaining such numbers, they attempted to reach out to black immigrants in their community with the message of personal holiness and provide an avenue for them to join the church.[101]

At the same time that these contributions and commitment to Nazarene ministries transpired, some Afro-Caribbeans sought to reach out and "win" others by giving to the "needy" in their community. For instance, when reflecting on the early days of Beulah's congregational life, Braithwaite noted:

> The outreach of the congregation at 31 Utica Avenue included an annual Flower Service to benefit the needy, a "Pound Service," in which members contributed a pound of foodstuff to distribute to the poor, and Open Air Meetings, to bring the Word to the unchurched. Bandages were prepared for use in hospitals, while the Sunday School and Young People's Society grew nearly, winning boys and girls to the Lord and swelling the ranks of the members. Everyone looked forward to Anniversary Day and the parade gave another avenue of witness with the church's banners.[102]

As the quote reveals, "witnessing" and "winning" others not only included giving to the "needy" but also through the church's active contribution to an annual Sunday school parade that was held every year in Brooklyn during the late 1920s and early 1930s. At this parade, Beulah's children and leaders, along with other large African American churches and youth organizations like Concord Baptist Church, Berean Baptist Church, Bethel African Methodist Episcopal Church, the Boys and Girls Scouts, would create large floats and elaborate banners inscribed with religious scriptures and slogans. As the floats and banners paraded through the streets, youth would march beside them and sing religious songs as community and political leaders watched their performances. In June of 1930, the *New York Amsterdam News* captured the pageantry of one of these parades. The periodical's detailed description of the event is worth quoting at length:

> Thousands thronged the thoroughfares of Brooklyn last Thursday afternoon, some waving flags, other cheering as an unprecedented number of Sunday school children marched to the even tempo of "Onward Christian Soldiers," the occasion being the annual parade of the Brooklyn Sunday School Union ... this one hundred and first, witnessed 310 Sunday schools with a number

---

[101]Church of the Nazarene Research Center, "Membership Status and Attendance of Free Gospel Church of the Nazarene—New York District." http://app.nazarene.org/FindAChurch/viewReport.jsp?reportId=21196&orgId=4318. (accessed 04 August 2010).

[102]Brathwaite, 3. *New York District Church of the Nazarene, Sixteenth Annual Assembly Journal,* 24 and Bowman, 15. According to Clarence Taylor, Beulah was like many other holiness and Pentecostal churches in Brooklyn in the mid to late 1920s and early 1930s in that they attempted to meet some of the physical needs of those in their communities. For further reference Taylor, 53-65.

estimated to be over one hundred thousand children stepping to the tune of band and drum corps . . .

This vast number was divided into 26 sections and those in which children of the group made very impressive showings were the Stuyvesant and the Clinton sections. In the former, there were St. Philip's P.E., Brown Memorial Baptist, Bethel A.M.E., Berean Baptist, Bethany Baptist, Beulah Church of the Nazarene and Mount Sinat Baptist . . . Each of these churches carried impressive looking floats and banners, inscribed on some of which were such lofty precepts as "Lord Save Us, We Perish, Hark the Herald Angles Sing," etc . . . These groups were reviewed by Mayor James Walker and other city officials since it is the custom to award prizes to the Sunday schools making the best showing.[103]

As the article alludes to, these churches, along with Beulah, provided a public display of religious commitment to young people and children in the borough of Brooklyn. Not only that, but it shows that Beulah joined with other black churches to create a religious event where municipal leaders could recognize how African American and West Indian churches were celebrating one aspect of collective black religious life in Brooklyn. To state the matter differently, Beulah, like those such as Berean, St. Philips, and Bethany not only sought to "witness" to others, but to also celebrate the religious lives of children in a way that could not be fully expressed or appreciated within the four walls of the church. Furthermore, Beulah's involvement represents their dedication during the late 1920s and early 1930s to "witness" to others beyond the domains of their church.

This religious and evangelistic "dedication" was fueled in part by Beulah's ongoing commitment to minister to children, youth, and adults. As it was mentioned previously, Beulah, and other West Indian Nazarene churches maintained active Sunday school chapters after they were organized in an effort to evangelize and disciple young people in their communities.[104] In 1932, for instance, Miller Memorial reported having a total of 140

---

[103]"Sunday School Kiddies' Parade, Again Made Splendid Showing Among Great Throng of Marchers," *New York Amsterdam News*, 11 June 1930. See also, Brathwaite, 4.

[104]This assertion is bolstered by a report by The Brooklyn Federation of Churches. In the report, the interdenominational Protestant body stated that the black Nazarene congregations were committed to outreach to local youth by maintaining vital youth Sunday school ministries. For further reference see, Brooklyn Federation of Churches, *The 1932 Brooklyn Church Year Book* (Brooklyn, NY: Brooklyn Federation of Churches, 1933), 10, Box 9, Folder 1, The Brooklyn Historical Society, New York (Brooklyn). See also, Louis B. Bryan, "Concord Baptist Church Sunday-School," 1-2, June 1937, Federal Writers' Project, Reel 2, Folder B, Schomburg Center for Research in Black Culture, New York (Harlem) and Brooklyn Federation of Churches, *Brooklyn Protestantism, 1930-1945: A Study of Social Changes and Church Trends*

Sunday school members, while Beulah had over 70 members that attended Sunday school.[105] At the same time, Free Gospel had a Sunday school attendance of 55 and many of those were youth and children.[106] A year later, the church had a similar record of attendance, while Miller Memorial and Beulah each had 140 and 197 who were enrolled in Sunday school classes.[107]

This commitment to Sunday school is just one example of how West Indians sought to carry out the evangelistic mission of the denomination during the 1920s and early 1930s among black immigrants in New York City. Through maintaining such traditional Nazarene ministries like NYPS and WFMS, black Nazarenes in Brooklyn sought to evangelize those in their communities in a time when the denomination was foregoing national black evangelization. Not only that, West Indian Nazarenes also extending the presence of their congregations and the denomination in New York by giving to black Barbadians and West Indians that were poor and impoverished through collecting food and raising money, by maintaining an active deaconess ministry, and by uplifting the religious and cultural accomplishments of black children in the borough of Brooklyn. Aside from this, at the international level, they assisted Nazarene hospitals in addressing medical needs and supported missionary work at home and in the Caribbean. Thus, even though they did not attempt to address some of the systemic racial, political, and economic issues that shaped and impacted blacks in their communities and in the Diaspora, they attempted, at various points, to "reach" out in a fashion that was not limited to personal piety but in a way that was spiritually, culturally, and physically relevant to black immigrants in their communities and for other persons around the globe.

Moreover, like the African American churches in Kansas, the ministerial activities of Beulah, Miller, and Free Gospel placed them as active partici-

---

made by The Committee for Cooperative Field Research for The Brooklyn Church and Mission Federation and Cooperating Denominations (Brooklyn, NY: Brooklyn Federation of Churches, 1946), 71-77, Box 5, Folder 1, The Brooklyn Historical Society, New York (Brooklyn).

[105]Brooklyn Federation of Churches, *The 1932 Brooklyn Church Year Book*, 156.

[106]Church of the Nazarene Research Center, "Membership Status and Attendance of Free Gospel Church of the Nazarene—New York District."

[107]In the 1920s, black Nazarene congregations, like white churches in New York and around the country, continued to have higher Sunday school membership than total congregational membership. Of course, like before, this unequal pattern was largely caused by the evangelistic emphasis of Sunday schools and the moral, ethical, and theological requirements for church membership. For further reference see Church of the Nazarene Research Center, "Membership Status and Attendance of Beulah Church of the Nazarene—New York District" and Church of the Nazarene Research Center, "Membership Status and Attendance of Community Worship Center—New York District." http://app.nazarene.org/FindAChurch/viewReport.jsp?reportId=21196&orgId=4331. (accessed 04 August 2010).

pants in how the denominational grew and expanded in one of America's largest urban centers before the CN completed its first twenty-five years of existence. Not only that, but their commitment to participate in district leadership alongside other white congregations allowed Afro-Caribbeans to bolster the vitality of the CN in New York as they helped decide how various ministries and committees on the district would evangelize, minister, and disciple those in and around New York. As such, it enabled them, like African Americans who helped spread the evangelistic message of the denomination in Hutchinson, to become agents and participants in the development of the CN in the United States in a period when the denomination did not systematically evangelize blacks. By doing this, both West Indians and African Americans, from two different geographical locations and ethnic backgrounds, embraced the message and mission of the denomination and laid the foundation for black Nazarene life before the CN closed the chapter on its first twenty-five years of existence.

Chapter Two

From the Midwest to the Northeast: African American and West Indian Ministry in Kansas and New York, 1934–1946

Continued Black Nazarene Contributions in Kansas and Brooklyn

By the time the 1930s began, African Americans in Kansas and Afro-Caribbeans in New York City set poised to continue their contribution to denominational life and the evangelistic and holiness mission of the CN. Their earlier efforts of sitting on district committees, evangelizing those in their communities and maintaining Nazarene ministries had placed various black ethnic as active participants alongside their white peers in the earlier stages of the denomination's growth. As the denomination would grow numerically and as leaders around the country continued to articulate the importance of evangelizing the world with the message of personal holiness, this participation would continue.

Before the beginning of the 1930s, the denomination's total membership stood around 63,000 members. However, by 1936 that number more than doubled to 136,227. Also, from 1932 to 1936, Sunday schools increased from 202,908 to 270,531 (33%) and NYPS membership for the entire denomination expanded to 56,934, which was a 62% increase from 1932. Furthermore, total WFMS membership went from 24,880 to 37,452 during the same period.¹ Likewise, by 1946, the total membership of the denomination in the United States and throughout other places around the globe numbered 197,502 and Sunday school attendance stood at 225,639.² At the same time, WFMS grew to 40,975 in the United States and giving for foreign missions rose from a total of $731,923 in the period from 1936-1940 to $1,389,824 for the years between 1940-1944, which was an improvement of 90%.³

Of course, as these gains took place, denominational leaders continued to preach, teach, and advocate for the importance of evangelizing the world and living a holy life. Like previous decades, ecclesiastical heads believed that the main goals of the denomination were to reach the masses with the personal holiness message of the Bible that called one to shun "worldly" sins such as immodest dress, public bathing, unholy amusements, and other personal "immorality" and in turn, live a "sanctified" life so that one could evangelize others in the name of Jesus Christ.⁴

This type of ecclesiastical and theological emphasis was exemplified in a December 1937 issue of the *Herald of Holiness*. In it, the Missionary Secretary for the denomination, C. Warren Jones, admonished Nazarenes to develop a passion to evangelize Americans with the message of scriptural holiness. He noted that the "church as a whole" was "sound asleep" and that they had failed to develop a "consuming passion" to evangelize ordinary Americans with the message of personal holiness. Jones reiterated this position and made known his concern about what he perceived to be a lack of zeal for domestic missions when he asked, "Why this condition? Lack of soul passion on the part of the church. No concern and no responsibility. My

---

¹William T. Purkiser, *Called Unto Holiness: The Story of the Nazarenes, The Second Twenty Five Years, 1933-1958*, v. 2 (Kansas City: Beacon Hill Press, 1983), 107, 123. Like the CN, many other predominantly white holiness churches continued to grow during this period. For example, the total membership of the Church of God (Anderson, IN) grew from 38,249 to 56,911 and the Christian and Missionary Alliance expanded from 25,930 to 43,536. Similarly, Pentecostal churches like the Church of God (Cleveland, TN) went from 21,377 to 52,206 and the Assemblies of God grew from 47,950 to 148,043. For further reference see, Mark A. Noll, Nathan Hatch, George M. Marsden, David F. Wells, and John D. Woodbridge, ed., *Eerdman's Handbook to Christianity in America* (Grand Rapids, MI: William B. Eerdmans Publishing Company, 1983), 411; Sydney Ahlstrom, *A Religious History of the American People* (New Haven, CT: Yale University Press, 1972), 920 and Mark A. Noll, *The Work We Have to Do: A History of Protestants in America* (New York: Oxford University Press, 2002), 100-101.

²Dale E. Jones, "Average US Churches Sizes, 1908-2010," March 1, 2011. Research Services, Global Ministry Center, Lenexa, KS.

³Purkiser, 157.

⁴Floyd Cunningham, Stan Ingersol, Harold E. Raser, David P. Whitelaw, ed., *Our Watchword & Song: The Centennial History of the Church of the Nazarene* (Kansas City: Beacon Hill Press, 2009), 241.

Lord, how will we as Nazarenes get by at the judgment? This field is before us." In order to combat these conditions and to help "red-blooded Nazarenes" become fervent evangelistic devotees, Jones stated that the church needed to overcome the temptation to be indifferent and develop a passion for home missions:

> The tendency is to take an indifferent, careless attitude; take the path of least resistance; do something, but do not get excited. So many are making excuses . . . God has commissioned us. It can be done, providing we get a vision and become obsessed with a burning, consuming passion . . . A passion is needed; a consuming fire . . . We will not do much to save the teeming millions of America without an inborn passion.[5]

Likewise, when Jones and the Department of Home Missions and Evangelism gave their quadrennial report to the Tenth General Assembly three years later, they stressed the need for the denomination to continue giving and supporting home missions so that the "gospel of Jesus Christ" could help to transform the "spiritual decay" of American society. In their report, they noted that:

> Let us repeat it, "America is in need." She is suffering from moral and spiritual decay . . . We have been called as Nazarenes to do something about it. The church, that we as members and delegates represent, is not an accident. God has called us to the Kingdom for just such a day . . . As John the Baptist was called for his day and the Wesleys were God's men for their century, just so we are an evangelizing agency arrived in time to fulfill a peculiar mission in the earth, that of heralding forth the unsearchable riches of gospel truth; sending the gospel to all men.[6]

At the local level in Kansas, congregations heard similar theological, ministerial, and evangelistic sermons given by district leaders and foreign missionaries. Churches and ministers listened to stories and messages about missionary activities in Africa and about the importance of creating new evangelistic methods to reach those throughout the state of Kansas. These sermons were designed to convince parishioners and pastors that they had a responsibility and duty to evangelize and start new Nazarene churches in their towns and communities. Not only that, but they were designed to stir district delegates to continue giving their time, money, and energy to district committees and boards that were necessary to fulfill the twin goals of the denomination, which were to "save" others and to help

---

[5]C. Warren Jones, "Home Missionary Passion," in *The Herald of Holiness* (December 4, 1937): 10. Church of the Nazarene Archives, Lenexa, KS.

[6]*The Manual of the Tenth General Assembly of the Church of the Nazarene* (1940): 358. Church of the Nazarene Archives, Lenexa, KS.

sanctify those who had come to believe in the message of individual holiness.⁷

Black Nazarene women and men like E.J. Brockett heard such admonitions and committed themselves to help the predominantly white districts carry out its commitment to international evangelism by leading and continuing Hutchinson, Second's WFMS and by legislating alongside other white Nazarenes about how to best support foreign missions. For example, Brockett, as Hutchinson's WFMS voting representative to the Kansas District Assembly in 1937, voted and agreed with the rest of the white district members that they should continue to help support missionary work around the world by giving money to world missionary funds, hosting guest missionary speakers, and reading Nazarene missionary literature.⁸

Like Brockett, black laity like Mrs. Bessie Reece carried out this evangelistic emphasis in Plainville, KS by leading and maintaining Plainville, Second's NYPS chapter and by participating in the leadership of the district NYPS—the main ministry that the denomination and churches around the country continued to use to evangelize and disciple teenagers. Furthermore, in an effort to "sanctify" youth and others that had been evangelized, members of Hutchinson, Second, like Clifford Johnson (a licensed minister) sat on the district's Sabbath Observance Committee, which, as the name describes, was a committee designed to make sure that churches and members observed the "sanctity" of the Sabbath and upheld certain ethical boundaries that pointed to evidence of living a holy life. For instance, aside from admonishing Nazarenes in Kansas not to take "the name of God in vain," they also stated that one should abstain from consuming alcohol, gossiping, should dress modestly, avoid the theater, circus, and lotteries, evangelize others, "do good to the bodies and souls of men," feed the hungry, visit the sick, and faithfully uphold the sanctity of the Sabbath day. In fact, to be united with the CN, the committee stated that one had to promise not to profane "the Lord's Day either by unnecessary labor, or business."⁹

---

⁷*Kansas District Church of the Nazarene, Twenty-Eighth Annual Assembly Journal* (August 1937), 32-33. Church of the Nazarene Archives. Lenexa, KS; *Kansas District Church of the Nazarene, Twenty-Ninth Annual Assembly Journal* (August 1938), 26. Church of the Nazarene Archives. Lenexa, KS and *Kansas District Church of the Nazarene, Thirtieth Annual Assembly Journal* (August 1939), 21. Church of the Nazarene Archives, Lenexa, KS.

⁸*Kansas District Church of the Nazarene, Twenty-Eighth Annual Assembly Journal*, 31.

⁹W.T. Purkiser, *Called Unto Holiness: The Second Twenty-five Years, 1933-1958*, vol. 2 (Kansas City: Beacon Hill Press, 1983), 65 and *Kansas District Church of the Nazarene, Twenty-Fifth Annual Assembly Journal* (August 28 to September 2, 1934), 6-7, 12, 20, statistical index. Church of the Nazarene Archives, Lenexa, KS.

During the same time, members and leaders from Hutchinson, Second remained committed to local evangelism by sustaining Sunday school ministries up until the time that their senior minister, Allen Pollard, moved to Seattle, WA in 1938. During his ministerial tenure in the late 1930s, the church consistently had more Sunday school members than regular church adherents. In 1937, for instance, the church had a total church membership of 13, but a Sunday school enrollment of twenty-five, of which a majority were adolescents and adults. A year later, shortly before Pollard left the congregation, the church possessed the same numbers.[10]

As an outreach ministry, Sunday school at Hutchinson, Second—like other Nazarene churches around the country—continued to use Sunday school as a method to reach out to those in their local community that did not attend church. Like earlier years, membership continued to include those who actively attended or who were home bound and were physically unable to attend weekly sessions. Most of the lessons tended to last about one-hour and students, regardless of age, were taught biblical stories. They also received information about the ministries of the church and were exposed to the theological teachings of the denomination.[11] By providing this space and time to explore the Bible and theology, Hutchinson, Second and other congregations on the Kansas District hoped that they could evangelize and strengthen their membership rolls, even if Sunday school membership did not always translate into a higher church membership.

Sunday school membership for most Nazarene churches during the late 1910s to early 1930s remained higher than church membership in large part because of the individual requirements for church membership and, this continued to be the reality throughout the 1930s and 1940s. To be a member of the congregation, one had to adhere to avoid a host of such things like consuming liquor and alcohol, using tobacco, reading "secular" literature, dressing immodestly, or attending "frivolous" entertainments. Aside from this, members had to actively support the ministries of the church, embrace the doctrines of the denomination, attend all worship services, evangelize others, and testify to living a holy life. If one performed all these functions, then they could join the church. Largely because of these realities, many Sunday school members around the country continued to avoid church membership and this probably led to why African Americans in Kansas, like white other Nazarene congregations on the Kansas district,

---

[10]Ibid., statistical index and Kansas District Church of the Nazarene, Twenty-Ninth Annual Assembly Journal, statistical index.

[11]The Manual of the Eleventh Annual General Assembly of the Church of the Nazarene (1948), 80-82. Church of the Nazarene Archives and Stan Ingersol, Nazarene Roots: Pastors, Prophets, Revivalists & Reformers (Kansas City, MO: Beacon Hill Press, 2009), 146-148.

had a larger proportion of Sunday school membership than church members in the late 1930s.[12]

For instance, on the Kansas District in 1938, many average sized white Nazarene churches had Sunday school members who didn't join the church. At Emporia CN in Emporia, KS there were 36 church members and 52 Sunday school members and by the end of the year, only three new people from the Sunday school body joined the church. Likewise, at the Junction City CN, the church had a congregational membership of 30 and 82 people that attended Sunday school. Despite the large Sunday school attendance, not one person from the total Sunday school body joined the church that year. In similar fashion, during the same year at Manhattan CN in Manhattan, KS, there were 24 church members and 31 Sunday school attendees, but not a single new person from all the Sunday school attendees became congregational members. Furthermore at Hays CN in Hays, KS, the church had a total church membership of 24 and 49 people who regularly attended Sunday school. Yet, for that year, the church only received 4 new members from those that were a part of the Sunday school ministries.[13]

In short, what this shows is that African American Nazarene Sunday school patterns in Kansas were very similar to those of white congregations in Kansas and around the country. They attempted to reach out and evangelize those in their community, but their efforts, like that of other white Nazarenes, did not always translate to church membership. Yet, low membership numbers in church did not stop African American pastors and laypersons in Kansas from attempting to spread the message of the denomination or from contributing to district leadership and ministries.

---

[12]Stan Ingersol, singersol@nazarene.org. "Sunday School Attendance for the Church of the Nazarene." Private e-mail message to Brandon Winstead. 10 October 2010.

[13]Church of the Nazarene Research Center, "Membership Status and Attendance of Emporia Church of the Nazarene—Kansas District." http://app.nazarene.org/FindAChurch/viewReport.jsp?reportId=21196&orgId=2935. (accessed 01 April 2011); Church of the Nazarene Research Center, "Membership Status and Attendance of Junction City Church of the Nazarene—Kansas District." http://app.nazarene.org/FindAChurch/viewReport.jsp?reportId=21196&orgId=2953. (accessed 01 April 2011); Church of the Nazarene Research Center, "Membership Status and Attendance of Hays Church of the Nazarene—Kansas District."
http://app.nazarene.org/FindAChurch/viewReport.jsp?reportId=21196&sIDType=rpt&orgId=2963. [accessed 01 April 2011] and Church of the Nazarene Research Center, "Membership Status and Attendance of Manhattan Church of the Nazarene—Kansas District." http://app.nazarene.org/FindAChurch/viewReport.jsp?reportId=21196&orgId=2944. (accessed 01 April 2011).

At the same time that African American pastors and laypersons in Kansas were contributing to denominational life and the evangelistic mission of the denomination, West Indian Nazarenes continued to carry out the evangelistic mission that they heard preached and taught by white missionaries and denominational leaders. For instance, numerous foreign missionaries like Rev. Jaroszewicz of Poland and Rev. and Mrs. John Duryea of Jerusalem came and spoke to the DA in 1938 about their work around the globe in an effort to gain monetary and spiritual support from congregations and leaders on the New York district. They showed pictures of their overseas work, and encouraged the congregations to help them bring "the message of salvation to the world."[14]

At the same DA, ecclesiastical leaders encouraged those in attendance to give to international missionary work, to read books and other accounts about foreign missions, and to remain passionate about evangelism at the local level. One of the General Superintendents, for example, Dr. J.W. Goodwin, stated that New York Nazarenes should face the "tremendous challenge" of "reaching" their neighbors by creating and utilizing new evangelistic methods. If they would not "cling to old ideas and methods but seek out God's method and do something new," then they could establish "at least fifty churches in and around New York with many cottage prayer meetings." Later on in the assembly, Goodwin delivered a sermon in which he told the assembly that it needed to reach "the ripened fields" of humanity. A contemporary observer summarized Goodwin's challenge by stating,

> Doctor Goodwin's message had the same tone of home missions as had the entire assembly. He spoke from the text, "Lift up your eyes and look on the fields, for they are white already to harvest." He exhorted us to lift our eyes beyond the immediate surroundings of our lives and catch a vision of the ripened fields beyond.[15]

At the same assembly, G.B. Williamson, the president of Eastern Nazarene College, gave a sermon that focused solely on the importance of persons giving their time, money, and talents, to "adapt the gospel of Jesus Christ" to those who lived in metropolitan New York. His main concern was to address how the church could spread the message of Christ and the CN to urban dwellers. Williamson's message and the commitment of district members to heed his challenge was captured in the following words,

> Dr. G. B. Williamson, president of Eastern Nazarene College, spoke from Romans 1:15. He pointed out the drawing power of the gospel of Christ, and

---

[14]*New York District Church of the Nazarene, Thirty-First Annual Assembly Journal* (April 1938), 18-27. Church of the Nazarene Archives, Lenexa, KS.

[15]New York District Church of the Nazarene, *Thirty-First Annual Assembly Journal* (April 1938), 13, 26. Church of the Nazarene Archives, Lenexa, KS.

he stated that in every place it is treated fairly it draws all men. The gospel of Jesus Christ is adapted to the lives of human beings. Are we, in the great metropolitan area, convinced that what we have is what men want, what they need, and why they must have? Are we ready to lay down our lives that they may share this experience of salvation that we enjoy? God is not limited in His power. God is still looking for men and women who will give their all. We all knelt in prayer for a wider vision and a greater burden for souls. Doctor Goodwin pronounced the benediction.[16]

Later on, after hearing this sermon, important black ministers on the district, like Levi Franklin and Lawrence Wallace, lent support to this evangelistic emphasis by preaching evangelistic sermons at the assembly, such as the one given by Franklin about "the story of Zacchaeus." In that message, Franklin communicated that like Zaccheaus, Nazarenes should see the necessity of communing with Jesus so that they could be empowered to spread "Christ's salvation to the world."[17]

In an effort to help the New York District carry out these evangelistic challenges of white and black leaders, West Indian Nazarenes voted and legislated on district matters, sat on district committees, and sustained traditional Nazarene evangelistic ministries like Sunday schools and NYPS and NWMS chapters. For instance, members of Franklin's congregation (there were 44 members by 1935), such as Darwell King, and Mrs. Rhoda Gittens headed up the church's NYPS and the WFMS chapters. In addition to this, Mrs. Christine Gosvenor and Miss Viola Bowen, two female leaders in the congregation, contributed to district leadership by voting at District Assembly and Gittens participated in helping the district support international and local missions by sitting on the Foreign Missions and the Deaconess and Rescue Work/Social Welfare and Orphanage district committees.[18]

By serving on these committees and as a licensed deaconess, Gittens was able to help lead some of the ministries at Beulah and make decisions regarding how the district would evangelize and minister to the poor, sick, and dying.[19] In particular, Gittens, alongside other white women like Emma Brown, Dora Youngs, Ella Wightman, Mrs. Cecil Coline, Mrs. Pearl Cashbit, and Mrs. Mary E. Warren, felt empowered to encourage the church and "Spirit-filled women" to relieve the suffering of the poor by visiting and evangelizing the disenfranchised. In 1933, Gittens, and the rest of the licensed and consecrated deaconesses on the New York District, emphasized this concern:

[16]Ibid., 17.
[17]Ibid., 27.
[18]*New York District Church of the Nazarene, Twenty-Eighth Annual Assembly Journal* (April 1935), 3-15. Church of the Nazarene Archives, Lenexa, KS.
[19]*The Manual of Eleventh General Assembly of the Church of the Nazarene*, 116-117.

We, the deaconesses of the New York District submit the following report:

Feeling the call of God upon us to do the Lord's work by visiting the sick and afflicted, relieving the distressed, and encouraging the discouraged ones, and, living in an age when it is necessary and commendable to go out into the byways and hedges and compel them to come in,

We feel that the work of the deaconesses should be emphasized and that the great need of Spirit-filled women to do this work should be pressed upon our young women when they are considering their vocations. We desire our pastors to recognize and encourage deaconess work in their churches and occasionally to hold a service in the interest of this work.[20]

In similar fashion to Gittens, women at Miller Memorial like Miss Ethel Greenridge and Mrs. Lillian Hardy contributed to local black evangelism by heading Miller's NYPS and WFMS and helping to increase the church's Sunday school membership to 128 by 1935. Moreover, women from Miller Memorial were sent as voting delegates to the DA in the same year to vote and legislate on ecclesiastical matters pertinent to the overall mission of the New York District. For instance, Miss Lillian Wilson and Miss Leonora Dowleyne were sent to the DA to vote on the election of district officers, district committee decisions, and other church issues. Dowleyne also sat on the district's Sabbath Observance, Temperance, and Prohibition Committee. By sitting on these committees and voting on ecclesiastical matters, Dowleyne and Wilson, like Gittens, revealed their commitment to furthering the mission of the denomination while also remaining committed to addressing some of the social issues that they felt impacted the life of those in their communities and in the neighborhoods surrounding other Nazarene churches on the New York District.[21]

At Free Gospel, the situation was very similar in terms of how ministers and laity, both male and female, helped to strengthen the ministry of their church and the denomination in the mid 1930s. For instance, in 1935, under the pastoral leadership of Lawrence King, the church's membership stood at 46, while Sunday school enrollment hovered at 115, and the church's NYPS and WFMS each had 35 members. Moreover, in the span covering 1933-1935, Free Gospel increased their total church giving by almost $100.00 from $874.00 to $972.00. This amount of giving covered such things as Sunday school supplies, outreach events, pastoral expenses, and missionary expenditures.[22]

---

[20]New York District Church of the Nazarene, Twenty-Sixth Annual Assembly Journal (April 1933), 38. Church of the Nazarene Archives, Lenexa, KS and New York District Church of the Nazarene, Twenty-Eighth Annual Assembly Journal, 11-15.

[21]New York District Church of the Nazarene, Twenty-Eighth Annual Assembly Journal, 13-15.

[22]Ibid., statistical index, New York District Church of the Nazarene, Twenty-Seventh Annual Assembly Journal (April 1933), statistical index. Church of the

In addition to this, Free Gospel also continued to participate in the decision making process of the district. In the middle of the decade, for instance, female leaders from Free Gospel's NYPS and WFMS such as Miss Mabel Catlyne and Mrs. Ethel Holder, voted and participated in the governing affairs of the district's NYPS and WFMS. Catlyne doubled her duties by serving as one of only nine consecrated deaconesses on the New York District. Because Catlyne held such a position, she, like the above-mentioned Gittens, was able to preach, visit the sick, administer the sacraments, evangelize the poor and sick, and contribute to the overall mission of the denomination in New York City. In short, Catlyne, because of her status, could perform any task that King and the local church board deemed her capable to do and because of this, Catlyne provided the necessary leadership for Free Gospel to minister in the borough of Brooklyn.[23]

At the same time, King was helping the district NYPS fulfill its evangelistic goals. In 1935, the NYPS decided that it wanted, among other things, to see a ten percent increase in membership, hold at least fifty devotional meetings, have the district president attend the General Assembly, engage in at least one "special" outreach project, require each member to read the Bible throughout the year, establish a library for each local society, and take a monthly offering for foreign missions. King, along with white committee members like H. Blair Ward, Martha Haselton, John Warren, Stanley Brooks, Ralph Horst and Hazel Wertman wanted the NYPS to fulfill some of these goals so they recommended five financial suggestions, which read as follows:

> 1. That we plan to provide for the General Assembly expenses of our District President and for the district expense fund by paying at the rate of one penny per member per month, this money to be sent monthly to our N.Y.P.S. treasurer.
>
> 2. That we as a District N.Y.P.S. raise $500 for Home Missions campaign above the District Church budget, this money to be paid to our N.Y.P.S. treasurer.
>
> 3. That each local society assume a portion of the unified or General Budget of the local church.

Nazarene Archives, Kansas City, MO and New York District Church of the Nazarene, Twenty-Ninth Annual Assembly Journal (April 1935), statistical index. Church of the Nazarene Archives, Lenexa, KS.

[23]*New York District Church of the Nazarene, Twenty-Ninth Annual Assembly Journal*, 11. Later on the chapter, the research will analyze how women from the black Brooklyn congregations used their ability to acquire leadership roles in their local congregations and on the New District to help bolster the work of their churches and denomination during the 1930s and 1940s.

4. That money raised for District and General Budget be paid through the regular church channels.

5. That all money be raised systematically and the treasurer be authorized to remind the local treasurers regularly as he finds such a reminder.[24]

This instance of King's contribution, along with the numerous examples mentioned above, signify the willingness of black Barbadians and West Indians to improve Nazarene ministries on the district and to improve their churches' "outreach" to those in their communities during the mid 1930s. By doing this, they remained committed to help the denomination meet many of its evangelistic goals in the northeast section of the United States and this course of contribution would continue to define the narrative of among Afro-Bajans as the years would unfold.

At the 1938 assembly, for instance, after Rev. Greene of Miller Memorial opened the WFMS convention by leading the "group in a fervent season of prayer," Miss Carlotta Graham, a black immigrant from Barbados, a former member of Miller Memorial and missionary to Trinidad, spoke to the assembly about her conversion in New York and "her divine call home to her own country where she was greatly blessed and used of the Lord in the work on the islands." She closed her message by asking for the "prayers and financial support of the people of New York District."[25] After hearing this, West Indian women like Miss Jones of Miller Memorial sang songs like "Something Has Happened to Me" in an effort to galvanize those gathered to support the evangelistic work in Trinidad. Likewise, a few years later, the WFMS president from Beulah, Mrs. Rhoda Gittens, gave an "inspiring" testimony to the assembly in order to inspire them to give more money and energy to local and international missions.[26]

In similar fashion, at the 1946 WFMS convention, women like Mabel Catlyne, Gittens, and Florence Wolcott attended the convention and voted and legislated on how the district body would allocate several hundred dollars raised to support foreign missions in India, Africa, Cape Verde Islands, and China. In addition to this, when the district WFMS wanted to highlight certain local chapters that had "exemplary reports," they called on Gittens to detail and share experiences from what they had accomplished

---

[24]Ibid., 53.

[25]For further information on Graham and her missionary labors see Henderson Carter, *Moulding Communities, Touching Lives: A History of the Church of The Nazarene in Barbados, 1926-2008* (Kingston, Jamaica: Ian Randle Publishers, 2008), 23-24, 33-35; The District of the Church of the Nazarene Trinidad and Tobago, *History of The Church of the Nazarene Trinidad and Tobago* (Barataria, Trinidad: Christian Printers, 2008), 54-60.

[26]Ibid., 51-53 and *New York District Assembly, Thirty-Fifth Annual Assembly Journal* (April 1942), 44-47. Church of the Nazarene Archives, Lenexa, KS.

over the past year in an effort to inspire other chapters to promote the evangelistic mission and vision of the WFMS.[27]

Aside from this, Afro-Carribean women continued to increase the membership numbers of the New York District's WFMS. For example, in 1939, the membership numbers for Miller Memorial WFMS stood at 31, but three years later that number increased to 52. Moreover, at Beulah, the membership increased by one during the same amount of time from 35 to 36 and at Free Gospel, WFMS membership moved from 29 at the end of the decade to 42 by 1942. Two years later, Miller Memorial had the highest WFMS membership of all the West Indian churches with 50 members. Beulah was second with 40 and Free Gospel was not far behind with a total membership of 39.[28] By 1946, Miller Memorial still led the way among the Afro-Carribean congregations with a total WFMS membership of 40 members, while Free Gospel and Beulah each still had 36 full time WFMS members in their congregations.

These WFMS membership contributions of the Afro-Caribbean congregations may seem miniscule to the casual reader, but in comparison to the white churches on the New York District, their numbers were quite significant. In 1944, out of the twenty-eight congregations that had active WFMS chapters on the district, Miller Memorial had the largest membership. In fact, the congregation that had the second largest membership on the district was Norwalk CN, a white congregation in Norwalk, CT with 41 members. Furthermore, even though Beulah and Free Gospel were behind Miller Memorial in terms of membership, they still possessed the third and fourth highest WFMS members on the entire New York District.[29] Likewise, in 1946, Miller Memorial did not have the largest WFMS membership on the district, but they were only second behind the white Dover CN in Dover, NJ, which had 42 members. In that same year, only two other white congregations on the district of twenty-eight churches had higher WFMS membership than Beulah and Free Gospel—Norwalk CN (37 members) and Richmond Hill CN in Richmond Hill, NY (39 members).

West Indian women also continued to help the denomination financially support foreign mission work amidst the days of the Great Depression and during and after WWII. In 1938, for instance, the women at Free Gospel raised $120.00 for world missions. Similarly, at Miller Memorial and Beulah, the WFMS chapters raised raise $220.00 and $144.00, totals that were comparable to other average sized white Nazarene churches in Brooklyn like Utica Avenue Church of the Nazarene and Brooklyn Hoople Church of

---

[27]*New York District Assembly, Thirty-Ninth Annual Assembly Journal* (April 1946), 40-41. Church of the Nazarene Archives, Lenexa, KS.

[28]*New York District Assembly, Thirty-Seventh Annual Assembly Journal* (July 1944), statistical index. Church of the Nazarene Archives. Lenexa, KS.

[29]Ibid, statistical index.

the Nazarene.³⁰ Furthermore, in 1944, the black WFMS chapters in Brooklyn continued to give significant amounts to foreign missions in comparison to the twenty-five white WFMS groups on the New York District. In fact, of the $4,961.00 raised for missionary work that year, the West Indian WFMS chapters contributed a total of $773.00. Of that amount, Free Gospel gave the lowest with an amount of $106.00 (seven white chapters gave lower amounts than Free Gospel), but Miller contributed $388.00, while Beulah gave $279.00. By giving these amounts, Miller and Beulah were the fourth and fifth highest giving WFMS groups on the district.³¹ Likewise, two years later, all the twenty-eight WFMS chapters on the New York District raised a total of $6,007.00 to support missionaries and foreign missions. Of that amount, Miller Memorial, Beulah, and Free Gospel contributed $862.00. By doing this, Miller Memorial ranked as the fifth highest financial contributor to the district WFMS, while Beulah placed eighth.³²

At the same time that West Indian women performed such actions in an effort to support global evangelism, other black Nazarenes continued to sit on district committees that were committed to local evangelism. For example, women like Miss Keturah Pilgrim, who was sent from Brooklyn Free Gospel as a voting delegate to the DA in 1938, sat on the jurisdiction's Home Missions and Church Extension Committee. Also, Rev. King and Rev. Franklin were committee members of the Campmeeting Committee, a conglomerate that was concerned with organizing services and revivals that could "save" souls and empower Nazarene members to evangelize and strengthen their churches. Also, two other women, Mrs. Rhoda Gittens (the same Gittens mentioned previously) and Miss Mable Catlyne (two consecrated deaconesses) helped churches on the New York District to expand their influence in their communities by sitting on the Deaconess and Rescue Work Committee. This board, as it was described earlier, was committed to evangelizing and ministering to the poor in their local communities and to assist with some of the educational and liturgical needs of their congregations.³³

In similar fashion, in 1944, West Indian women like Gittens, Catlyne, and Jennie Beatty continued to help the district decide on how to evangelize and

---

³⁰*New York District Assembly, Thirty-First Annual Assembly Journal*, 57; *New York District Church of the Nazarene, Thirty-Second Annual Assembly Journal*, statistical index; *New York District Church of the Nazarene, Thirty-Fourth Annual Assembly Journal* (April 1941), statistical index. Nazarene Archives, Lenexa, KS and *New York District Church of the Nazarene*, (April 1942), statistical index. Church of the Nazarene Archives. Lenexa, KS.

³¹*New York District, Thirty-Seventh Annual Assembly Journal*, statistical index.

³²*New York District Assembly, Thirty-Ninth Annual Assembly Journal*, statistical index.

³³*New York District Assembly, Thirty-First Annual Assembly Journal*, 12.

minister to the poor by sitting on the Deaconess and Rescue Work Committee. Furthermore, Lawrence Wallace, James Mosely, Rev. Levi Franklin, and Joseph Forde sat on one of the main evangelistic committees of the district, the Church Schools Committee. This committee legislated and decided the educational and evangelistic goals of Sunday schools. At the District Assembly, Wallace, Mosely, Franklin, and Forde decided that the district needed to be reminded of the evangelistic emphasis of Sunday schools by stating that the main goal of Sunday schools was to evangelize others.[34]

Like years prior, West Indian congregations also remained committed to evangelizing and "reaching" black teenagers by maintaining active NYPS chapters. In 1940, for instance, Free Gospel (by this time, Free Gospel had been renamed Bedford Zion), Miller Memorial, and Beulah had a combined total of NYPS membership of 117. At the same time, the combined church membership of all the congregations was 179, which means that a little over 65% of the churches were comprised of teenagers and those in the early to mid 20s.[35] By the end of WWII, the total number of NYPS members at Miller Memorial and Bedford Zion exceeded half of the total church membership of both churches (Beulah did not report their numbers to the District Assembly in 1945). In fact, at the latter congregation, of the 51 church members, 40 of them were reported to be active members of the local NYPS chapter. Likewise by 1945, Miller had a total church membership of 56 and 24 of those were active and contributing members to the weekly NYPS gathering.[36]

In addition to evangelizing and discipling youth through NYPS ministries, other Afro-Caribbean Nazarenes remained committed to domestic evangelism on the New York District by leading, sustaining, and growing Sunday school ministries in their congregations. Mosley, Wallace, and Forde were some of those who embodied this commitment. Mosley, in the year between 1938 and 1939 almost doubled the Sunday school membership of Free Gospel from 56 to 101, while the total membership increase of the congregation lagged far behind—38 in 1938 and 47 in 1939. During the same span of two years, Sunday school membership at Beulah increased from 166 to 177 and Miller Memorial moved from 129 to 160, even though their congregational numbers were smaller. In fact, in 1939,

---

[34] New York District Church of the Nazarene, Thirty-Seventh Annual Assembly Journal, 12, 28-29.

[35] New York District Church of the Nazarene, Thirty-Third District Assembly Journal, statistical index.

[36] New York District Church of the Nazarene, Thirty-Eighth District Assembly Journal, statistical index.

Beulah had a total of 62 members while Miller had 65 on their membership roll.[37]

Several years later, a similar pattern held sway. In 1941, Beulah had a Sunday school membership of 164 and a total congregational membership of 64. Likewise, at Miller Memorial, 65 regularly attended Sunday morning worship, while 143 men and women of all ages joined the ranks of the Sunday school ministry. Three years later, the amount of Sunday school members (the total was 156) was still more than double the total amount of congregational members at Miller Memorial. Free Gospel was not much different when the membership totals were counted in 1941 and 1944. In the former year, there were 41 congregational members and 121 on the Sunday school membership rolls and in the latter, there were a total of 56 church members and 125 who regularly attended Sunday school. Likewise, in 1946, Miller Memorial had 64 church members and 106 Sunday school members, while Beulah 68 members and a Sunday school membership of 136. At the same time, Free Gospel had a church membership of 51 and 100 who were Sunday school members. The same held true for the newly formed West Indian congregation of East New York CN who had a Sunday school membership of 66, a number which was significantly higher than their congregational membership.[38]

Of course, like their African American and white contemporaries in Kansas, West Indian Sunday school membership continued to remain higher than their church membership and this was not particular to the black congregations in Brooklyn. For instance, in 1944, large white churches on the New York District on Dover CN had 116 church members, but a Sunday school membership of 164. At the same time, the white congregation of East Rockaway CN had a church membership of 108 and 175 Sunday school members. Two years later, both congregations still had higher Sunday school members than church members and almost every other white congregation maintained the same pattern.[39]

Again, like previous decades and like Nazarene churches in general and the black and white congregations in Kansas in particular, Sunday school membership among white and black churches on the New York District usually remained higher than church membership primarily because of the moral and ethical requirements for church membership and due to the fact

---

[37]Ibid., statistical index and New York District Church of the Nazarene, Thirty-Second Annual Assembly Journal (April 1939), statistical index.

[38]New York District Assembly, Thirty-Fourth Annual Assembly Journal, statistical index; New York District Assembly, Thirty-Seventh Annual Assembly Journal, statistical index and New York District Assembly, Thirty-Ninth Annual Assembly Journal, statistical index.

[39]New York District Church of the Nazarene, Thirty-Seventh Annual Assembly Journal, statistical index and New York District Church of the Nazarene, Thirty-Ninth Annual Assembly Journal, statistical index.

that one could be an official Sunday school member without ever having to officially join the church. Thus, in similar fashion to the African American congregations in Kansas, the West Indian churches in New York were like their white peers in that they continued to evangelize and teach numerous individuals in their Sunday schools and many joined those classes, but those who attended did not always take the next step to officially join the church.[40]

In sum, the congregations in Brooklyn and Kansas continued to contribute to the mission and ministries of the Kansas and New York districts and expand the evangelistic mission of the denomination both abroad and at home. On these districts, they contributed to district leadership and maintained (like previous years) traditional Nazarene ministries like Sunday schools, NYPS, and NWMS chapters in order to evangelize and disciple those around the globe and in their communities.[41] At the same time that West Indian congregations performed such actions, it should be remembered that a few Afro-Caribbean ministers attempted to expand their ministerial activities beyond official church ministries by reaching out to youth during a heightened time of juvenile delinquency, by participating in interdenominational worship services, and by addressing some of the economic and racial concerns facing blacks in Brooklyn and around the country. By doing this, they sought to "reach out" to others through non-Nazarene ministries and to become socially active in their communities in the late 1930s and 1940s.

Levi Franklin and William Greene's Social Outreach in New York City

Even though most Nazarenes in the late 1930s and 1940s continued to equate holiness with individual piety and did not seek to find creative ways

---

[40]Cunningham, Ingersol, Raser, and Whitelaw, 449-450.

[41]For a further look into the complexity of economic concerns and realities that developed during this time see, Howard Zinn, *A People's History of the United States: 1492-Present* (New York: HarperCollins Publishers, 2003), 387-397 and William J. Duiker and Jackson J. Spielvogel, *World History: Comprehensive Volume*, 2nd ed. (Belmont, CA: Wadsworth Publishing Company, 1998); Stacy Mitchell, "Union in the North Woods: The Timber Strikes of 1937," *Minnesota History* 56, no. 5 (Spring 1999), 262-277; Thomas E. Blantz, "Father Haas and the Minneapolis Truckers' Strike of 1934," *Minnesota History* 42, no. 1 (Spring 1970), 5-15; Carol Quirke, "Reframing Chicago's Memorial Day Massacre, May 30, 1937," *American Quarterly* 60, no. 1 (March 2008), 128-157; Donald G. Sofchalk, "The Chicago Memorial Day Incident: An Episode of Mass Action," *Labor History* 6 (Winter 1965): 3-43 and John Hope Franklin and Alfred A. Moss, Jr., *From Slavery to Freedom: A History of African Americans,* 7th ed. (New York: McGraw-Hill, Inc., 1994), 384-385.

to carry out social outreach by addressing systematic social concerns—such as unemployment and war—that pressed upon the nation during the Great Depression and WWII, leaders, pastors, or laity were not officially circumscribed from addressing issues. Thus, when compelled, a few Nazarene leaders spoke about the need for the denomination to extend its evangelistic outreach to the world by becoming more socially active. For instance, in 1935 during the height of the Great Depression, the managing editor of the denominational magazine, *The Herald of Holiness*, spoke out on the church's lack of social involvement stating that the church had done "nothing for society as a whole" and that Nazarenes were more concerned with avoiding evil than doing good.

Around the same time, others took concrete moral action against what they perceived to be systematic social concerns in the United States. In 1940, for example, denominational leaders provided a registry for several hundred Nazarenes that wanted to register as "conscientious objectors" to World War II. Moreover, in the same year, denominational leaders at the General Assembly took a more socially active stance against international racism by officially condemning anti-Semitism.[42]

Likewise, Rev. Levi Franklin of Beulah chose to extend his outreach activities by becoming more socially active and connected with some of the pressing social concerns in Brooklyn. For instance, throughout the late 1930s and early 1940s Bedford-Stuyvesant (Bed-Stuy)—a neighborhood where many black families lived in Brooklyn and the location of all the black Nazarene churches—saw an increase in the amount of crimes committed by youths and adolescents. Many young people, unconcerned with trying to learn at inferior schools and frustrated by increasing poverty, unemployment, and familial strains, committed robbery, vandalism, and other acts of violence.[43] In the *New York Amsterdam News*, it was reported that black youth roamed the streets intent on protecting themselves and harming others. The article underscored this point by noting,

> Groups of young boys armed with penknives of all sizes and other weapons roam the streets at will and threaten and assault passer-bys and commit muggings and hold-ups with increasing frequency. Gangs of hoodlums armed with such knives and weapons commit hold-ups, stabbings, homicides and other serious crimes.[44]

Problems like this became so pronounced that in November of 1943, Mayor LaGuardia and the New York City Police Department were charged

---

[42]Cunningham, Ingersol, Raser, and Whitelaw, 237, 329-331.

[43]"Seek Efficient Bedford Teachers: Local Group Begins Drive to Help Area," *New York Amsterdam News*, 24 March 1945; "School Conditions Assailed," *New York Amsterdam News*, 3 February 1945 and Taylor, 107-110.

[44]"Cops Itch to Mop Up Brooklyn: La Guardia Moves to Prevent Terrorism Against Negro Citizens," *New York Amsterdam News*, 20 November 1943.

with letting "lawlessness" and "the growth of gangsterism" go unchecked in Brooklyn's "Little Harlem." The authorities sought to combat these charges by commissioning additional 420 detectives and policemen into Bed-Stuy in order to "augment district officers."[45] In addition to this, non-profit organizations, schools, churches, and ministers sought ways to curb the violence by holding mass community meetings in an effort stop petty crimes in the neighborhood and in the school, setting up youth leadership programs, showing educational movies for parents on Saturday mornings, building recreation facilities and hundreds of playgrounds for youth and parents. Dr. Seymour Rothschild helped the group by convincing six theatres in the community to show educational movies for parents on Saturday mornings.

In an effort to assist these efforts, Franklin labored alongside civic leaders, entrepreneurs, church members, and other ministers to create youth programs that tried to alleviate juvenile delinquency. For example, in the winter and summer of 1945, Franklin attended meetings with other prominent leaders of the community to come up with a comprehensive plan to tackle juvenile crime. At one of the gatherings, churchwomen, ministers, and other civic and community representatives (the list of public and community leaders who attended were Police Captain Ralph Demartino, Mrs. Constance Baker, Rev. John M. Coleman of St. Phillips Protestant Episcopal Church, Attorneys Charles Kellar and Clarence Johnson, Rev. A.L. Scott, Congressman Eugene Keogh, Assemblyman Starky, Herbert T. Miller, executive secretary of the YMCA, and Mrs. Ada B. Jackson, the chairperson of the Inter-racial Assembly) gathered at the home of Mrs. Margaret V. Brown to plan how they might "gather the support of the public" as they sought to coordinate a juvenile delinquency strategy. In outlining the purpose of the meeting, Mrs. Brown and Rev. Franklin stated that agencies such as churches, the YWCA, YMCA, and Block Associations needed to collaborate and work together to develop a "well rounded plan" that would help bring about racial and familial unity in Bed-Stuy.[46]

Aside from this involvement, ministers like Franklin and William Greene of Miller Memorial sought to "reach" local blacks and to become more socially active by preaching at black interdenominational services and by promoting and supporting black owned businesses. For instance, in 1938, Greene and Franklin preached, alongside other black pastors, at black holiness churches like "the Christian Mission Church." Furthermore, in 1943, Franklin was one of the featured speakers at the third anniversary

[45]Ibid.

[46]See "Parents' Group Enlists Aid of Public in 'Curb Crime' Effort," *New York Amsterdam News,* 14, November 1942; New Setup Seen in Bedford Area," *New York Amsterdam News,* 12 February 1944 and New Playground Opened at Monroe-Ralph Avenue Site," *New York Amsterdam News,* 27 January 1945.

celebration of "The Church of the Redeemer, Methodist."[47] In addition to this, Rev. Franklin and Beulah invited other black churches and choir groups to sing and worship with them during special occasions. On Easter Sunday of 1945, a choir group named the Universal Choir Group came and performed at Beulah during the Sunday morning service.[48]

As these actions took place, Franklin, unlike many other Afro-Caribbeans that set up businesses with the intention of catering only to the West Indian communities in places like Brooklyn and Harlem, actively supported national black owned businesses like the Victory Mutual Insurance Company. The Victory Mutual Insurance Company was based out of Chicago and was founded in 1920 by Anthony Overton, a former entrepreneur of bathroom items and the founder of the first black owned bank, Douglass National Bank. By the late 1930s, the company had expanded to be one of only three black insurance companies headquartered in the North that served clients in both the North and South (the other two were Liberty Life Insurance Company of Chicago and Northeastern Life Insurance Company of Newark, New Jersey). Victory Mutual had offices and clients in thirteen different states both the North and the South and with large assets (at one point, the company's stock was valued at $200,000.00, its assets amounted to $572, 238.19, possessed liabilities of $340, 824.53, and had a surplus of $31,413.66, one of the highest totals of all black owned insurance companies) and with offices in both northern and southern states to cover both southern blacks and the increasing black migrants in the North, Victory Life was able to cover many African Americans and Afro-Caribbeans around the United States.[49]

Because of this financial strength, Rev. Franklin was probably aware that Victory Life could provide a needed financial and racial service to black constituents in New York and around the country. That is why when Dr. P.M.H. Savory, the president of Victory Life, came to speak, in 1937, at a ten-day ceremony in Brooklyn commemorating "the seventy-four years of Negro Achievement and Race Relations," Franklin was in attendance to support his efforts. During the engagement, Franklin heard Savory discuss how his company could strengthen black businesses, provide "great economic" levering for new black entrepreneurial endeavors, and help employ "thousands" of young black men and women around the country. After he finished, Franklin, along with other city politicians and black ministers, applauded Savory's appeal to economic and racial unity by speaking on the value of recognizing the cultural achievements of blacks,

---

[47]"Church Group Offers Prayers for Minister," *New York Amsterdam News*, 13 August 1938.

[48]"Beulah Church of the Nazarene," *New York Amsterdam News*, 31 March 1945.

[49]Carter G. Woodson, "Insurance Business Among Negroes," *The Journal of Negro History* 14, no. 2 (April 1929): 202-226.

supporting black businesses and racial unity, and remaining loyal "to God, to race and to country."[50]

Aside from Victory, Franklin also backed black food companies such as the Brown Bomber Baking Company. When Brown Bomber took out an ad in the *New York Amsterdam News* in the winter of 1943, it claimed to be the largest owned and operated "Negro Baking Company" in America. Not only that, but it also asserted that its "enriched bread" was needed for every member of black families—"from school child to housewife to war worker"—because it provided the necessary "vitamins" and "mineral essentials for really good nutrition." It went on to extol how its nutrition could enhance the lives of black families by stating that its "enriched bread is wholesome, fresh daily, and deliciously good."[51] As one who endorsed such claims, Franklin, along with ministers and community members like Rev. James B. Adams, Rev. S. H. Williams, Rev. V.H. Williams, and David Lane, a mortician, placed his name under the list of sponsors of the company. By doing this, Franklin publicly supported a black owned business that claimed to be concerned about the overall well being of black families throughout New York.

In addition to this, Franklin continued his social involvement by addressing some of the systemic issues facing black Brooklynites and others from the African Diaspora. In the early 1940s, for instance, Rev. Franklin joined the Interdenominational Ministers Alliance (hereafter referred to as IMA). The body was an interdenominational organization of black Brooklyn pastors designed to help improve the physical, religious, and social conditions of African American and West Indians who lived in the borough of Brooklyn and to support issues facing blacks around the country. Throughout the tenure of its existence, the IMA conducted annual Emancipation Day services, held food drives, raised legal funds, backed Army desegregation efforts, supported certain black elected officials, and assisted families who suffered from the effects of the Great Depression.[52] Moreover, during Franklin's tenure as the IMA's secretary in the mid 1940s,[53] the organization labored to improve local municipal services by

---

[50]"Hundreds Help Boro Celebration," *New York Amsterdam News*, 12 June 1937.

[51]"Eat Brown Bomber Bread and Rolls at Every Meal," *New York Amsterdam News*, 5 January 1943.

[52]"To Celebrate Emancipation January First," *New York Amsterdam News*, 30 December 1944; "Escaping Brooklyn," *New York Amsterdam News*, 18 March 1944; "Dr. Eldridge Gets Special Activities GOP Position," *New York Amsterdam News*, 30 September 1944; "Brooklyn Church Bulletin," *New York Amsterdam News*, 30 September 1944 and "Negro Freedom Rally Duck Alien 'Isms' in Program," *New York Amsterdam News*, 19 April 1947.

[53]Franklin was installed as secretary in 1944. See "Rev. S. Eldridge Installed As President Of Alliance," *New York Amsterdam News*, 11 March 1944 and "Church Honors Levi Franklin," *New York Amsterdam News*, 11 February 1950.

working with councilman J. Daniel Diggs to improve bus service in Bed-Stuy. In addition to this, they met with city hospital officials and persuaded them to improve ambulatory services for black residents and to lift a ban that barred city hospitals "from issuing contraceptive devices."[54]

As an active participant of the IMA during the mid 1940s, Franklin also became involved in the international struggle for black national autonomy when he, along with other black pastors of the IMA such as S.T. Eldridge of Berean Baptist Church, Gardner C. Taylor of Concord Baptist Church, C.L. Franklin of Mount Lebanon Baptist Church, Rev. Garrison Waters of Newman Memorial Methodist Church, William Orlando Carrington of First AME Zion, Rev. S.H. Williams of Varick Memorial AME Zion, and Rev. John Coleman of St. Phillips Episcopal, sent a letter to the United Nations protesting the governmental policies of the "Union of South Africa" (which is now the country of South Africa.) In the correspondence, the group protested the racist and colonizing efforts of "Christian Jan Smuts, Premier of the Union of South Africa, with reference to the annexation of certain territories in South West Africa." John Foster Dulles, the noted American politician, who, at that time, was the advisory chairman of the United States' delegation to the UN, responded positively to their letter. He let the IMA know that the United States sub-committee had already approved to oppose "the incorporation of Southwest Africa in the Union of South Africa."[55]

Even though available evidence suggests that Franklin was the only black Nazarene minister or lay person in New York that became involved in such efforts, records show that William Greene, along with Franklin, maintained a social awareness by occasionally keeping abreast of black nationalistic struggles around the world. For instance, in February of 1936, Lij Tasfaye Zaphiro, an Ethiopian Envoy to the United States came to speak to a crowd of almost 1,500 people at Mt. Carmel Baptist Church, a large African American congregation located in Bed-Stuy. At the gathering, Franklin, Greene, the Rt. Rev. Edmund Robert Bennett of the African Orthodox Church, Rev. A.M. Schemper of Gethsemane Baptist Church, and Rev. J.N. Carrington of the host congregation were just a few of the ministers present from West Indian and African American churches. In addition to their presence, member guards of the Universal Negro Improvement Association, a semi-religious Black Nationalist organization

---

[54]Clarence Taylor, *The Black Churches of Brooklyn* (New York: Columbia University Press, 1994), 121.

[55]"Inter-Ministerial Alliance Sends Protest Against Smuts," *New York Amsterdam News*, 28 December 1946 and "About Religion and Education in our City of Churches," *New York Amsterdam News*, 4 January 1947 and Taylor, 97, 116-117 and 238.

founded by the Jamaican born Marcus Garvey, were in attendance and they helped to escort Zaphiro to the front of the church.

As he began to speak, Zaphiro discussed the ongoing attempts to colonize Ethiopia (which started in October of 1935). Zaphiro stated that Italy was "the aggressor" and that Ethiopia's emperor, Haile Selassie, had made numerous attempts to prevent war from happening. However, because Italy did not cease its ongoing aggression, the speaker stated that Selassie and other Ethiopians were continuing to fight for the "right to life, liberty and the pursuit of happiness." He went on to note that Ethiopians needed resources and support from blacks around the world so that it could preserve its national autonomy. Thus, Zaphiro made an appeal to those present to help the struggle of their brothers and sisters in Ethiopia. He asserted that Ethiopians were in fact black and that if the country lost the struggle to Italy, then "the colored man's voice in this world will be hushed forever." Because of Zaphiro's impassioned argument and his ability to persuade the black crowd that Ethiopia's struggle was, in essence, their struggle, those in attendance gave a total of $327.32 to purchase a hospital building and medical supplies for Ethiopians wounded in the war.[56]

Despite this, however, most black Nazarenes on the New York District did not take similar actions in the social and religious domain as those taken by Franklin and Greene. As a result, none of the black congregations in Brooklyn took systematic steps to participate in social activism or join organizations that tackled systemic issues that impacted the lives of blacks in Brooklyn or other black communities around the country. Instead, as the narrative has shown, like their white and African American Nazarene contemporaries in Kansas and around the country, Afro-Caribbean Nazarenes in Brooklyn continued to primarily focus their energies on promoting the work of the denomination around the globe, strengthening the ministries of their churches and districts, and evangelizing those in their local communities with the message of personal holiness.

By embracing such a stance, the black Brooklyn churches, like African Americans in Kansas, made efforts to be faithful contributors to the local and international mission of the CN from the mid-1930s to after WWII. As black immigrants in New York City, West Indians worked alongside white churches to strengthen district leadership and ministries, evangelize those in their communities, and support domestic and international missions. Likewise, as black participants on a predominantly white district in the Midwest, African Americans at Hutchinson, Second and Plainville, Second embraced the personal holiness theology and evangelistic mission of the denomination up until they were left with no pastoral leadership in the late 1930s. How these groups continued this participation in the following years

[56]"Brooklynites Cheer Ethiopia's Envoy," *New York Amsterdam News*, 22 February 1936.

amidst shifting racial and evangelistic realities in the denomination will soon be outlined. But first, attention must be drawn to those African Americans who joined the CN as segregated members and how their actions amidst national ecclesiastical segregation adds to our understanding of the CN's historical relationship to black churches in the United States.

Chapter Three

Ecclesiastical Segregation and Black Participation, 1947-1958

African American Evangelization on the Colored District, 1947-1952

Black Nazarenes throughout the country embraced the theological particularities of the denomination and worked to strengthen the ministries of their churches and contribute to the mission and thrust of the denomination on their own volition during the first few decades of its existence. They utilized their finances and resources to support foreign missions, pay their ministers, sustain Sunday school outreach, give food to the hungry, provide clothes for poor community members, and support other "outreach" ministries in their communities. As they made these efforts, black congregations were governed by local districts and were not placed in a segregated jurisdiction where they were separated in a racially homogeneous governing body. However, as the country moved into the post-WWII Era, the denomination placed a different form of ecclesiastical governance on African American Nazarenes—one premised on the notion of racial segregation—and left West Indians to be governed by the New York District alongside white congregations. Yet, despite this jurisdictional and racialized transition in the denomination, African Americans continued their contribution to Nazarene ministries and evangelism throughout the United States during the late 1940s and 1950s.

The plans to segregate and evangelize African Americans under a national jurisdiction began to germinate at the 1940 General Assembly. At the gathering, Dr. C. Warren Jones (the same Jones mentioned in the previous chapter), the executive secretary of the Department of Home Missions, spoke to the General Board and stated that serious discussion needed to begin regarding black evangelization on a national scale. He noted that,

> When it comes to the Negro race, we have done nothing. We have a few and very few missions for the colored people, of which there are 12,000,000 in the United States. We have talked and promised ourselves to do something but that is as far as we have gotten. We seem to fail when it comes to consistency. We keep thirty-five missionaries in Africa and spend $40,000 a year to evangelize 1 1/3 million people and neglect the millions of the same face in the homeland. We would not do less for Africa, but do you no think we should do something for the black man of our own land? They may be black but they go to make up the human race were surely included in the "all nations' of the Great Commission."[1]

Jones' evangelistic convictions pushed the General Assembly to adopt a resolution to lay plans for "evangelization of the American Negro and the establishment of churches among them and that this work be inaugurated at the earliest possible date."[2] "The earliest possible date," however, did not come within the proceeding days and months of the annual gathering. Instead, the General Assembly and the Department of Home Missions chose to postpone organizing a national evangelistic plan until the next General Assembly, which was held in 1944 in Minneapolis, Minnesota. At the assembly, the Department of Home Missions sent a memorial to the General Board[3] requesting,

> In as much as there are thirteen million colored people in the United States (one out of every ten person being colored) we urge the Department of Home Missions and Evangelism and the General Board to take definite steps toward the evangelization of these people, toward the establishment of Nazarene churches for colored people, and to appropriate necessary funds for the accomplishment of the task.[4]

---

[1]The Manual of the Tenth Annual General Assembly of the Church of the Nazarene (June, 1940), 118. Church of the Nazarene Archives, Lenexa, KS.

[2]Ibid., 119.

[3]The General Board (hereafter referred to as GB) was created by the General Assembly (the supreme elective and legislative body in the CN) of the denomination in 1923. The main function of the GB was to oversee the work of six major denominational departments: Foreign Missions, Church Schools, Department of Home Missions and Church Extension (later termed Home Missions and Evangelism), Publication, Ministerial Relief, and Education. In 1932, it was decided that the General Board would meet every January to give reports and assess the work of each subcommittee. For further reference, see William Purkiser, Called Unto Holiness: The Second Twenty Five Years, 1933-1958, vol. 2 (Kansas City: Beacon Hill Press, 1983), 32-51.

Within a few weeks, the memorial was passed and the Board of General Superintendents agreed to allocate funds to set up "The Colored District" (hereafter referred to as CD). Shortly after its founding, the General Board appropriated $5,600.00 from the Home Missions Budget and by 1947, white leaders had worked alongside other blacks to start a few "black missions" and churches that whites "supervised" and "oversaw" in various places like Alabama, Chicago, and New Orleans. Moreover, in the same year, churches were in operation from West Virginia to California, with the largest ones located in Indianapolis, IN (19 members), Mashulaville, MS (20 members), Columbus, MS (16 members), Oakland, CA (15 members), and Institute, West Virginia (57 members). The pastors of these churches were Warren A. Rogers, C.C. Johnson,[5] Clifford R. Johnson (the former pastor of Hutchinson, Second CN), and R.W. Cunningham.[6]

Over the next four years, more congregations were added to the CD. In fact, by the time the CD was dismantled in 1952, two more congregations of thirty-one and nineteen were in operation in San Antonio, TX and Oklahoma City, OK. Also, by the end of that year, a church of twenty-eight was operating in a rented building in Detroit and two small Los Angeles congregations had purchased property and developed Sunday school ministries. In fact, by 1953, Sunday school enrollment outdistanced membership numbers for almost all African American churches. For instance, at Chicago Central, membership was only 11, but they had a total Sunday school membership of 58. Likewise at Indianapolis First Colored, they had a total church membership of 16, but 102 were on the Sunday school rolls. Other churches were similar such as Oakland Bethel CN (38 church members as opposed to 157 in Sunday school), Institute CN (112 Sunday school members and 32 church members) and Oklahoma City Alice Street CN (46 Sunday School members and 19 church members).[7]

---

[4]The Manual of the Eleventh General Assembly of the Church of the Nazarene (June 1944): 123. Church of the Nazarene Archives, Lenexa, KS.

[5]C.C. Johnson oversaw and pastored both the work at Mashulaville, MS and the church in Brookhaven, MS until 1958. The next year, the ministry at Mashulaville was dissolved, but Johnson continued to pastor the latter congregation until 1962. Shortly thereafter, the church ceased operation. See, Gulf Central District Church of the Nazarene, Seventh Annual Assembly Journal (April 1959): 6-7. Church of the Nazarene Archives, Lenexa, KS and Gulf Central District Church of the Nazarene, Seventh Annual Assembly Journal (July 1962): 7-11. Church of the Nazarene Archives, Lenexa, KS.

[6]Journal of the Second Annual Conference of the Colored District Church of the Nazarene (November 1948): 13-14. Church of the Nazarene Archives, Lenexa, KS.

[7]For further reference see Gulf Central District Church of the Nazarene, First Annual Assembly Journal (February 1953): 11-12. Church of the Nazarene Archives, Lenexa, KS.

Sunday school numbers among these congregations continued to remain greater than church membership during this time because Sunday school members, like previous decades, did not have to embrace the many individual moral requirements such as avoiding the consumption of alcohol, using tobacco, working on the Sabbath, reading "secular" literature, listening to "worldly" radio programs, wearing "immodest dress" or clothing, taking the name of God in vain, and attending the circus, theatre, and ballroom.[8]

Not only that, but as in preceding years, to be an official member of the denomination, one had to contribute to the ministry of the church, believe in all the doctrines of the denomination, regularly attend all worship services, actively evangelize others, and testify to having experienced the second work of grace—personal sanctification. If one carried out these requirements, then they could join the church. Yet, as one could imagine, these standards continued to deter many Sunday school members (whether black or white) from joining a local congregation and it probably contributed to why many African American congregations, like white Nazarene congregations around the country, had a larger proportion of those who attended Sunday school than church members (in 1956, the average church membership in the CN was 65, while Sunday school membership was 89).[9]

Even though this trend persisted and although there wasn't a single African American congregation that had over fifty members (the average membership of a Nazarene church in 1953 was 64—a relatively small average number)[10], there were still fourteen registered ministers on the CD in 1952, nine of which were actively pastoring churches in the North, South, and West—Rufus Sanders (Chicago Friendly CN), Warren A. Rogers (Detroit Jubilee CN), Clarence Jacobs (Indianapolis First Colored CN), O.B. Whiteside (Los Angeles Marshall Memorial CN), Clifford R. Johnson, the former licensed minister of Hutchinson, KS, (Oakland Bethel CN), D.A. Murray (New Orleans Bethel CN), C.C. Johnson (Brookhaven CN [Mississippi]), Leslie Casmere (San Antonio West End CN), and R.W. Cunningham (Charleston West Institute CN [West Virginia]).[11]

Although these statistics and names point to the presence of African American churches and ministers on the CD, the majority of the legislative

---

[8]Stan Ingersol, singersol@nazarene.org. "Sunday School Attendance for the Church of the Nazarene." Private e-mail message to Brandon Winstead, 10 October 2010.

[9]Ibid and Dale E. Jones, "Average US Churches Sizes, 1908-2010," March 10, 2010. Research Services, Global Ministry Center, Lenexa, KS.

[10]Jones, "Average US Churches Sizes, 1908-2010."

[11]*Gulf Central District Church of the Nazarene, First Annual Assembly Journal*, 12.

and executive power over African American churches, missions, and Sunday schools in the North, West, and South was held by white ecclesiastical leaders throughout the duration of the CD. For instance, J.B. Chapman, a white pastor and church head assumed ultimate jurisdiction over the CD in 1947. Along with Chapman, S.T. Ludwig, the Executive Secretary of the Department of Home Missions and Evangelism was appointed and remained secretary over the district for years to come until Rev. Dr. Hardy C. Powers replaced him as the primary supervisor in 1949.[12]

By maintaining this system of governance, the denomination took a paternal approach to evangelizing and organizing black congregations. For example, in the policy covering the establishment of the CD, the Board of General Superintendents made sure that white District Superintendents on local districts where the black churches resided made organizational and jurisdictional decisions regarding African American congregations:

> The organization of new churches among the colored people is to be carried out through the regular Districts now covering the fields, the District Superintendents of the various districts being authorized and instructed to organize such churches wherever in their judgment the organization is advisable. When organized, the new churches are to be assigned to the Colored District and their statistics inserted in the minutes of the Colored District. Insertion in this list of authorized churches is to be by order of the District Superintendent from the District in which the church is located. [13]

When it came to the licensing and ordaining of black ministers, the same approach applied. Officially, the policy stated that,

> Recognition of orders for colored preachers, the licensing and ordaining of such preachers and other matters affecting the roll of the new District are to be on order of the regular Districts in which the colored churches are located. But the ministers so recognized, licensed and ordained shall be placed on the rolls of the new District and not on the rolls of the regular Districts involved. License shall be by voted of the board of General Superintendents and signed by the Chairman and the Secretary of the Colored District. Ordination may be by a General Superintendent assisted by the District Superintendent of the District on whose recommendation the

---

[12]Department of Home Missions and Evangelism, "Colored Work: Annual Report to the Board of General Superintendents and the Members of the General Board," (January 1950): 1-2. Church of the Nazarene Archives, Lenexa, KS.

[13]Board of General Superintendents, "Policy Covering the Setup and Organization For Colored Work As Authorized By the General Assembly," (Sept. 1944): 1. Church of the Nazarene Archives, Lenexa, KS; S.T. Ludwig, "Report of the Present Status of the Colored Work," (Sept. 1947): 1. Church of the Nazarene Archives, Lenexa, KS; Taylor, 149 and Purkiser, 198-199.

ordination takes place and such credentials shall be signed by the General Superintendent officiating and by the Secretary of the Colored District.[14]

This type of administrative governance toward African American churches was practiced by the denomination throughout the duration of the CD and it seems to have discouraged African Americans from taking complete ownership over how black evangelization would take place at the national level. For instance, when the CD met for the first time in 1947,[15] black Nazarenes did not address how they should contribute or make decisions regarding evangelization among African Americans, nor did white leaders raise the question about how African Americans could take the ultimate lead in developing a national evangelization plan. Likewise, at the district's next annual gathering on November 20-21, white leaders like Dr. Hardy Powers, the DS of the CD, stressed the importance of developing black pastors and evangelizing African Americans around the country without providing space to discuss whether blacks would take the lead in helping to meet these goals. In short, he reiterated the importance of how black and whites needed to make individual sacrifices in order to evangelize and increase the presence of black Nazarenes around the country.[16]

Such beliefs and ecclesiastical governance continued to impact churches on the CD throughout the following years as almost all of the officers that held positions of legislative and executive power on the jurisdiction were white and all the churches and Sunday schools reported their membership numbers and financial expenditures to these representatives. For instance, black ministers like C.C. Johnson and D.A. Murray kept alive small southern churches in the early 1950's, but they, along with other black churches, continued to be supervised by local white District Superintendents. Moreover, in 1952, white District Superintendents supervised all of the thirteen African American churches that reported membership numbers to the CD.[17] Thus, even though African Americans led the affairs of local congregations and contributed to the ministerial development of the CD, they were afforded little opportunity to vote on or speak about how African Americans figured in the final decisions regarding black evangelization or on other administrative concerns pertinent to African American congregations.

---

[14]Board of General Superintendents, 1.

[15]Even though the Board of General Superintendents agreed to start the conference in 1944, the first district meeting did not take place until 1947.

[16]*Journal of the Second Annual Conference of the Colored District Church of the Nazarene*, 8.

[17]See *Gulf Central District Church of the Nazarene, First Annual Assembly Journal*, 12.

In short, what these actions reveal is that through the administrative structure of the CD, there was an attempt to oversee black churches by having them report to local white District Superintendents. At the same time, African American churches were segregated on a national basis under the jurisdiction of the CD. As a part of this structure, black ministers and leaders were not afforded the opportunity to fully govern the affairs of the segregated jurisdiction and the same held true when the denomination decided to build and form Nazarene Bible Institute (hereafter referred to as NBI)—an all black theological training school—in 1948.

Hardy Powers was concerned with recruiting and training African American ministers and he, along with other white denominational leaders, felt that a racially homogeneous Bible college would help bring this desire to fruition. They searched for the best possible location to make this happen and found it in Institute, WV, a suburban area located next to the city of Charleston, WV. Institute was chosen because it housed the strongest "colored" church in the southeast. A committee nominated by the Board of General Superintendents also found that it would be suitable to start "a colored Bible Training School" because it "had the active support" of the local District Superintendent and because it was located across the street from "West Virginia State College for Negroes." In their estimation, this location provided an ecclesiastical and educational base to reach out to the "over two thousand students" that were enrolled at the school.[18]

Based on these recommendations, Powers, the committee, white denominational leaders, and the Department of Home Missions and Evangelism decided to buy two lots across the street from the college. After clearing the land, the Board of General Superintendents borrowed $19,000 from the "Reserve Army Fund"—along with funds raised from white leaders, pastors, and laity on the West Virginia District—to begin construction on a large brick edifice (brick was chosen to match the aesthetics of the college buildings). Over time, these leaders helped finish construction of the building sometime before the beginning of 1949.

As planners who took principal financial responsibility and direction over the construction of NBI, white leaders also assumed primary leadership and decision-making power over the Bible school in its first few years of existence. For example, Dr. E.E. Hale, a former chaplain during World War II and "white churchman," was appointed the first president of the school in June 1948. In addition to Hale's appointment, whites made up all of the inaugural Board of Trustees. At the first trustees' meeting on January 11, 1949 in Kansas City, Missouri, all of the seven members were white ministers and denominational leaders: Hardy C. Powers (the same

---

[18]S.T. Ludwig, "Some Facts Concerning the Situation at Present," (1948): 13. Church of the Nazarene Archives, Lenexa, KS and S.T. Ludwig, "Report of Individual Churches," (1948): 8. Church of the Nazarene Archives, Lenexa, KS.

Powers mentioned above and a General Superintendent), S.T. Ludwig, Gene Phillips, E.O. Chalfant, E.C. Oney, E.E. Hale, and A.K. Bracken. During the gathering, it was also decided that Bracken would serve as chairman, Oney as Vice-Chairman, Ludwig as Secretary, and Roy F. Smee, another white Nazarene, as the board's Treasurer.[19]

By 1951, the situation regarding white leadership had changed little. Of the seven Board of Trustee members only one was an African American— R.W. Cunningham. Cunningham, the pastor of Institute CN, was recruited to be an instructor at NBI but was not able to have direct control or governance over the curriculum of NBI or its financial direction. Nonetheless, he was allowed the opportunity to become a board member and to let the board know "the general attitude of the colored people toward the program."[20]

Thus, during the first few years of existence and until R.W. Cunningham assumed the presidency of the school in 1955, black Nazarenes played a minimal role in contributing to the decision-making processes of NBI.[21] Even when Rev. Clarence Bowman, a black graduate of Nyack Missionary College in New York and Gordon Conwell College in Boston, came to the school to serve as Dean of Men for the college in 1951 and although Rev. Warren Rogers joined the board in the early 1950s, many of the decisions were still made by white denominational leaders that struggled to deal with some of the "problems" at NBI. For instance, at the fifth annual meeting of the Board of Trustees meeting on January 13, 1953 in Kansas City, President Hale told of his frustrations:

> The year which has just past had been one of discouragement so far as the school alone is concerned ... As we began four years ago, we know that we were entering a field and attempting to start a school that would be fraught with many problems, possibly more than have been faced by any other institution to be started in the life of our beloved Zion. And, may we say here that our anticipations of problems, both as to numbers and sizes, were very conservative when compared with what we have encountered.[22]

As he went on to describe the problems he and the school encountered, Hale particularly noted the difficulty of recruiting black students to NBI:

> Many thought that our door yard would be quickly filled with young people seeking an entrance. However, most of us did not expect this, but were not quite prepared for the small response which we did get toward

---

[19]S.T. Ludwig, "Minutes of the Board of Trustees Meeting, Nazarene Bible Institute," (January 11, 1949): 1-3. Church of the Nazarene Archives, Lenexa, KS.

[20]S.T. Ludwig, "Third Annual Board Meeting of the Trustees of Nazarene Bible Institute," (Januray 9, 1951): 1-3. Church of the Nazarene Archives, Lenexa, KS.

[21]Ibid., 1-3.

[22]E.E. Hale, "Report of the President, Nazarene Bible Institute," (January 13, 1953): 1. Church of the Nazarene Archives, Lenexa, KS.

student enrollment . . . It will be recalled that two years ago an effort was made to challenge each district to find and support at least one student. All such efforts have failed to produce the enrollment we desire.[23]

After delivering these words, Hale went on to detail that the school only had twelve total students enrolled during the previous fall semester. Of those twelve, only one was not a "resident of the community or a part time student from West Virginia State College."[24]

Hale felt that these low numbers were caused by several factors: (1) the desegregation of higher education in the North and in the Border States, (2) NBI's lack of close proximity "to the Deep South," and (3) it's "circumscribed curriculum." In order to overcome these limitations, Hale stated that all those who were concerned with NBI needed to work harder and visit more churches so that more black students could be recruited. He underscored this by stating,

It now seems safe to say, that, with a little more effort on the part of all those who have responsibility, a little stronger appeal during next summer, and a few more of our Pastors and people getting stirred up over this matter, that be next we should have not less than twenty or twenty five dormitory students . . . if this could be accomplished, many of our greatest troubles would be over.[25]

Despite his sincerity and recommendations to labor more diligently, however, Hale and the rest of the white leaders never questioned if, or how, blacks could provide the solutions to their problems. Hale and others saw "the colored work" as a "mission field" that needed to be harvested via the decisions of white leaders. Black leaders, pastors, and educators like Cunningham, Rogers, and Bowman were not asked to head committees to systematically address the dearth of black students at NBI nor were they voted as chairman or vice-chairman of the Board of Trustees before Cunningham took the office of President in 1955. In short, their power was limited as to how far they could lead in addressing the financial and educational institutions of NBI.

Furthermore, even though West Indian pastors and congregations had an active presence in Brooklyn, there is no evidence to suggest that they were ever consulted or considered as partners in the ministry at NBI. People like Hale, Bowes, and General Superintendent Vanderpool were bent on targeted African Americans that attended the few Nazarene churches around the country and the students that attended West Virginia Negro College. Targeting, therefore, the Afro-Caribbean churches in Brooklyn for

---

[23]Ibid., 2-3.
[24]Ibid., 2.
[25]Ibid., 3-5.

possible student enrollment or educational leadership fell outside the purview of what whites considered relevant to the "colored work" and one is only left to wonder how a possible relationship with the West Indian congregations in New York could have strengthened NBI during its early days of existence.

Yet, lack of ultimate power and control over the affairs of the CD and NBI and how the denomination addressed black evangelization on a national scale did not prevent African Americans from contributing to denominational life around the country.[26] Even though they remained small congregations, African Americans led Sunday schools, started NWMS and NYPS chapters and participated in laying the educational foundation for training African American pastors at NBI. Thus, despite enduring segregation with limited decision-making power under the jurisdiction of the CD, African Americans around the country labored to expand the

---

[26]Around this same time, the lack of ultimate decision making power on the CD and at NBI was different from African Americans in other predominantly white Protestant and holiness bodies like the Methodist Church and the Church of God (Anderson, IN). In those bodies, they were able to control the ministerial and governmental affairs of their congregations around the country. For example, when the Methodist Episcopal Church and the Methodist Episcopal Church, South united in 1939 to form the Methodist Church, the Plan of Union stated that African American churches and annual conferences would be governed by a segregated jurisdiction called the Central Jurisdiction. Under this plan, black congregations and ministers could elect their own bishops that could vote at the General Conference, speak out on racial concerns, endorse minority legal protection, and oversee and govern the operations of their own journal (called *The Southwestern Advocate*).[26]

Likewise, by the end of the 1940s, blacks within the Church of God (Anderson, IN) continued to use the racially autonomous West Middlesex Campground in West Middlesex, Pennsylvania to address the needs of black congregations. Established in 1917, the West Middlesex Campground served as an annual gathering place for African American congregations in the Church of God (Anderson, IN) where black pastors and lay members would gather to worship, celebrate, and discuss other educational, evangelistic, and polity concerns of African American congregations. Through this annual gathering, blacks used their money and resources to speak out on ecclesiastical racism and establish a Board of Education, a Foreign Missions Board, a National Youth Fellowship (1921), a Youth camp (1949), and a semi-monthly publication called the *Shining Light Survey* (June 1932). For further reference see James Massey, *African Americans and the Church of God (Anderson, IN): Aspects of a Social History* (Warner Press: Anderson, IN, 2002); James Thomas, *Methodism's Racial Dilemma: The Story of the Central Jurisdiction* (Nashville: Abingdon Press, 1992); Peter Murray, *Methodists and the Crucible of Race, 1930-1975* (Columbia, MO: University of Missouri Press, 2004) 34-35; J.H. Graham, *Black United Methodists: Retrospect and Prospect* (New York: Vantage Press, 1979), 80-82 and Dwight Culver, *Negro Segregation in the Methodist Church* (New Haven, CT: Yale University Press, 1953), 60-67

presence of African Americans in the denomination during the late 1940s and 1950s. This participation would continue when the CN decided, in 1953, to place all the black congregations in the South under one racially homogenous district called the Gulf Central District (hereafter referred to as GCD) and place those outside the South under the governance of local districts.

Sectional Segregation and The Beginnings of the Gulf Central District, 1953-1958

After the CD was dissolved at the end of 1952, the General Board and the Board of General Superintendents decided to establish the GCD as a jurisdiction that would govern all churches in the southern portion of the United States and place all other churches outside the South under the jurisdiction of their local geographical districts. In the beginning, the GCD was like the CD in that all the district officers were white pastors and denominational leaders. D.I. Vanderpool, one of the General Superintendents, served as head officer, Dr. John Stockton as treasurer, Alpin P. Bowes as District Secretary and Rev. Leon Chambers as DS. Chambers (a native of Alabama) was appointed to this position because he expressed to denominational leaders his "desire" to develop black ministries in the South. Thus, after he graduated from Nazarene Theological Seminary in the early 1950s, Chambers was chosen as DS.[27]

Of course, there is evidence to suggest that Chambers' "desire" was influenced by his assumption that the "cultural instability" of African Americans needed to be redeemed. He never made this view public in any of the district minutes, but he did echo these sentiments two decades later when he was asked by R.W. Hurn to reflect upon his time as DS on the GCD. In that correspondence, he stated that, "Black people are (in a) class and status conscious among themselves . . . The black population is in a state of cultural instability . . . The cultural instability of the black people could be the greatest opportunity of the church."[28]

Nevertheless, Chambers' paternalism did not impede black pastors from giving him their advice on how to improve black evangelization. In 1955, pastors like C.C. Johnson and D.A. Murray told Chambers that he would need to recruit more black ministers if he wanted to establish more congregations in the South. Chambers listened to their counsel and

---

[27]Roy F. Smee, "Missionary Societies Pray for U.S. Chinese and Negro Work," *The Herald of Holiness*, 20 August 1958, 16-17. Church of the Nazarene Archives, Lenexa, KS.

[28]Leon Chambers to Dr. R.W. Hurn, 25 July 1972, transcript in the hand of Leon Chambers, Church of the Nazarene Archives, Lenexa, KS.

recommended to recruit and develop more pastors.²⁹ By the time of the District Assembly, those recommendations turned into actual numbers. The district ordained Lula Williams (the female pastor at Meridian Fitkins Memorial CN in Meridian, MS) and Joe Edwards (the minister at Oklahoma City Alice Street CN in Oklahoma City, OK) as elders, which brought the grand total to three on the district. Along with them, three other persons were licensed as ministers —Leslie Casmere (San Antonio West End CN, San Antonio, TX), C.C. Johnson (Columbus CN, Columbus, MS), and E.W. Wilson (Shawmut Bethel CN, Lanett, AL).³⁰

By 1957, the ministerial situation remained the same but the total number of churches had increased to thirteen. Organized congregations were in operation in Brookhaven, MS, Calvert, AL, Columbus, MS, Columbus, TX, Memphis, TN, Meridian, MS, Miami, FL, Nashville, TN, New Orleans, LA, Oklahoma City, OK, Richmond, VA, San Antonio, TX, and Lanett, AL. On top of this, missions and Sunday schools were established in Chattanooga, TN, Concord, NC, Mashulaville, MS, and Newport News, VA. At the same time, another person was ordained as an elder—C.C. Johnson—and the list of licensed ministers grew to seven—Leslie Casmere (San Antonio West End), Roland Chopfield (Chattanooga mission station), R.S. Green (San Antonio West End), David C. Moore (no official placement), Boyd L. Proctor (Richmond Mt. Zion CN), Lawrence Reddick (Miami Overcoming CN), and Henry Terry (Memphis Friendship CN).³¹

By asserting their views and by starting and maintaining these churches, those on the GCD contributed to the ministerial and congregational development on the district even though white leaders like Leon Chambers and Alpin P. Bowes held most of the highest decision-making appointments on the district. Moreover, even though congregational and ministerial growth was miniscule in the 1950s (by 1958, membership total on the GCD numbered 178, which was 300 less than the total number of black Nazarenes outside the South),³² African Americans started new Sunday school missions and congregations and licensed and ordained black ministers across the South.

Aside from this, African Americans on the GCD acquired positions of district leadership and helped to build the organizational framework of the GCD. For example, in 1954, blacks served on two of the ministerial boards that

---

²⁹Ibid, 3-4 and *Gulf Central District Church of the Nazarene, Third Annual Assembly Journal* (Feb 28-March, 1955): 14-15. Church of the Nazarene Archives, Lenexa, KS.

³⁰Ibid, 4-5.

³¹*Gulf Central District Church of the Nazarene, Fifth Annual Assembly Journal* (April 25-26, 1957): 4-7, 11. Church of the Nazarene Archives, Lenexa, KS.

³²For further reference see, *Gulf Central District Church of the Nazarene, Sixth Annual Assembly Journal* (March 1-2, 1958): 18-21. Church of the Nazarene Archives, Lenexa, KS.

reviewed and recommended those who would be ordained and licensed as ministers. Melza Brown, D.A. Murray, and Leslie Casmere sat on the District Advisory Board and black ministers like Clarence Bowman and R.W. Cunningham were on the Orders and Relations, and Ministerial Studies Board. Over the next two years, African American pastors continued to serve on these boards and Cunningham maintained his position as president over NBI.[33]

Furthermore, by 1957 and 1958, women continued to serve as two of the six district officers. Arthur Jackson (a member of Memphis Friendship CN) was the president of the Nazarene Foreign Missionary Society (hereafter referred to as NFMS)[34] and Lula Williams (the acting pastor of Meridian Fitkin Memorial Church of the Nazarene) headed up the District Church School Board. As head of the primary educational board on the district, Williams, along with the rest of the committee, often sent recommendations to the district in an effort to improve evangelization in the South. For instance, on April 26, 1957, Williams and the board recommended that,

> 1. In order to bring new members into our Sunday schools and reach new families in our church communities, we recommend that each church appoint a committee to survey the community and take a religious census of families attending no church and children not attending Sunday school.
>
> 2. We recommend that each N.Y.P.S sponsor religious education courses for youth to be taught on youth level and give Christian Service Training credit cards from the Christian Service Training Commission in Kansas City.
>
> 3. We recommend that the missionary societies be responsible for sending at least one student to Nazarene Bible Institute this fall.
>
> 4. We recommend that representatives be invited from Nazarene Bible Institute to visit the church in the month of June and stimulate interest in the various communities surrounding our churches.

---

[33]Cunningham accepted the presidency of the NBI on January 11, 1955. For further reference see, Alvin P. Bowes, "Annual Meeting of the Board of Trustees of Nazarene Bible Institute," (January 7, 1954); 1-3. Church of the Nazarene Archives, Lenexa, KS and Alvin P. Bowes, "Annual Meeting of the Board of Trustees of Nazarene Bible Institute," (January 11, 1955): 2-4. Church of the Nazarene Archives, Lenexa, KS.

[34]The Nazarene Foreign Missionary Society was originally called the Women's Foreign Missionary Society and had active branches an almost every Nazarene district by the late 1950s. It changed its name in 1952 in an effort to recruit and enlist men to the society. They were relatively unsuccessful and by 1958, it continued to be dominated by females. For more information see, W.T. Purkiser, *Called Unto Holiness: The Second Twenty-five Years, 1933-1958*, v. 2 (Kansas City: Beacon Hill Press, 1983), 256.

5. We recommend that a vacation Bible school be held in each church and that Bible teaching be emphasized.[35]

Such statements reveal that Williams was committed to evangelism and to raising awareness about the need to develop and train pastors at NBI. There were a few ministers on the GCD during the mid to late 1950s and Williams and her counterparts understood the importance of overcoming this shortage. This particular concern is what drove her and the board to make the above recommendations and why, at the next district assembly, they stated,

> 1. The constituent churches of the Gulf Central District, under the authorization of the district, be required to conduct Christian Service Training courses in their churches at least once a year.
>
> 2. That consideration be given to fostering vacation Bible schools in all of the churches and that, where it is possible, trained workers if extra workers are essential.
>
> 3. That each church of the district be responsible for sending one boy and one girl, eighteen years of age or over, to our Nazarene Bible Institute annually for youth rallies.
>
> 4. That Nazarene Young people be encouraged to make caravan trips to the Nazarene Bible Institute annually for youth rallies.
>
> 5. That Rev. R.W. Cunningham's educational tours be continued in order to maintain the interest of the churches on our district in the Institute and that time be give for two meetings at each church that would desire it.[36]

In addition to this, Williams and other pastors recorded the highlights of the conference and reported them to *The Herald of Holiness* (the denominational magazine), urged churches to pay their budgets, led committees on evangelism, took an active role in meetings, and participated in district worship. In certain services, Joe Edwards, Clarence Bowman, and Arthur Jackson sang songs such as "He's the One," "Joshua Fit the Battle of Jericho," "Close to Thee," "I Need the Prayers," and "How Great Thou Art." Also, Roland Chopfield and C.C. Johnson occasionally preached, while R.W. Cunningham gave reports on the affairs of NBI.

Moreover, at the annual assemblies, pastors like D.A. Murray, Leslie Casmere, Warren Rogers, and Lula Williams delivered papers that focused on evangelism, on training African American pastors and lay workers, and on improving church finances. At the 1954 district assembly, Murray read a work entitled, "Revivals," while Casmere and Rogers took the opportunity

---

[35]Gulf Central District Church of the Nazarene, Fifth Annual Assembly Journal, 17-18.

[36]Gulf Central District Church of the Nazarene, Sixth Annual Assembly Journal, 22.

to deliver their papers called, "Evangelizing Our People," and "Financing Our Churches." At the following assembly, Williams made public her commitment to strengthen black Sunday schools by reading her paper, which was termed, "Building the Sunday School." Rogers followed her address by reading his work entitled, "The General Work of a Pastor."[37]

Through such efforts and by committing themselves to the evangelistic mission of the CN in the early to mid 1950s, southern black Nazarenes chose to focus on evangelization instead of addressing the segregated structure of the GCD—even though the 1956 General Assembly (GA) made an official statement against racism that read that, " . . . world-wide discrimination against racial minorities [must] be recognized as being incompatible with the Scriptures' proclamation that God is no respecter of persons." In short, like previous decades, black (and white) leaders and laity on the GCD remained primarily concerned with evangelizing others, strengthening church budgets, increasing Church and Sunday school membership, training black pastors, and improving the overall structure and strength of congregations on the GCD. Racism and segregation, whether in society or in the denomination, were publicly ignored and even if black pastors or congregants had preached on or discussed these concerns, those voices were not heard outside their local congregations and communities. Therefore, it seems that southern black Nazarenes endured ecclesiastical segregation because, like most other Nazarenes, their overall commitment was geared towards holiness evangelism and improving the overall life and direction of their congregations.

By doing this, black Nazarenes, like most other Nazarenes, carried on the social conservative tradition of the church that tended to shy away from addressing social concerns. Even when social action was addressed by ecclesiastical heads in the late 1940s and 1950s, it was never done without mentioning the end goal—saving souls. For example, towards the end of the 1940s, J.B. Chapman stated that "revival" and evangelization would bring about social change because through evangelization God could "save" individuals who would "bear upon . . . domestic problems" "and save . . . people from the twin evils of divorce and race suicide." Aside from this, evangelization would help those in society abstain from personal taboos such as "mixed bathing," attending plays, watching television, and attending movies. Thus for Chapman and others, social transformation meant that

---

[37]Gulf Central District Church of the Nazarene, Fourth Annual Assembly Journal, 11-15; Gulf Central District Church of the Nazarene, Third Annual Assembly Journal, 11; Gulf Central District Church of the Nazarene, Fourth Annual Assembly Journal, 11-13; Gulf Central District Church of the Nazarene, Fifth Annual Assembly Journal, 12-14 and Gulf Central District Church of the Nazarene, Sixth Annual Assembly Journal, 14-17.

individuals and congregations worked to evangelize a society that was not aligned with the denomination's ethical or personal holiness standards.[38]

Despite positions like this in the denomination, churches were not officially prohibited from addressing broader social, political, racial, or economic issues. Congregations or pastors could be socially active, but it depended on their own initiative and most congregations in the United States did not choose this path. Instead, they decided to focus their congregational energies in the direction of missions and evangelism, both at home and abroad and African Americans on the GCD weren't much different.

At the same time, it must be remembered that African Americans did not merely accept their second-class membership on the GCD. Instead, through participation on GCD boards, committees, and worship services, through their theological and ministerial commitment to local evangelism, and through their calls to recruit and train more black pastors, African Americans (both males and females) in the mid to late 1950s had an impact on the life and direction of churches on the GCD and to the expansion of the denomination among African Americans throughout the southern United States.

African American Churches Outside the South, 1952-1958: A Brief Synopsis

Like their counterparts in the South, African Americans in the North, South, and West continued to contribute to denominational evangelization and the expansion of the CN among blacks after the CD was dissolved in 1952. For example, when churches like Oakland Bethel returned to their geographical districts, they were able to sit on district committees, boards, vote on legislative matters at district assemblies, and send voting delegates to the General Assembly in 1956. In 1954, lay men and women like William Harper, Milverdia Edmond and Ann Long served as presidents of the church's Sunday school, NYPS, and NFMS departments. As leaders of these ministries, they were able to help decide how the district would go about improving the overall direction of each ministry. Furthermore, because they were governed like their white counterparts and not segregated under the rubric of another jurisdiction, Bethel was able to send a voting lay delegate to the Northern California DA, which they did by sending Cynthia Weir as their congregational representative.[39]

---

[38]William T. Purkiser, Called Unto Holiness, V. 2: The Story of the Nazarenes, The Second Twenty-Fiver Years, 1933-1958 (Kansas City, MO: Beacon Hill Press, 1983), 160-161 and 266-272.

[39]North California District Church of the Nazarene, Forty-Ninth Annual Assembly Journal (May 1954): 5, 13, 85-87. Church of the Nazarene Archives, Lenexa, KS.

Like Bethel, congregations such as Indianapolis 29th Street CN contributed to ministries of the Indianapolis District. In 1955, they had a Sunday school superintendent named "L." Farly that attended DA and a female NYPS president named Rose Mae Patterson.[40] Moreover, during the same year, smaller churches on the Chicago Central, Eastern Michigan, Los Angeles, New England, and West Virginia districts also sat on district committees, sent voting delegates to their annual assemblies, and had NFMS and NYPS chapters that bolstered their districts' membership numbers.[41]

In addition to this, most of the congregations outside the GCD were able to further develop the effectiveness of such ministries like Sunday school. For example, at the beginning 1953, Sunday school attendance in congregations like Bethel stood at 82. However that number jumped to 131 (its total church membership stood at 80) in 1958.[42] In similar fashion, at Institute, Sunday school membership stood at 120 in 1952. Within a matter of a few years that number increased by almost 30 to 148 in 1958.[43]

Simultaneously, African American churches outside the South continued to recruit and train black leadership to the denomination after they joined their geographical districts. In 1954, calls to train and appoint black ministers to churches helped African Americans gain 17 licensed and ordained black and African American ministers in states like Illinois, California, New York, and West Virginia—a number that would remain the same by 1958. By improving in this manner, churches in the North and West helped to raise the total church membership of all African American churches outside the South, contribute to their districts' ministries, and improve the financial giving of their districts. At the start of 1954, for example, there were fifteen "colored" churches outside the South that had a total membership of 409, an average Sunday-school attendance of 703, a total giving of $34,196.00, and an aggregated property value of $217,500.00. Four years later, the total membership number increased to

---

[40]Indianapolis District Church of the Nazarene, Thirtieth Annual Assembly Journal (August 1955): 17, 29. Church of the Nazarene Archives, Lenexa, KS.

[41]None of the churches on these districts had congregational membership over fifty. For further reference, see Gulf Central District Church of the Nazarene, Third Annual Assembly Journal (February 1955): 7-8. Church of the Nazarene Archives, Lenexa, KS.

[42]Gulf Central District Church of the Nazarene, First Annual Assembly Journal (February 1953): 8-9. Church of the Nazarene Archives, Lenexa, KS and Gulf Central District Church of the Nazarene, Sixth Annual Assembly Journal (March 1958): 11. Church of the Nazarene Archives, Lenexa, KS.

[43]Church of the Nazarene Research Center, "Membership Status and Attendance of Institute—West Virginia South District." http://app.nazarene.org/FindAChurch/viewReport.jsp?reportId=107639&sIDType=rpt&orgId=9569. (accessed 20 March 2011).

487. At the same time, Sunday school enrollment grew to 819, while total giving for all congregations reach $45,972 and property value was assessed at $283,264.00.[44]

As this evangelistic contribution transpired by African Americans throughout the United States, West Indians in New York and Cape Verdeans in Massachusetts, continued (or began for Cape Verdeans) their contributions to denominational evangelism and congregational growth among blacks in the Northeastern United States. Unlike their African American counterparts, these two groups were not subjected to the same segregated practices and changes that took place under the CD and then the GCD. Instead, they continued to minister and evangelize their communities with the message of Christian holiness as congregational participants on the New York and New England districts.

West Indians and Cape Verdeans: Expanding the Black Immigrant Church in New York City and Massachusetts, 1947-1958

In the late 1940s and 1950s, the West Indian churches in Brooklyn, continued to hear, embrace, and contribute to the evangelistic and personal holiness message of the general church and denominational leaders. In 1948, for instance, Dr. G.B. Williamson, a General Superintendent, gave a sermon at the New York DA in which he stated, "a spiritual church is a growing church, and that is an indication that it is spiritual." He went on to assert that if Nazarene churches were going to exhibit this growth, then they needed to maintain a "burden" for home and foreign missions. After noting this, he gave a prayer in which he asked God to "intensify our burden and soul passion" for missions and to "revive Thy work in the midst of the years." The following day—July 2, 1948—he emphasized this point when he challenged the assembly to maintain a balance between "personal Holiness" and "the vision of the lost World." He claimed that holiness people could be equipped with "power of the Holy Ghost" and that this "Divine energy," if drawn upon, could help the churches on the New York District reach "the world."[45]

After hearing the words of Williamson, the Church Extension Committee and the New York District's WFMS gave recommendations to expand the

---

[44]Gulf Central District Church of the Nazarene, Second Annual Assembly Journal (February 1954): 6-8. Church of the Nazarene Archives, Lenexa, KS and Gulf Central District Church of the Nazarene, Sixth Annual Assembly Journal, 7-9.

[45]New York District Church of the Nazarene, Forty-First Annual Assembly Journal (July 1948): 4, 17, 32. Church of the Nazarene Archives, Lenexa, KS.

mission of the denomination at the local and international levels. In their report, they stated that,

> We recommend that the churches make a more earnest effort to pay monthly their District Budget to facilitate the Home Mission work. We further recommend that each pastor encourage, and each church sponsor some Home Mission enterprise such as cottage prayer meetings or afternoon Sunday Schools in neighboring communities in order that we might carry out the suggestion of our General Superintendent that the New York District establish twelve new churches during the next quadrennium.[46]

The leader of the latter group, Augusta Vischer (the District President of the WFMS), seconded this motion by making her own overtures toward fulfilling Williamson's evangelistic desires. At the beginning of the WFMS convention, she "read the Word from Acts 10:2" and noted that if the world was "going to know Him," then "it will be through us." After hearing these words, the district body made a resolution to "go on to greater heights and deeper depths for Christ and His cause this coming year."[47]

Of course, the WFMS presidents from the black Brooklyn churches were in attendance and voted to approve these resolutions. By voting, they gave their approval to support foreign missions. At the same time, their congregations endorsed and supported denominational evangelism at the local level. In 1948, when a motion was made to increase the District Church School dues of Beulah, Free Gospel, and Miller, the congregations accepted the motion. They allowed the increases in order to pay for materials that could strengthen the effectiveness of their local Sunday schools.[48]

Likewise, in the same year, members and leaders from Free Gospel helped to start another worshipping community in Long Island. According to the Home Missions report of the district, members from Free Gospel "located a building at Wyandanch, Long Island," and "finished arrangements with the Wyandanch Colored Civic Association to use the building for Sunday school and Church services." It went on to note that "Our Colored Churches in Brooklyn are all back of the project and it looks prospective for a new church."[49]

---

[46]Ibid., 32.

[47]Ibid., 45-46.

[48]Interestingly enough, of the twenty-nine churches that had their dues increased, there were only four churches that had a higher mandate to give than either Beulah or Miller. The two congregations were recommended to give $11.90 and $11.20 for the year while the white churches of Dover, East Rockaway, Kingston, and Richmond Hill were required to give $15.40, $15.00, $13.20, and $12.90. See, Ibid., 34.

[49]Ibid., 29.

In short, recommendations, resolutions, and evangelistic labors such as these revealed West Indians continued commitment to denominational evangelism and improving their membership numbers and outreach ministries. For instance, in 1948, Miller had a total of 65 church members and a Sunday school membership of 65. Similarly, Beulah had a sum of 73 members that regularly attended Sunday morning worship and 70 persons that filled the Sunday school rolls. At the same time, Free Gospel was not as large as the other two congregations, but they still had 34 church members and 40 regular Sunday school attendees.[50] However, over the course of the next few years, the collective numbers of these churches continued to grow. By 1951, Beulah, Miller Memorial, Bedford Zion (formerly known as Free Gospel,)[51] and Wyandanch CN[52] had a total of 207 church members, 209 who regularly attended Sunday school, and 38 that were on the membership rolls of the NYPS. Seven years later, the numbers increased across the board. The total church membership for all the congregations was 239 and Wyandanch alone added 19 new members by the time the District Assembly gathered in the summer of 1958. Similarly, the Sunday school attendance of all the congregations in that year totaled approximately 300, while the NYPS membership for the four churches was 74.[53]

While this happened, black laity and ministers continued their contributions to district leadership. In 1948, William Greene sat on the Orders and Relations Board and helped decide who would be ordained, receive their minister's license or be commissioned as an evangelist. Moreover, Rev. Levi Franklin persisted in assisting with district leadership by sitting on the Education Committee and the Foreign Missions Committee,

---

[50]Ibid., 34, 37, statistical index.

[51]*New York District Church of the Nazarene, Forty-Second Annual Assembly Journal* (July 1949): 6, 25. Church of the Nazarene Archives, Lenexa, KS. This name change coincided with the purchasing of the building in which they worshipped. For quite some time, the congregation held services, Sunday school, and other ministry events in a rented edifice at 550 Washington Avenue, Brooklyn, New York. With the purchase of the building, the structure at Washington Avenue became the congregation's permanent home.

[52]The Wyandanch congregation was officially organized in 1950 as a way to evangelize West Indian Nazarenes that were migrating to Long Island in the post-WWII years. The first pastor, Eugene Hazard, was one of the founding members and ordained elders of Bedford Zion. For further information about Wyandanch's organization, see *New York District Church of the Nazarene, Forty-Fourth Annual Assembly Journal* (July 1951): 31. Church of the Nazarene Archives, Lenexa, KS.

[53]*New York District Church of the Nazarene, Forty-Fourth Annual Assembly Journal*, statistical index and *New York District Church of the Nazarene, Fifty-First Annual Assembly Journal* (July 1958): statistical index. Church of the Nazarene Archives, Lenexa, KS.

while James Jessamy, the pastor of Free Gospel, and Lawrence Wallace, the lay minister of the newly formed Brooklyn East New York CN, sat on district committees like the Ministerial Relief and Pastoral Support Committee and the Publishing Interests Committee.[54]

Meanwhile, women and young people from the West Indian congregations actively contributed to the youth and deaconess ministries of the district. Young persons like Herbert Nicholls, Grace Thorpe, Iris Atkinson, and Millicent Jones led the local chapters of the NYPS at Beulah, East New York, Free Gospel, and Miller Memorial, while women such as Geneatha Harris, Florence Vaughn, Mabel Catlyne, and Florence Walcott led each of the above mentioned congregations' WFMS chapters. At the same time all the churches' voting delegates that year were women—Mable Barnett, Viola Bowen, Keturah Pilgram, Miriam Clarke, and Edith Clarke—and of the seven consecrated deaconesses on the New York District, three of them were Afro-Caribbean—Mabel Catlyne, Gertrude Forde, and Rhoda Gittens. Likewise, when the Deaconess and Rescue Work Committee gathered in 1948, several Afro-Caribbean women from the black Brooklyn churches were chosen as voting representatives.[55]

This type of active contribution to district leadership continued to persist throughout the 1950s. When the District Assembly minutes were recorded in 1955, Afro-Caribbean Nazarenes sat on committees such as the Ways and Means Committee, the Home Missions and Church Extension Committee, the Publishing Interests Committee, the Church Schools Committee, the Deaconess and Rescue Work Committee, the Memorials Committee, the Sabbath Observance Committee, and the Memorials Committee. The congregations also sent voting delegates to District Assemblies and Levi Franklin and Eugene Hazard, a former member of Bedford Zion and pastor of Wyandanch CN, received votes from the delegation to be sent as representatives of the district to the 1956 General Assembly in Kansas City, MO.[56]

Likewise, three years later, lay delegates from all five West Indian congregations attended DA and voted on matters related to church governance, Sunday school, evangelization, and foreign missions. Persons like Rev. Franklin, Mabel Catlyne, Walter Hazard, Lawrence King, Clarence Jacobs (the former pastor of the African American congregation in Indianapolis and minister of Miller Memorial), and James Jessamy sat on assembly committees. Furthermore, persons like Mabel Catlyne, Lillian

---

[54]New York District Church of the Nazarene, Forty-First Annual Assembly Journal, 20-21.

[55]Ibid., 11-13.

[56]New York District Church of the Nazarene, Forty-Eighth Annual Assembly Journal (July 1955): 11, 14-16, 20-21, 28-29. Church of the Nazarene Archives, Lenexa, KS.

Franklin, Lillian Corbin, Ophelia Mayers, Dorothy Howell, Louise Davis, Johanna Houston, and Albert Braithwaite were sent to the DA representatives of their local chapters of the NYPS and the NFMS (formerly called the WFMS). [57] By filling these positions of leadership, young people and women worked alongside male ministers and laypersons to help lead their churches' commitment to improve Nazarene ministries on the predominantly white New York District.

At the same time, one pastor, Franklin, continued to work alongside other ministers and organizations outside the CN to not simply promote black evangelism, but to address social issues that impacted blacks in New York and throughout the country. For instance, in the late 1940s, Franklin maintained membership in the Interdenominational Ministerial Alliance (IMA), an interdenominational organization of Brooklyn ministers that addressed issues of racism throughout the United States. As a member and secretary of the organization in the summer of 1947, he helped the group send a resolution, which condemned lynching, to political leaders in Washington D.C. and Albany, New York. The resolution, which was recorded by Franklin and approved by Dr. R.G. Waters, the pastor of the large African American Newman Memorial Methodist Church in Brooklyn, noted that,

> We view with great alarm a situation that has created the greatest concern in the life of the Negro in this country. The Federal and State courts of this country must find a way to stop the un-American practice of killing without giving a man or woman the right to consider themselves innocent until, by a court of justice, they are proven guilty. Lynching is a foul blot on our Democratic form of government, a stain on our way of living that makes America reproachful in the eyes of a civilized world. The Inter-Denominational Ministerial Alliance decries this hideous specter as the shame that creates fear and distrust on the part of 15,000,000 people, whose sole protection is the decision of an intelligent Christian conscience which embodies the declaration, 'Do unto others as you would have them do unto you.'[58]

Because of his membership and participation in the IMA, Franklin associated with other IMA ministers that were socially conscious, like the young black Presbyterian minister Milton A. Galamison. Galamison, the pastor of Siloam Presbyterian Church, often preached about the social implications of the Christian Gospel in the late 1940s and 1950s. During Franklin's tenure, Galamison gave such sermons like, "The Social Significance of the Crucifixion," on March 13, 1949. In that sermon, he stated that Jesus' death was a result of his preaching and teaching against

---

[57] New York District Church of the Nazarene, Fifty-First Annual Assembly Journal, 22-23, 33.

[58] "Negro Ministers Protest Lynchings," The Brooklyn Daily Eagle, 14 June 1947.

the "collective social evil" and "organized corruption."⁵⁹ In addition to this, Galamison reiterated in another sermon entitled, "The Tie That Binds," that one of the primary purposes of the church and its Christian leaders was to oppose "evil" in all its systemic forms and to help those who were oppressed to achieve freedom.⁶⁰

Aside from Galamison, other IMA ministers embodied a socially conscious Christian ethic. Gardner C. Taylor was one of those. He was the pastor of Concord Baptist Church and a vocal member of the Democratic Party that developed close ties with Mayor Robert Wagner, served on an advisory group to improve city services, and became a member of the Board of Education in 1958. Likewise, the president of the IMA in the late 1940s to mid 1950s, the Rev. C.L. Franklin of Nazarene Congregational Church, challenged the organization to speak out when racial injustice threatened the lives of African Americans.⁶¹ In short, by maintaining membership in the IMA, Franklin associated with such individuals that actively struggled for school integration, better medical service for Bed-Stuy residents, and attacked local and national racism.⁶²

Yet, aside from these instances, written evidence for such social activism among black leadership and laity is almost nonexistent. The overall commitment of the Brooklyn ministers and lay leaders was to carry out the mission of the denomination to those in their communities. In other words, evangelism was the primary focus of ministers and laity and thus, the energies of congregations were spent on "reaching" those in their communities through evangelistic efforts. As a result, engagement in local or national civil rights action was not primary to the West Indian congregations in New York.

In this way, the majority of black Nazarenes in New York, much like their white and African American constituents around the country, resembled the predominant social views in the CN in the late 1940s and 1950s. Instead of addressing complex social issues, most West Indians chose to focus on local evangelism and outreach. The activist activities of those like Franklin were not the norm of Afro-Caribbean pastors and congregations throughout this period. Attacking national or ecclesiastical racism, unemployment, housing conditions or other social concerns was not

---

⁵⁹Milton A. Galamison, Sermon: The Social Significance of the Crucifixion, Exodus 6:1-13, written at Siloam Presbyterian Church, Brooklyn [23 March 1949], Milton A. Galamison Papers, Box 2, Folder 7, Schomburg Center for Research in Black Culture, New York (Harlem).

⁶⁰Milton A. Galamison, Sermon: The Tie That Binds, written at Siloam Presbyterian Church, Brooklyn [05 June 1955], Milton A. Galamison Papers, Box 3, Folder 17, Schomburg Center for Research in Black Culture, New York (Harlem).

⁶¹Clarence Taylor, *The Black Churches of Brooklyn* (New York: Columbia University Press, 1994), 121.

⁶²Ibid, 121.

the primary concern of West Indian churches or their ministers. The primary goal, like others on the New York District and around the country, was to evangelize others, both at home and abroad, with the denominational message of Christian salvation and personal holiness.

This evangelistic or "outreach" goal was not only promoted in traditional Nazarene ministries like NYPS, NFMS, and Sunday school, but also in certain ecumenical activities and creative ministries of local congregations. For instance, Franklin, aside from his pastoral duties and activities in the IMA, held interdenominational worship services that promoted black evangelization and historical black achievement. In addition to this, he often preached evangelistic sermons on the radio for the Brooklyn Church and Mission Federation.[63]

Like Franklin, the Rev. James Jessamy of Bedford Zion, participated in ecumenical events such as the annual celebration of the New York Bible Society (hereafter referred to as NYBS). NYBS, which was formed in 1809, was an interdenominational missionary organization that focused on "trying to provide every person" in New York City with a Bible that was written "in his own language" and "at cost prices to those able to pay, and free to the poor." In an effort to make sure that the society could meet this end, African American and West Indian churches would hold annual worship celebrations to raise money and awareness about the work the organization was doing in the black neighborhoods of "Brooklyn, Queens, and Richmond."

At the annual celebration in 1950, Rev. Jessamy helped to lead the service alongside such prominent African American ministers like Rev. Galamison, Rev. Taylor, Rev. C.L. Franklin, and Rev. J. Henry Carpenter. Galamison presided over the service, while Taylor and Carpenter gave greetings to the assembly. When they finished, Franklin introduced the speaker of the night, the Rev. Father Charles E. England, Rector of St. Augustine Protestant Episcopal Church. After the sermon, Rev. Jessamy gave the benediction right before the 200 voice Interdenominational Choir

---

[63]Because of these labors, along with his long-time participation in Bedford Ministers Association and the IMA, when a poll was taken by the *New York Amsterdam News* in 1949 to discover who was the most influential Black Brooklynite, Rev. Franklin finished 21st and was also one of only six ministers that made the final list of 30. For further reference see "Feted," *New York Amsterdam News*, 04 February 1950; "Church Honors Levi Franklin," *New York Amsterdam News*, 11 February 1950; "About Religion and Education," *New York Amsterdam News*, 04 January 1947; "Cite Record Of Poll Winners," *New York Amsterdam News*, 08 January 1949. It is interesting to note that Franklin's notoriety in the community was also recognized in 1952 when the *New York Amsterdam News* mentioned him as one of the more well know black Brooklynites that vacationed at "Richard's House" in Saratoga Springs, New York. For further details see, "Brooklynites at Richard's House," *New York Amsterdam News*, 23 August 1952.

led the assembly in singing the recessional hymn entitled, "Lead On, O King Eternal."[64]

Likewise, at the youth level, persons like Grace Braithwaite, a child of Barbadian immigrants and young adult member of Miller in the 1950s, participated in Brooklyn Day—the annual interdenominational Sunday school parade held by black and white Brooklyn congregations. As Braithwaite notes, in the early to mid 1950s, the event was so large that it became a "holiday" for black and white children of Brooklyn. It was a time, she recalls, where the children could wear "their very best Sunday dress" and make their own elaborate floats that celebrated the theme of the annual parade, such as "The Lord is the Way, the Truth, and the Life," or "Jesus Christ is the Hope of the World." By doing this, Braithwaite notes that she was able to have "fun" and celebrate the collective work of Sunday schools across Brooklyn. She alludes to this point, commentating that,

> The event was a wonderful day for us because we all got involved in the parade. We all marched up and down the main avenues. We went down as far as we could, turned around and came back and we came back to our own churches and we sang and we had ice cream and cake and it was great fun … all the churches on anniversary day.[65]

Aside from this, Braithwaite and Ludwick Jones, a long-time member of Miller Memorial, maintain that the Nazarene churches in the borough of Brooklyn encouraged young people in their congregation to attend an interdenominational group called the "National Young People's Association." This group was led by Afro-Caribbeans from holiness and Pentecostal traditions that held worship services for youth throughout the year. Specifically, in the summer, the organization would hold outdoor youth revivals for weeks on end and because of this, Braithwaite claims states that many black Nazarenes and other young people were able to hear and accept the Gospel and avoid trouble by staying "off the streets."[66]

In addition to ecumenical activities, Braithwaite notes that in the 1950s, deaconesses at churches like Bedford Zion, Miller Memorial, and Beulah CN

---

[64]"The New York Bible Society: 141st Anniversary Celebration and Universal Bible Sunday Observance at First African Methodist Episcopal Zion Church, December 3, 1950," Milton A. Galamison Papers, Box 94, Folder 14, Schomburg Center for Research in Black Culture, New York (Harlem) and "The New York Bible Society: 142nd Anniversary Celebration at the Concord Baptist Church, December 2, 1951," Milton A. Galamison Papers, Box 94, Folder 14, Schomburg Center for Research in Black Culture, New York (Harlem).

[65]Grace Braithwaite, personal interview with Brandon Winstead, Brooklyn, New York, September 17, 2009. Brandon Winstead's Private Collection, Kansas City, KS.

[66]Ibid. and Ludwick Jones, personal interview with Brandon Winstead, Brooklyn, New York, September 18, 2009. Brandon Winstead's Private Collection, Kansas City, KS.

helped to expand the "outreach" mission of the black churches by "witnessing" and taking care of some of the laity's and community member's physical needs. Specifically, Braithwaite claims that when church members and their family members who did or did not attend church, would return home from the hospital, deaconesses would visit and make sure that some of their medicinal and physical needs were met. Also, she maintains that if a church member or someone they knew in the community had a baby, they would help provide some of the essentials needed to raise the child during the first few months of infancy.[67]

Furthermore, Jones notes that when he immigrated to Brooklyn from Barbados in 1957, many laypersons at Miller Memorial tried to "reach out" to those outside the church by establishing an informal credit union to Barbadian immigrants. As he recalls, immigrants and church members and certain other individuals that were recommended by church members could contribute to and borrow from the large monetary fund when they needed a down payment to purchase property, whether commercial or residential. Because of this practice, Jones notes that many at Miller Memorial "were able to purchase properties" and "it worked good for a lot of folk." Not only that, but he notes that some outside the church became members because they received financial assistance through the credit union.[68]

Nonetheless, what these examples reveal is that West Indians in Brooklyn contributed to the leadership of the denomination on the New York District, started new churches, improved their NFMS, NYPS, and Sunday school ministries alongside white congregations on their district. Not only that, but ministers like Franklin worked to address systemic issues around the country and he, along with other ministers and laity, participated in ecumenical activities and organizations in order to expand the evangelistic efforts of the black congregations in New York. In addition to this, in an effort to "reach out" to those in their communities, they continued and began local ministry initiatives to address some of the physical and economic needs of black immigrants in the late 1940s and 1950s.

However, West Indians weren't the only immigrants of African descent during this period that carried out the mission of the denomination in the northeastern United States. In 1949, the New Bedford Portuguese CN was established in New Bedford, MA as a fully participating and voting congregation of the New England District. The church started as an outreach ministry of Adelina Domingues who immigrated to New Bedford sometime in the 1930s or 1940s and joined the CN (shortly after she arrived, Domingues started attending the white Nazarene church along

---

[67]Braithwaite, personal interview with Brandon Winstead.
[68]Jones, personal interview with Brandon Winstead.

with her husband, John Manuel Domingues—also a native Cape Verdean[69] who had come to accept the personal holiness teachings of the CN before immigrating to the United States).[70] After becoming a devotee of the CN, she began holding a weekly Bible study in her home at 95 Jenney St., New Bedford, MA in 1948. According to a congregational history, Domingues knocked on the "doors of 2,000 homes" of Cape Verdean immigrants in an effort to get them to attend her meetings so that a "Nazarene mission" could be founded amongst the couple thousand mulatto or "African Portuguese" that had settled in New Bedford's South End as early as 1860. Within a few months her labors bore fruit and the Rev. Turpel, the pastor of the white New Bedford congregation, wrote the "by-laws of the first organized Cape Verdean Mission in the United States."[71]

Shortly thereafter, at the New England District Assembly, it was noted that this young congregation "was born in New Bedford, Mass . . . with twenty-three charter members." J.C. Albright, the District Secretary, went

[69]The term "Cape Verdean" refers to those of either African or African/Portuguese (i.e. mulatto) descent who were from the West African islands that were an extension of Portugal's colonial empire since the late 15th century. However, in 1975, the conglomeration of islands won their independence and established, "The Republic of Cape Verde." Hence, the term is historically retroactive and is used to designate those who migrated from the islands to the states during the late 19th century to the mid 20th century. For a brief overview of the events surrounding Cape Verde's nationalistic struggle and the historical use of the term "Cape Verdean," see Marilyn Halter, *Cape Verdean American Immigrants, 1860-1965* (Champaign, IL: The University of Illinois Press, 1993), 2-20, 34.

[70]John Domingues became a Nazarene after hearing the preaching of John José Diaz, a native Cape Verdean, American immigrant, and member of the Association of Pentecostal Churches of America (hereafter referred to as APCA). After accepting the message and teachings of the organization, he was commissioned and sent as a missionary to his native island in February 1901. While on the mission field, the APCA joined the CN thus making Diaz the first missionary to Cape Verde. He eventually retired from his post as missionary in 1938 and moved back to Pawtucket, Rhode Island. Although not mentioned by denominational historians, pictures of Diaz from the early 20th century reveal that his physical characteristics were sub-Saharan Africa making him not only one of the first missionaries for the denomination, but also the first "black" missionary for the CN. For further reference see, Unknow Author, "In Memoriam, Rev. John Dias, 1873-1964, Cape Verde Islands," in *The Other Sheep* (March 6, 1965): 11. Church of the Nazarene Archives, Lenexa, KS; *New England District Church of the Nazarene, First Annual Assembly Journal* (May 1908): 8. Church of the Nazarene Archives, Lenexa, KS; J. Fred Parker, *Mission to the World: A History of Missions in the Church of the Nazarene Through 1985* (Kansas City, MO: Nazarene Publishing House, 1988), 191-192 and Unknown Author, "Nazarene Roots, The Ties That Bind: Part 1," in *The Herald of Holiness* (October 15, 1988): 11. Church of the Nazarene Archives, Lenexa, KS.

[71]Unknown Author, "Recorded History of the Portuguese Nazarene Church," Church of the Nazarene Arcives, Lenexa, KS and Halter, 38-46, 164-170.

on to extol the work of Domingues and stated that the church had "purchased a lot in a good location" and that Rev. Manuel Chavier had "been appointed pastor and is enthusiastically pushing the work."[72]

Chavier came to the church by the recommendation of one his former Sunday school teachers in Rhode Island who "remembered his pupil of promise, now a college student." When the members heard this recommendation and invited Chavier to preach, "they were deeply impressed by his delivery" and "spiritual charisma." Thus, they called a meeting of the church, and they voted to have Chavier as their inaugural pastor "if he were willing to work there and felt the call to minister among his people in this city." Chavier accepted and immediately "rolled up his sleeves," focused on ministering to the Cape Verdean community, and quickly helped to strengthen the ministerial presence of his congregation on the New England District.[73]

In particular, Chavier and other Cape Verdeans in New Bedford (like their counterparts in Brooklyn) sat on district committees, voted on legislative and ecclesiastical concerns at district assemblies, sustained Sunday school, NFMS, and NYPS ministries, and became evangelistically active in the Cape Verdean community of New Bedford. In 1952, some of Chavier's congregants like Mrs. Lydia DePina, Jonathan DePina, and Frank Johnson headed up the NFMS and NYPS and sat on the district Sunday School Committee. Likewise, in 1956, Agnes Roderiques attended the DA of the New England District as a Sunday school delegate and Reinaldo Balla represented the congregation's NYPS to the district body. Meanwhile, by the following year, Chavier sat on the Home Missions and Church Extension Committee and Diah Lomba was on the committee for Foreign Missions.[74]

Because of involvement in such active ministries, the membership numbers of the church and Sunday school continued to improve. Within eight years of its founding, the church had more than doubled its membership to fifty and it also had 79 Cape Verdean women, men, children, and teenagers who regularly attended Sunday school—a number that was almost double what it had been in 1949. By the following year, they added another member to the congregation and another 40 members to the Sunday school roster, which brought the total to 119.

---

[72]New England District Church of the Nazarene, Forty-Second Annual Assembly Journal, (June 1949): 44. Church of the Nazarene Archives, Lenexa, KS.

[73]Unknown Author, "Recorded History of the Portuguese Nazarene Church."

[74]New England District Church of the Nazarene, Forty-Fifth Annual Assembly Journal (June 1952): 15, 25-30, 36-37. Church of the Nazarene Archives, Lenexa, KS; New England District Church of the Nazarene, Forty-Ninth Annual Assembly Journal (May 1956): 30-37. Church of the Nazarene Archives, Lenexa, KS and New England District Church of the Nazarene, Fiftieth Annual Assembly Journal (June 1957): 19, 29, 39-47. Church of the Nazarene Archives, Lenexa, KS.

Although these numbers may seem small or miniscule, when compared to some average size white churches on the district in 1958, the New Bedford Portuguese Church of the Nazarene's membership and Sunday school numbers were anything but insignificant. For instance, Framingham CN in Framingham, MA, a church that had been in operation since the late 1920s, had 71 church members and 76 Sunday school members. Likewise, Nashua CN in Nashua, NH, possessed a church membership of 38 and a Sunday school attendance of 47. On the New England district, other churches like Newport CN in Newport, VT had 58 church members and 77 people that regularly attended Sunday school while Yarmouth CN in Yarmouth, ME possessed a church membership of 54 and a Sunday school membership of 109.[75]

Of course, there were other churches like Lowell First CN in Lowell, MA, that had almost 200 members during this time, but these congregations were far and few between. Most remained under 100 members and churches like New Bedford Portuguese were an average reflection of both church and Sunday school membership. In this regard, the Cape Verdean membership numbers were not small, but average and they reflected how they participated and contributed to the overall church and Sunday school membership numbers on the New England District.[76]

At the same time that Cape Verdeans contributed to district leadership and maintained traditional Nazarene ministries like NFMS, NYPS, and Sunday school, the church also offered additional ministries for the congregants and the community. Ministries like Vacation Bible School were started in the summer time for children in the community and a "Dorcas

---

[75] Church of the Nazarene Resource Center, "Membership Status and Attendance of Framingham Church of the Nazarene—New England District." http://app.nazarene.org/FindAChurch/viewReport.jsp?reportId=21196&orgId=8199. (accessed 28 March 2011); Church of the Nazarene Resource Center, "Membership Status and Attendance of Nashua Church of the Nazarene—New England District." http://app.nazarene.org/FindAChurch/viewReport.jsp?reportId=21196&orgId=8222. (accessed 28 March 2011); Church of the Nazarene Resource Center, "Membership Status and Attendance of Newport Church of the Nazarene—New England District." http://app.nazarene.org/FindAChurch/viewReport.jsp?reportId=21196&orgId=8229. (accessed 28 March 2011) and Church of the Nazarene Resource Center, "Membership Status and Attendance of Yarmouth Church of the Nazarene—New England District." http://app.nazarene.org/FindAChurch/viewReport.jsp?reportId=21196&orgId=8229. (accessed 28 March 2010).

[76] Church of the Nazarene Resource Center, "Membership Status and Attendance of Lowell First Church of the Nazarene—New England District." http://app.nazarene.org/FindAChurch/viewReport.jsp?reportId=21196&orgId=8212. (accessed 28 March 2010).

Society" was inaugurated so that young and older women could learn to sew for themselves and for others. In addition to this, a "Men's Fellowship" that sponsored "various programs" was founded along with a youth choir, a "Contemporary Choir," and an adult choir. Moreover, an "Outreach Program" was established and shortly thereafter, the ministry had an "impact" that was "felt in the community" as they carried out "Christ's Great Commission of 'preaching the Gospel to every creature.'"[77]

Sponsoring ministries like this with the intent of evangelizing and improving the religious life of the Cape Verdean community did not end with the collective actions of the church. It also extended to the personal actions of Rev. Chavier. For example, at the same time that he pastored New Bedford Portuguese CN, Chavier (an educated pastor who received theological degrees from Gordon College and Eastern Nazarene College by the early 1950s), taught English at a local junior high school called Normandin Jr. High School. As a teacher and educator, Chavier was noted, by local authorities, to be an important contributor to the moral, educational, and religious lives of New Bedford's Cape Verdean youth in the 1950s.[78]

In sum, by performing in such ways, Cape Verdeans, along with Afro-Caribbeans and African Americans around the country, sought to extend the mission and message of the denomination among blacks of African descent throughout the United States during the late 1940s and 1950s. As this chapter has revealed, black churches, whether placed under a segregated judicatory or on geographical districts and regardless of their ethnicity, geographical location, or historical experience, embraced the evangelistic thrust of the denomination and focused their energies on evangelizing and discipling those in their communities through supporting traditional Nazarene ministries, foreign missionaries, and by creating local ministry initiatives. As this transpired, some of the congregations sought to address (or continued to address) certain physical, social, educational, and economic concerns that impacted those in their communities. They took it upon themselves to tackle these concerns so that the churches could be more effective in "reaching out" to those in the congregations and local communities. In this way, they sought to live out their faith that could make a difference in the lives of those in their churches and communities.

At the same time, as African American and black churches supported and participated in denominational life during this period, they did not form substantial ecclesiastical relationships across ethnic lines.

---

[77]New England District Church of the Nazarene, Fiftieth Annual Assembly Journal, statistical index and New England District Church of the Nazarene, Fifty-First Annual Assembly Journal (June 1958), statistical index.

[78]"1969 Achievement Award, Rev. Manuel Chavier," The Cape Verdean, July 1969. Church of the Nazarene Archives, Lenexa, KS.

Geographical location, ethnic differences, social particularities, and historical experiences seem to have divided the various groups from cooperating with one another during this period. Not only that, but because of these issues, the various groups, for reasons unbeknownst to the modern researcher, did not join together to see how they could strengthen the collective black presence of the church or address ecclesiastical racism that limited African American decision making power on the CD and the GCD.

Yet, black Nazarenes continued their evangelistic and denominational work. Whether it was the West Indian churches in Brooklyn, the Cape Verdean congregation in Massachusetts or the African American churches in Mississippi, Oklahoma, Tennessee, Louisiana, Texas, Illinois, Michigan, California, or West Virginia, black Nazarenes played a pivotal part in strengthening the CN in the late 1940s and 1950s. Moreover, even when African Americans remained segregated under a national or regional jurisdiction, they continued to participate in denominational activities, improve their local ministries, train and educate black ministers, and support foreign missions. Thus, black groups throughout the country experienced different ecclesiastical practices and different levels of racism within the denomination, but they nonetheless continued to embrace the personal holiness message of the CN, participate in denominational life and expand the presence of the denomination among a divergent of black communities during this period.

In the years following 1958, such a dynamic would continue to shape black Nazarene churches throughout the nation as Afro-Carribeans, West Indians, and African Americans carried out the evangelistic mission of the denomination in their local communities. However, as West Indians, Cape Verdeans, and African Americans outside the South did this, southern blacks continued to minister under the guise of the racially segregated GCD.

Chapter Four

African American Nazarenes, Social Conservatism, and Evangelistic Growth from 1958-1969

"Evangelize the Negro": Continued Participation on the Gulf Central District

On the last day of the Sixth Annual Assembly of the GCD, Warren A. Rogers was presented by Chambers as the new DS. After the presentation, it was noted that Rogers "brought a stirring message from Acts 1:8" and that after his sermon concluded, the altar was "filled with seekers." Several weeks before Rogers gave this oration, the Board of General Superintendents appointed Rogers to his new position. [1] Rogers received this offer because he had been born and raised in the Deep South[2] and because he had developed his reputation as an efficient minister that was committed to personal holiness evangelism. By the time of his appointment, he had already successfully pastored two black Nazarene churches in Indianapolis,

---

[1] This appointment came after Chambers tenured his resignation in early 1958.

[2] Rogers was born in Winnsboro, LA in 1917. After four years, the family moved to the Mississippi Delta and worked on a variety of cotton plantations in and around Alligator, MS and Clarksville, MS. Sometime before 1941, Rogers moved to Akron, Ohio, where he became a member of the Kenmore CN. For further reference, see Warren Rogers to to R.W. Hurn, 09 September 1972, transcript in the hand of Warren Rogers. Church of the Nazarene Archives, Lenexa, KS and Bowman, 43.

IN and in Detroit, MI. Rogers first pastored the Indianapolis congregation, where he helped the church acquire property and attain a small, but established membership (19 members were registered in 1948). After stabilizing that church, he then moved to Detroit and over the following years, he helped Detroit Jubilee CN become a stable congregation.[3]

When Rogers became DS in 1958, he sought to strengthen the GCD like he had the churches in Indianapolis and Detroit. In order to accomplish this end, Rogers immediately established a district newspaper so that communication on the jurisdiction could be improved. The name of the paper was entitled, *The Gulf Central Informer* (hereafter referred to as GCI), and its main purpose was to keep pastors and laity informed about what was happening on the district throughout the year. During his first year of administration, Rogers also held four holiness revivals at Memphis Friendship CN, at West Side San Antonio CN, at Chattanooga Alton Park CN and in Orlando, FL. He believed that these revivals would help revive and sanctify the spiritual condition of blacks in these churches and would empower others to establish new African American congregations. At the end of 1958, this belief turned into reality, as his revival preaching helped the Chattanooga congregation increase its membership by five, from five to ten and as it helped to lay the foundation of the congregation that would be established in Orlando at the end of the year.[4]

By holding revivals and by visiting various locations and churches throughout the district, Rogers also helped to organize two other churches and increase membership on the district by thirty-six, which brought the total to two-hundred and eighteen. Moreover, his efforts encouraged sixteen additional people to join the NYPS and the NFMS. In other words, during his first year as DS, Rogers was able to further the work of the district by helping to start new churches and by evangelizing in various black communities around the South. However, it is important to remember that other black pastors and laity contributed to the strengthening of the district during the late 1950s and early 1960s. For example, in an article written in February 12, 1958, Rev. Joe Edwards of Providence CN in Oklahoma City, OK, asked all Nazarenes to pray for; (1) more black holiness evangelism (2) more African American churches to be established, (2) funds to improve church structures, and (3) additional African American

---

[3]Unknown Author, "Report of Individual Colored Churches, Indianapolis, Indiana," (1948): 6. Church of the Nazarene Archives, Lenexa, KS and *Gulf Central District Church of the Nazarene, First Annual Assembly Journal*, 7-9, 14.

[4]*Gulf Central District Church of the Nazarene, Sixth Annual Assembly Journal* (March 1-2, 1958): 19. Church of the Nazarene Archives, Lenexa, KS; *Gulf Central District Church of the Nazarene, Seventh Annual Assembly Journal* (April 4-5, 1959): 5, 20-21. Church of the Nazarene Archives, Lenexa, KS. See also, Warren Rogers, "What the General Budget Means to Our Negro Work," *The Herald of Holiness*, 18 March 1959, 11. Church of the Nazarene Archives, Lenexa, KS.

preachers. Edwards emphasized the importance of praying for these things when he asserted,

> When people pray they will see the urgent need of more churches and Sunday schools in our district among our people. When people pray, they will want to enter into that colaboring (sic) God to bring into existence the things we pray for. This is my prayer for 1958. We need more churches, better church buildings, and more preachers of our race; but most of all we need more people of my race who are willing to suffer and die for this great cause...For it is the will of God that black men and women, too, be saved and sanctified in our Southland, where more than ten million of the seventeen million Negroes live.[5]

Edwards' statements reveal the importance that he placed on the continuing need to develop more racial autonomy within the district. He believed that this could be attained by training black laity to take on a more active role in their congregations and by developing African American pastors who could effectively evangelize black southerners with the holiness message of the denomination.

In the early 1960s, many on the district heeded Edwards' call. By 1961, for instance, Arthur Jackson headed the NFMS, Archie Williams[6] chaired the District Church School Board, and Roland Chopfield led the NYPS. Likewise, Rogers, along with Edwards, Jackson, Chopfield, and R.W. Cunningham, oversaw and led the District Advisory Board and the Orders and Relations and Ministerial Studies Board.[7] This growth in black leadership also took place on the various district committees. By the third year of Rogers' administration, there were seven more assembly committees in operation, which brought the total to twelve[8] and all but one—the committee on Publishing Interests—was chaired by an African American.

Throughout the early to mid 1960s, these boards and committees expanded and were led by black pastors and laity. In 1962, for instance, the District Advisory Board did not have a single white minister or ecclesiastical head on its committee and the Orders and Relations and Ministerial Studies only had one white member—Alpin P. Bowes—on its board. Also, licensed black ministers or laity headed all of the twelve committees in operation. The list of chairmen included Archie Williams, Roy L. Fralin, Joe Edwards, Charles Johnson, "Mrs." Roy L. Fralin, Roland

---

[5]Joe Edwards, "When People Pray," *The Herald of Holiness*, 12 February 1958, 6. Church of the Nazarene Archives, Lenexa, KS.
[6]Williams was the newly licensed minister who pastored the three-year-old congregation in Orlando.
[7]*Gulf Central District Church of the Nazarene, Ninth Annual Assembly Journal* (August 3, 1961): 5. Church of the Nazarene Archives, Lenexa, KS.
[8]The names of those committees were Church Schools, Education, Evangelism, NFMS, Home Missions, Memoirs, NYPS, Nominations, Public Morals, Publishing Interests, Resolutions, and Ways and Means. See Ibid., 23-26.

Chopfield, Eddie Burnett, Edward Greene, Boyd Proctor, and Warren Rogers.[9] In that same year, the NFMS added five more officers to its organization. Instead of operating with just a President, persons now held titles of Vice President, Secretary, Treasurer, Secretary of Study, and Secretary of Publicity and Star Society. By the following year, the NYPS followed the lead of the NFMS and elected a Vice-President (Charles Johnson), a Secretary (Roy L. Fralin), and a Director of Junior Fellowship ("Mrs." Archie Williams).

During this same time, these enlarged groups began to ask local congregations to develop their own missionary and youth societies. At the 1962 District Assembly, the district NYPS challenged churches and ministers to develop youth ministries so that more young people could develop their knowledge of the Bible and so their energies could be "channeled to God." They emphasized these two points in their recommendations:

> 1. We encourage each pastor to properly organize an N.Y.P.S. If you have a sizable group of young people, you are by the constitution of the NYPS to divide them into three classes: junior (ages 4-11), teen (ages 12-19), young adult (ages 20-40)....We sincerely feel our youth should get together annually, or once every two years....This we feel is a must to have fellowship with our youth. We commend that you meet together once per week, but keep your meeting where God can approve, and please give them an active part in your regular service. The tireless energy of youth must be channeled to God.

> 2. The pastor and local church president must be responsible. Bible study should remain in our N.Y.P.S. If what you are doing is not a problem, you are either not doing your best or it is not worth doing. Remember our goal—300 by 1963.[10]

Similar requests to build up the constituency of local chapters, to increase financial budgets, and to evangelize southern blacks were made by the NFMS in the early to mid 1960s. For example, at the 1961 District Assembly, they made the following recommendations,

> 1. A monthly missionary meeting be held in every church...

> 2. Finances Alabaster offering for the September Alabaster services. Every church try having a regular African *Umbongo* Thanksgiving offering. Challenge the people to raise all the General Budget offering in November, then have an overflow offering at Easter time. Begin to announce the

---

[9]In 1962, Rogers headed up the Nominations Committee, the Ways and Means Committee, the District Advisory Board, and the Orders and Relations and Ministerial Studies Board. See, *Gulf Central District Church of the Nazarene, Tenth Annual Assembly Journal* (July 13-14, 1962): 24-30. Church of the Nazarene Archives, Lenexa, KS.

[10]Ibid., 27.

missionary offering early. Have the preacher preach on the plight of the lost world. Encourage people to pledge.

3. Goals for the year: Every Nazarene observe the sky watch. Every member strive to win a soul. Buy one Memorial Roll. Every church raise their General Budget. Every church have in full a Prayer and Fasting society.[11]

Likewise, three years later, Arthur Jackson and the Nazarene World Missionary Society (hereafter referred to as NWMS) (formerly the NFMS) challenged every congregation to increase their membership, purchase missionary books, hold at least one monthly missionary meeting, pray for missionaries, and increase their giving to world missions. When it came to actual numbers, the committee recommended that by the beginning of 1965, there should be at least 20 societies, 450 members, 250 prayer and fasting members, 200 *Other Sheep*[12] subscriptions, 50 junior readers, and $200.00 in Alabaster offering.[13]

These calls for greater participation were bolstered by the fact that committees like the NWMS had experienced financial and membership growth during the first half of the decade. In 1959, total giving for the NWMS stood at $68.00. However, by 1962 (the first year that the GCD held a NWMS convention) that total jumped to $588.00, which was more than the combined sum of the Sunday school department and the NYPS. During the same year, the NWMS had 13 societies and 166 members. By 1964, total societies for the NWMS had increased by three and overall membership had swelled to 337. Jackson attributed this growth to God, but acknowledged that the NWMS had to continue to grow and improve if they were going to "save" and "sanctify" more people.[14]

Even though total membership numbers in these committees and in the churches were affected by the decision to remove all five Florida churches from the jurisdiction of the GCD,[15] membership continued to remain steady. For instance, in their report at the Fifteenth Annual District Assembly, Jackson and her committee stated that there were 226 NWMS members on the district. At the following assembly, membership increased to 266 and a

---

[11]Gulf Central District Church of the Nazarene, Ninth Annual Assembly Journal, 24-25.

[12]The Other Sheep was a monthly missionary journal that was started in 1911. For further reference, see Purkiser, 41-42.

[13]Gulf Central District Church of the Nazarene, Twelfth Annual Assembly Journal (August 13-14, 1964): 26. Church of the Nazarene Archives, Lenexa, KS.

[14]Gulf Central District Church of the Nazarene, Seventh Annual Assembly Journal, 31; Gulf Central District Church of the Nazarene, 35 and Gulf Central District Church of the Nazarene, Twelfth Annual Assembly Journal, 25-26.

[15]After being removed, the churches were governed by the district in which they were located. This decision to integrate the Florida churches will be discussed later on in the paper.

total of 13 societies were still supporting Nazarene missions around the globe.[16]

Jackson supported and encouraged this growth through some of her reports and writings for the NWMS. In some of her written pieces, she maintained that NWMS members needed to pray and fast if their work was going to expand and if they were going to help spread the message of personal holiness "among the people." In a small article written in July of 1966, she expressed these convictions when she stated that,

> Prayer and fasting are much needed these days. Through prayer and fasting we become strong in the Lord and in the power of His might. Prayers of intercession accompanied with fasting releases the hand of God to do wonders among the people. Problems are solved, difficulties overcome, and souls are won to Christ.[17]

In a brief article written two years later, she also challenged NWMS members to remember that Christ had called them to spread "the good news" among the inhabitants of the world:

> A ministry has been entrusted to us namely, to communicate the good news that man can be reconciled to God. As Christians we want to see people saved. How do we go about it? This is a person to person ministry. God is looking to the church through world missions to be a bright light shining in a world of darkness. We are responsible to God and man. God demands our best. The time has come that we must be courageous leaders, and point our people back to God.[18]

In order for black Nazarenes to fulfill this divine responsibility to evangelize persons around the world, Jackson stated that they had to trust in God's power. In another article written for the GCI, Jackson noted that if African American Nazarenes would draw upon the "Spirit" of "the Lord," then they would be able to expand the presence of the CN throughout the United States. She emphasized this point when she noted that, "With God's help, we can do all things!"[19]

In addition to Jackson, other women on the GCD's NWMS wrote about how African American men and women possessed a divine responsibility to

---

[16]Gulf Central District Church of the Nazarene, Fourteenth Annual Assembly Journal (September 1-2, 1966): 17-18. Church of the Nazarene Archives, Lenexa, KS; Gulf Central District Church of the Nazarene, Fifteenth Annual Assembly Journal (September 15, 1967): 27, 35. Church of the Nazarene Archives, Lenexa, KS and Gulf Central District Church of the Nazarene, Sixteenth Annual Assembly Journal (September 12, 1968): 25. Church of the Nazarene Archives, Lenexa, KS.

[17]Mrs. Arthur Jackson, "N.W.M.S.," The Gulf Central Informer 8, no. 1 (July 1966): 2. Church of the Nazarene Archives, Lenexa, KS.

[18]Mrs. Arthur Jackson, "N.W.M.S.," The Gulf Central Informer 10, no. 4 (February 1968): 3. Church of the Nazarene Archives, Lenexa, KS.

[19]Mrs. Arthur Jackson, "N.W.M.S.: Be a Star Society," *The Gulf Central Informer* 11, no. 1 (June 1969): 3. Church of the Nazarene Archives, Lenexa, KS.

evangelize others because Christ had come specifically to "save the world." Frances Greene and Mazella Riddick, the respective leaders of the NWMS in 1960, reflected this belief in a report they submitted to the District Assembly. In their statement they stated that, "Jesus loved and gave himself that all the people of the world might be saved. All of God's children should love and give, that this message might be preached to all nations." After this, they noted a racially specific challenge by stating that if the GCD wanted to be a "growing dynamic organization" that fulfilled the challenge of "spreading scriptural holiness among America's millions of colored people," then every church needed to have a missionary society that used their financial and spiritual resources to evangelize those with the message of individual holiness.[20]

The following year, the same committee stated that if every member of the NWMS wanted to "win a soul", then they needed to read the Bible and tell its stories with "life and freedom" so that those who heard them would have confidence and come to believe that God had come to "save" their souls from the "lost world." Not only that, but they asserted that if African American congregations in the South were going to increase their monetary giving and develop an ever-increasing desire to evangelize those in their communities and world, then black pastors had a responsibility to actively promote missionary efforts and "preach on the plight of the lost world."[21]

Like Jackson and others on the NWMS, those on the district's NYPS also contributed to the evangelistic thrust of the GCD. During this time, it challenged churches to work towards evangelizing youth so that more young people could be "saved" and incorporated into the life of southern churches. Roland Chopfield, the president of the NYPS, emphasized this urgent need in 1965 when he asserted that,

> We are especially emphasizing N.Y.P.S. work in our district. We must organize our society by gathering together the saved from 4 to 40. The way to start is to start, it is as simple as that. The time is now . . . All of this requires work, but work brings sums not subtraction, or division and bring joy and good reports at our meetings.[22]

Similarly, when Edward Husband (a recent graduate of NBI) became president of the committee in 1966, he challenged each church to organize a NYPS so that young people could receive salvation.[23] Like the NWMS and

---

[20]Gulf Central District Church of the Nazarene, Eighth Annual Assembly Journal, 28-29.

[21]Gulf Central District Church of the Nazarene, Ninth Annual Assembly Journal (August 1961): 24-25. Church of the Nazarene Archives, Lenexa, KS.

[22]Roland Chopfield, "N.Y.P.S. Meet in Orlando, Fla.," The Gulf Central Informer 7, no. 3 (June 1965): 1. Church of the Nazarene Archives, Lenexa, KS.

[23]Gulf Central District Church of the Nazarene, Fourteenth Annual Assembly Journal, 25.

the rest of the GCD, the overarching goal was to evangelize "souls." This was stressed in their reports to the district and in their annual conventions. For instance, at the 1968 yearly convention of the NYPS, Chopfield delivered a message entitled, "They Turned the World Upside," which allegedly "encouraged and inspired the convention" to carry on its evangelistic work with zeal and fervor.[24]

As these voices and challenges were being uttered, more local NYPS units were being formed and more young people were becoming members of those chapters. In fact, out of the nineteen churches that were operating in 1967, twelve of them had NYPS committees with a total of 298 members. Within the next two years, that number increased to 374.[25] As membership increased in the NYPS, Rogers was able to recruit more black students to attend NBI to prepare for Christian ministry. Rogers felt that the school was the "life line" for developing black leadership on the GCD.[26] That is why he traveled extensively and was able to encourage more young people to attend NBI. For example, when he finished his annual college tour in 1966, he reported that some 215 young people were interested in attending NBI with the explicit purpose of training for Christian ministry. Over time, those interests turned into commitments as enrollment was pushed to a total of 42 by 1968, which was a total increase of 36 since 1961.[27]

Of course, this financial and membership growth in youth and missionary societies and at NBI happened at the same time Rogers was laboring to recruit more pastors and as he was helping to start more churches and strengthen those already in existence. As it was mentioned previously, few pastors were recruited to the district during its first five years of existence. However, while he was DS, Rogers made it one of his primary goals to develop pastors that would lead and develop churches on the GCD. He realized that like any other newly formed religious body, the district would not survive unless it had stable clerical leadership. The challenge for Rogers, therefore, was to develop "trained and dedicated leadership" so that the churches could become more self-sufficient and better able to evangelize "the Negro people of the United States."[28]

---

[24]Ibid., 28 and Gulf Central District Church of the Nazarene, Sixteenth Annual Assembly Journal, 29-30.

[25]Gulf Central District Church of the Nazarene, Fifteenth Annual Assembly Journal, 20 and Gulf Central District Church of the Nazarene, Seventeenth Annual Assembly Journal (July 25, 1969): 15. Church of the Nazarene Archives, Lenexa, KS.

[26]Warren Rogers, "Nazarene Training College Tour," The Gulf Central Informer 10, no. 3 (August 1967): 1. Church of the Nazarene Archives, Lenexa, KS.

[27]Warren Rogers, "Nazarene Training College," The Gulf Central Informer 10, no. 6 (May 1968): 1. Church of the Nazarene Archives, Lenexa, KS and Gulf Central District Church of the Nazarene, Eleventh Annual Assembly Journal (July 1963): 19-20. Church of the Nazarene Archives, Lenexa, KS.

[28]Gulf Central District Church of the Nazarene, Eleventh Annual Assembly Journal, 19.

Because of this need, Rogers made a recommendation during his second year as DS to (1) create two new churches, (2) establish two self-sustaining congregations, and (3) enroll ten students at NBI by the following District Assembly. During the previous year, only one church, Providence CN in Oklahoma City, OK, was added to the list of existing churches that were self-supporting and that could sustain a full-time salary for its pastor.[29] Most of the congregations were small in number and thus were unable to employ a full time minister.[30] Rogers understood these difficulties, so he made it a point to commend the church in Oklahoma City when they were able to employ Joe Edwards as their full time pastor. At the same district assembly, Rogers also praised the San Antonio West End CN when they had generated enough funds to build a new church. He revealed his enthusiasm, noting,

> On Sunday, September 13, 1959, we had the thrilling experience of helping to dedicate our first new church building on the district. This was our San Antonio, Texas, West End Church, where Rev. Leslie Casmere is pastor. Our beloved general superintendent, Dr. Vanderpool, officiated in the affair, with Rev. Alpin Bowes; Rev. Hester, the district superintendent of the San Antonio District; Rev. Kornegay, pastor of San Antonio First Church; yours truly; and others sharing in this victorious service, with the house filled to its capacity. We are grateful to God for this achievement of San Antonio West End Church, for their exercised faith in this venture to present this beautiful and commodious building to God and the community.[31]

Over the following years, experiences like this would become more common on the district as more black pastors were added to the district and as more churches became self-sustaining. For instance, in 1961, twelve of the nineteen total churches—Calvert Faith CN (Calvert, AL), Chattanooga Alton Park CN (Chattanooga, TN), Columbus First CN (Columbus, TX), Concord Emmanuel CN (Concord, NC), Goulds First CN (Goulds, FL), Nashville Community CN (Nashville, TN), Providence CN (Oklahoma City, OK), Orlando Gorman Memorial CN (Orlando, FL), Richmond Woodville CN (Richmond, VA), San Antonio Morning Glory CN (San Antonio, TX), Winnsboro CN (Winnsboro, LA), and Lawton Grace CN (Lawton, OK)—paid their district budgets. Also, both Orlando Gorman and Richmond Woodville

---

[29]Gulf Central District Church of the Nazarene, *Eighth Annual Assembly Journal*, 22.

[30]Each church also was required to pay their district budgets, which added an extra burden to their financial difficulties. In fact, of the seventeen churches in existence in 1960, only eight paid their budgets in full. Of those eight, only the church in Oklahoma City had to pay $25.00 to both the general and district budgets. The rest of the congregations did not have to pay more than $20.00 to either budget. These figures alone seem to reveal that most of the churches on the GCD did not have enough members or enough income to support a full time pastor at the start of the 1960s. See Ibid., 26.

[31]Ibid., 21.

acquired their own church buildings and two more pastors—Roland Chopfield (pastor of Chattanooga Alton Park CN) and Ruben Davis (pastor of Concord Emmanuel CN)—were ordained as elders, which brought the district total to seven. Moreover, by the end of the assembly, Roger Bowman, Frank Bryant (pastor of Goulds First CN)[32], Eddie Burnett (pastor of Orlando Gorman Memorial CN), Roy Fralin (pastor of Nashville Community CN) and Charles P. Johnson (the newly appointed minister at Meridian Fitkin Memorial CN) were licensed as ministers. Because of their admittance, the GCD now had a sum of twelve licensed pastors who were ministering on the district.[33]

By 1964, the organizational and ministerial situation improved even more. Since 1961, three more churches had been formed—Memphis New Prospect CN (Memphis, TN), Taft CN (Taft, FL), and Orlando Praise Temple CN (Orlando, FL)—which brought the total to twenty-two. Church finances improved and all but eight congregations paid their budgets in full.[34] By the following year, all twenty-two churches were still in operation and the total membership of those congregations stood at 501, which represented over half of all "Negro" Nazarene members in the continental United States.[35] Moreover, at the district assembly, nine ordained elders were ministering on the district, while thirteen licensed pastors oversaw the work of various churches and ministries on the GCD.[36]

The following year would bring changes to the district after it was decided that all five of the Florida churches would be integrated and governed by the Florida District. Rogers and the GCD Advisory Board made this decision in May of 1966.[37] Although this cut into the overall strength of

---

[32]Both Goulds First CN and Lawton Grace CN were the two new churches formed in 1961.

[33]*Gulf Central District Church of the Nazarene, Ninth Annual Assembly Journal*, 5-30.

[34]*Gulf Central District Church of the Nazarene, Twelfth Annual Assembly Journal*, 19, 22.

[35]*Gulf Central District Church of the Nazarene, Thirteenth Annual Assembly Journal*, 21.

[36]That list of ordained elders included Winston Best, Eddie Burnett, Roland Chopfield, Ruben Davis, Joe Edwards, Charles Johnson, Warren Rogers, Archie Williams, and "Mrs." Lula Williams. Those recorded on the licensed minister roll were Leonard Adams, Leslie Casmere, "Mrs." Cora Dials, Raymond Harvey, Edward Husband, Mrs. Janie Johnson, Charles Jones, Christopher Joseph, Mrs. Norvell Lewis, Miss Joe Ann Marshall, Elonza Pugh, Earl Joe Walker, and Eddie Lee Walker. For further reference see, *Gulf Central District Church of the Nazarene, Thirteenth Annual Assembly Journal*, 6-10.

[37]*Gulf Central District Church of the Nazarene, Fourteenth Annual Assembly Journal*, 17 and Warren Rogers, "Florida Churches Transfer to Florida District," *The Gulf Central Informer* 8, no. 1 (July 1966): 1-2. Church of the Nazarene Archives, Lenexa, KS. It is important to note that around this time the United Methodist

the GCD, Rogers and the district were still able to organize two new churches during the same year—Johnson Chapel CN in Prentiss, MS and Rogers Chapel CN in Nashville TN—which brought the district church total to nineteen. Of those nineteen, all but one paid their budgets in full and their total giving equaled $27,972.00, which was about a fourth of all the money given by "black" churches in the United States.[38]

Until the GCD was dissolved in 1969, these numbers would remain relatively stable. In the proceeding year after the Florida decision, the district still had nine ordained elders actively ministering and a total membership of 455. Total giving for that year reached to about $37,000 and every congregation paid its general and district budgets in full.[39] Likewise, by 1969, nineteen congregations were still in operation with an overall membership of 532, which still represented almost a third of all black Nazarenes in the United States. Also, in its last year of operation, southern black Nazarenes gave almost $50,000 to local and global missions.[40]

What the Florida action and the above numbers reveal is that by the late 1960s, the GCD steadily grew, both financially and numerically, even though it was segregated from the rest of the southern white churches. At the same time, black pastors and laity made ministerial and financial decisions that impacted the life and direction of black southern congregations and were able to send voting delegates to legislate on ecclesiastical matters at various General Assemblies. These factors enabled leaders and laity on the GCD to direct the affairs of the jurisdiction, which, in turn, enabled district boards, committees, pastors, and parishioners to strengthen and develop their own ministries that could effectively contribute to Nazarene home missions.

African Americans on the GCD were able to attain these ends because of their continued dedication to personal "holiness evangelism." This approach was exemplified in Rogers' address at the 1960 District Assembly when he noted that one of the main objectives of his ministry was to evangelize African Americans. According to Rogers,

> To present my second report as district superintendent of the Gulf Central District in this eighth assembly brings me face to face, not only with the

Church was also trying to dismantle the Central Jurisdiction, which was the segregated conference that governed all the black churches in the UMC. After several years of debate, the denomination decided, on August 20, 1967, to gradually transition African American churches into their geographical conferences. For further reference on how certain events and persons impacted this decision, see Thomas, 137-147.

[38] *Gulf Central District Church of the Nazarene, Fourteenth Annual Assembly Journal*, 15-21.

[39] *Gulf Central District Church of the Nazarene, Fifteenth Annual Assembly Journal*, 20, 35.

[40] *Gulf Central District Church of the Nazarene, Seventeenth Annual Assembly Journal*, 15, 26.

submitting of my report, but also with the fresh awareness of the challenge, which has been the driving power in my very being, for the evangelization of my people.[41]

Similarly, at the following annual gathering, Rogers reminded Gulf Central Nazarenes of their "responsibility . . . for the evangelizing of more than ten million of my people of the Gulf Central District area." Then, he noted that if southern blacks were going to expand the "total Negro work" then they had to "mind God" and trust that God's spirit would enable them "to spread salvation . . . among the Negro people of the United States." He emphasized this by saying that,

> God is the enabling power if we will only employ Him. Must we see the resources of heaven untapped because we fail to fast and pray and exercise our faith? We have seen success in the past and we can today with God's help. Let us not be swallowed up by a lukewarm, passionless program, but rather accept the challenge of living in victory and winning souls for Christ. This is our day! I will mind God![42]

Likewise, when Rogers addressed the assembly six years later, he challenged those gathered to remain focused on their divine responsibility to evangelize African Americans despite "racial problems, conflicts in the labor world, religious differences, economic problems, and distresses on every hand." He emphasized this point when he claimed that,

> Fellow workers of Christ, are we living in the awareness that we are laboring in the day, but when the night cometh no man can work? These are the words of Jesus which are recorded in St. John's Gospel 9:4. Jesus indicated by making this declaration that the hour will come when it will be too late to find Him as Savior...Therefore, what we plan to do for God toward winning lost souls must be done quickly.[43]

After stating this, Rogers went on to assert that there were "more than 20 million Negro people inhabited in the United States" that needed to be "saved" and in order to "reach" them, a "spirit of evangelism" had to prevail in the lives of both black individuals and churches.[44]

In an effort to improve this "spirit of evangelism," Rogers occasionally preached at revivals outside the GCD so that he could help organizing and strengthen existing churches in the Midwest, North, and West. In 1965, he noted to the district assembly that he visited four churches outside of the GCD and conducted revivals in Detroit, Columbus, OH, Dover, DE, and

---

[41]Gulf Central District Church of the Nazarene, Eighth Annual Assembly Journal, 20.

[42]Gulf Central District Church of the Nazarene, Ninth Annual Assembly Journal, 16-17, 20-21.

[43]Gulf Central District Church of the Nazarene, Fifteenth Annual Assembly Journal, 15.

[44]Ibid., 15.

Muncie, IN, "in the interest of organizing churches."[45] Two years later, he maintained a similar policy in an effort to improve black evangelization and the "Negro work outside of the Gulf Central District." He noted that over the course of the year, he visited churches and Sunday school missions in various places like Saginaw, MI, Detroit, Kansas City, Pasadena, CA, Los Angeles, St. Louis, and Wichita, KS. These visits caused Rogers to become excited about the future of black evangelization and the establishment of additional churches outside the South. He underscored his enthusiasm when he noted that, "For the most part, I found the churches in the northern areas on the move for God, a spirit of revival and enthusiasm prevailed, and the future looks very encouraging."[46]

The same emphasis on preaching revivals and visiting black churches outside the South in an effort to enhance the possibilities of increasing African American evangelization remained a part of Rogers' activities in the final years of his tenure as District Superintendent of the GCD. In fact, in 1968 Rogers told how his revival services in areas like Los Angeles, Pasadena, and Rand, WV helped to add new black members to the CN. He underscored this by stating that, "These were . . . fruitful revivals, when many new people from the communities attended new members were added to these churches."[47]

In addition to these revivals, Rogers hinted that black Nazarenes needed to develop a more racially conscious expression of holiness evangelism among African Americans. At the Sixteenth Annual Assembly of Gulf Central, for instance, Rogers told delegates that if black evangelism was going to increase and the message of the denomination spread among African Americans then black Nazarenes needed to develop stronger ties among other African American churches in the United States. In particular, he noted that,

> To keep close contact with our churches and pastors in the northern area is to provide a bridge to involve a fellowship among all of our Negro pastors and people which will prove to be a great advantage when we are faced with pastoral exchange, the need for evangelists, Christian workers in other areas of our church work, and on the social level.[48]

Likewise, at the next and final annual gathering of black pastors and laity of the GCD, Rogers briefly stated how a more racially connected ecclesiology in the denomination could help improve black evangelization.

---

[45]*Gulf Central District Church of the Nazarene, Thirteenth Annual Assembly Journal*, 20.

[46]*Gulf Central District Church of the Nazarene, Fifteenth Annual Assembly Journal*, 17.

[47]*Gulf Central District Church of the Nazarene, Sixteenth Annual Assembly Journal*, 17.

[48]Ibid., 16.

For instance, after visiting several regional black Nazarene fellowships in the North and West, Rogers noted that southern churches should establish similar connections in an effort to enhance their efforts to evangelize African Americans in the South. Rogers felt that this was particularly important due to the fact that the GCD was going to be disbanded by the early part of 1970 and the remaining churches would need some sort of collective body to sustain black Nazarene life in the South. He stressed the importance of southern churches developing such a fellowship when he commented,

> We feel that these Regional Fellowships are vital in the interest of keeping close contact with our churches and pastors, for assisting in pastoral exchange, to provide fellowship for our people, for the recruitment of students to train for Christian leadership, to emphasize evangelism among the people . . . I would recommend that the camp meeting held here at Prentiss, Miss., should be continued for the spiritual good of the people who formerly comprised the Gulf Central District in the same interest which we have in mind for operating the two northern Negro area Regional Fellowships.[49]

In short, by the end of the 1960s, Rogers had developed a deeper sense of the need for racial solidarity among African Americans in the South. His interaction with churches in the North seemed to have persuaded him that regional racial fellowships among black Nazarenes could help improve the evangelistic presence of the denomination among African Americans in the South and North.

Nevertheless, as it pertains to collective black life in the denomination, Rogers, as leader of the GCD and as a prominent African American minister in the CN, did not publicly advocate for the establishment of a national black fellowship in the denomination, despite the fact that Rogers, along with the rest of the district, often included the West Indian congregations as part of the number of national black churches in their annual assembly minutes. For example, in the 1967 District Journal, the GCD leadership included the Brooklyn and Long Island churches in New York as part of the total black church membership of 977 outside of the GCD. Likewise in 1968, the Afro-Caribbean churches in New York were included as part of the total number of black churches registered by the GCD.[50]

Again, these brief inclusions by Rogers and other leaders on the GCD did not translate—like the previous decade—into an organized plan to establish ongoing relationships with those in New York and it did not equate to a concerted effort to join forces with either West Indians or Cape

---

[49]*Gulf Central District Church of the Nazarene, Seventeenth Annual Assembly Journal*, 14.

[50]Gulf Central District Church of the Nazarene, Fifteenth Annual Assembly Journal, 34 and Gulf Central District Church of the Nazarene, Sixteenth Annual Assembly Journal, 30.

Verdeans to help create a national fellowship of black churches. Such a relationship could have improved the decision making power of black churches, addressed denominational racism, or created a large voting block that could have promoted the needs of those from the African Diaspora.

Such actions were probably not taken because of the different locations, social settings, ethnic differences, patterns of segregation, and historical experiences that impacted the various groups. More importantly, however, the lack of organized movement by Rogers and other African Americans in the South was probably due, as it has already been revealed, to Roger's overarching focus on holiness evangelism among African Americans and his desire to improve the GCD's institutional strength and overall presence in the southern United States throughout the 1960s.

Yet, Rogers was not the only one who articulated and promoted such an evangelistic desire. In fact, aside from the pastors and leaders mentioned previously, certain female leaders and laity become proponents of this evangelistic spirit—especially after hearing Rogers' sermons and speeches at District Assemblies. For instance, after hearing Rogers' annual address to the District Assembly in 1961, women such as Lula Williams, the long time female pastor and leader on the district, challenged the delegation to realize their responsibility to evangelize black Americans through a sermon entitled, "Christian Service Training and Evangelism." When she completed her message, it was noted that it "was received heartily by everyone in doing greater work for our Master." In fact, the message moved some like Geneva Ann Robison and Inez Green to give testimonies about God's faithfulness in their lives and witness how "God's glory" had helped them fulfill their responsibility to win "souls for Christ."[51] Likewise, after Rogers' gave his address to the assembly in 1966, Janie Johnson, a female pastor on the district, expressed her appreciation to the DA for Rogers' leadership and his challenging sermon. Johnson stated that she was thankful for all the work Rogers did for the district and she also testified that she was grateful to "God for the outpouring of His Holy Spirit" that had challenged black Nazarenes to strengthen their resolve to evangelize others.[52]

Aside from this, at NWMS conventions women remained focus on communicating and supporting the evangelistic mission of the denomination and the GCD. At their convention gathering in 1966, for example, black women heard evangelistic sermons given by white female missionaries such as Dorothy Ahleman. In her homilies, Ahleman preached from biblical texts like Isaiah 45:2-3 and Acts 1:8 and stressed the importance of supporting missionary efforts around the world. After

[51]Gulf Central District Church of the Nazarene, Ninth Annual Assembly Journal, 15, 20-21.

[52]*Gulf Central District Church of the Nazarene, Fifteenth Annual Assembly Journal*, 13, 29.

hearing her message, Jackson and "Mrs." Eddie Burnett felt that God would continue to empower them to fulfill their responsibilities to evangelize others. They expressed this when they stated that, "We trust that God will continue to bless us as we endeavor to build His kingdom in the hearts of His people on earth."[53]

Likewise, at a different NWMS gathering, Jackson, Williams, Juanita McKinnon, Annie Mae Proctor, Betty Ruth Wilcox, Willie Mae Tatum, Bessie Moore, and Thelma Rowe heard a missionary from Argentina deliver an "inspiring message from St. Luke the twenty-fourth chapter and forty-fifth verse." They were "stirred by his message" and decided to take up an offering for the missionary. Not only that, but shortly thereafter, Jackson publicly stated that if black men and women would put their trust in God and work towards fulfilling their evangelistic responsibilities, then God would help African American Nazarenes "do much better" in their "lives, prayers, and efforts for other people lost in sin."[54]

Nonetheless, Roger's and other female and male leaders' desire was not to merely "save" southern blacks, but to help them become "sanctified" Nazarenes. One of the ways that they attempted to do this was through establishing various committees that would make recommendations on how to carry out evangelism and how to indoctrinate pastors and laity. Various entities like the Education Committee, the Evangelism Committee, the Home Missions Committee, and the Public Morals Committee were created to help meet these ends by stressing to churches the importance of evangelizing and developing the personal sanctity of black Nazarenes. In 1961, for instance, the Evangelism Committee had the following recommendations passed by the District Assembly, such as,

1. That each church endeavor to have at least two revivals per year.

2. That if the church is not able financially to support an evangelist, then the pastor should conduct his own revival.

3. That each church promote a personal evangelism program for witnessing for Christ.

4. That our worship should be with joy and blessing and freedom in the Lord.[55]

On top of holding evangelistic services, the Public Morals Committee suggested the following,

---

[53]*Gulf Central District Church of the Nazarene, Fourteenth Annual Assembly Journal*, 23-24, 28.

[54]*Gulf Central District Church of the Nazarene, Twelfth Annual Assembly Journal*, 25, 30-31.

[55]Gulf Central District Church of the Nazarene, Ninth Annual Assembly Journal, 24.

1. Each church in the Gulf Central District read and exhort at least once per month in a regular service from the church *Manual* concerning the moral standards of the church.

2. Each church should impress upon the minds of all Christians, and especially our youth, the importance of simplicity in hair dress and other manner of dress.

3. Each pastor should stress the danger and possible results of intemperate living.

4. Each church should warn the people about the danger of close relationship with unconverted people of low morals.[56]

Four years later, the district, along with these committees, remained committed to evangelizing, holding revivals, and developing the personal morality of black Nazarenes without addressing issues related to civil rights or racism. In fact, neither the Education Committee nor the Public Morals Committee made any recommendations on how to evangelize or express one's faith publicly during this time of social unrest. The former entity continued to stress the importance of holding revivals, while the Public Morals Committee suggested that:

1. Our pastors should read our *Manual* to our people each month, especially to our young people in the days in which we now live.

2. In all of our young people's meetings, we should not fail to warn them against immoral television programs and to read good material.

3. We should all stress to our young people about the kind of company they keep, and about their dress.[57]

Likewise, in the 1965 and 1966 editions of *The Gulf Central Informer*, Rogers did not state how black Nazarenes in the South were to engage issues related to racism in society or in the church. Instead, Rogers continued to stress the importance of creating new congregations, new church buildings, and "winning souls" for the "Kingdom of God."[58] In his report to the 1967 District Assembly, Rogers continued to relay the importance of "winning souls" to the audience when he stated that,

Fellow workers of Christ, are we living in the awareness that we are laboring in the day, but when the night cometh no man can work? These are the words of Jesus which are recorded in St. John's Gospel 9:4. Jesus indicated by

---

[56]Ibid., 26.

[57]Gulf Central District Church of the Nazarene, Thirteenth Annual Assembly Journal, 25-29.

[58]See, for instance Warren Rogers, "The District Superintendent's Notes," *The Gulf Central Informer* 7, no. 2 (June 1965) and Warren Rogers, "The District Superintendent's Notes," *The Gulf Central Informer* 8, no. 1 (July 1966). Church of the Nazarene Archives, Lenexa, KS.

making this declaration, that the hour will come when it will be too late to find Him as Savior, but instead He will be sitting in the judgment chair. Therefore, what we plan to do for God toward winning souls must be done quickly.[59]

Later on in that report, he also explained the importance of shunning "worldly styles" and living holy lives:

> The theory of salvation and sanctification is not enough, Gulf Central Nazarenes; but rather true holiness is required by God. It must be demonstrated in a spirit of forgiveness, meekness, love, long-suffering, compassion, seeking the salvation of others, suffering for righteousness' sake, the wearing of apparel as becoming to holiness, and taking on the whole likeness of Christ. More should be said from our Nazarene pulpits concerning Nazarenes who endeavor to keep up with the styles, fashions, and tempo of the world today...There is a middle-of-the-road position which we as holiness people must take, and the Word of God gives support...Taking holiness is not enough, but rather it is a life to be lived day by day.[60]

What these examples and quotes reveal is that Rogers, female leaders, pastors, and many others on the district were committed (like they had been in the previous decade), both in practice and theory, to spreading "scriptural holiness" among southern blacks without publicly challenging social or denominational racism. This is interesting to note, considering the fact that the Sixteenth General Assembly made an official pronouncement against racism. The statement read as follows,

> We, the members of the Sixteenth General Assembly of the Church of the Nazarene, wish to reiterate our historic stand of Christian compassion for men of all races. We believe that God is the Creator of all men and that of one blood are all men created. We believe that all races should have equality before law, including the right to vote, the right to equal educational opportunities, the right to earn a living according to one's ability without discrimination, and the right to public facilities supported by taxation.[61]

Similarly, other Nazarenes wrote to *The Herald of Holiness* in support of overcoming racism within the denomination. One article written by a white pastor in New York stated that racism often caused white Nazarenes from fulfilling the Christian commandment to "love they neighbor as thyself." Moreover, a laywoman named "Mrs." John Scott expressed her desire to see

---

[59]*Gulf Central District Church of the Nazarene, Fifteenth Annual Assembly Journal*, 15.

[60]Ibid., 16.

[61]W.T. Purkiser, "The Church Speaks on Current Issues," *The Herald of Holiness*, 5 August 1964, 12. Church of the Nazarene Archives, Lenexa, KS. In the same year, the Church of God (Anderson, IN), another predominantly white holiness body, also rendered a statement in support of civil rights legislation. See Massey, 118-119, for further details.

the church take a stronger stand on civil rights and even stated that the church's relative silence was not compatible with the "gospel of holiness."[62]

Around the same time, General Superintendent G.B. Williamson stated that Nazarenes should address the "race question" with a philosophy of "Meritocracy." For Williamson, "Meritocracy" was defined as a teaching that "embodies the idea that all men have equal right to life, liberty, and the pursuit of happiness, and that God is no respecter of persons." He expanded on this basic definition and revealed his belief in racial equality, stating,

> The character of the individual and his response to the light he has received are the criterion of judgment. Given the opportunity, people of all races have capacity for progress. "Meritocracy" includes the principle that nay person may lawfully live, lodge, eat, travel, and do business according to state of his prosperity. He may have equal opportunity to acquire knowledge to acquire knowledge and skill and hold any position of which he is capable. He shall not be excluded by law or practice from school, church, place, or privilege because of his color or race or position of previous servitude.[63]

In similar fashion, A.F. Harper, Executive Editor of the Department of Church Schools stated that Christ's teachings challenged Nazarenes to change America's unjust racial "social system." Harper underlined this position in *The Herald of Holiness*, noting,

> It seems to me that there are some issues in the current situation where the Christian attitude is clear. They are not debatable in the light of the teachings of Jesus. No man ought to be hindered in his efforts to earn a living for himself and his family simply because his skin is dark. No child with a dark skin ought to be deprived of an education that is open to a white child of equal ability. No young person whatever his color who wants to learn the way of God more perfectly would be excluded from the company of those whose call is to proclaim salvation to all men. No sincere Christian would *personally* be responsible for these kinds of sins against a fellowman. But the problem is that our *social system* does in fact quite often produce these wrong effects—and in a democracy *we have the ability to do something about the system.*[64]

Despite these sporadic claims, however, most leaders and laity in the CN continued to place their focus on evangelizing the world with the message of personal holiness and chose not to challenge the church to make a concerted effort to methodically address racism. Instead, the decision to

---

[62]William Goodman, "My Duty to My Neighbor," *The Herald of Holiness*, 24 February 1965, 9 and Mrs. John Scott, "Pro: Civil Rights," *The Herald of Holiness*, 7 April 1965, 18. Church of the Nazarene Archives, Lenexa, KS.

[63]G.B. Williamson, "Meritocracy," *The Herald of Holiness*, 22 July 1964, no pagination. Church of the Nazarene Archives, Lenexa, KS.

[64]A.F. Harper, "Toward Christian Understanding," *The Herald of* Holiness, 3 February 1965, 5. Church of the Nazarene Archives, Lenexa, KS.

systematically address such concerns continued to lie in the hands of individual districts and churches and as a result, most continued to focus on how racism needed to be overcome so that evangelism would not be thwarted. E.E. Barrett, a white pastor in Kankakee, IL, expressed this sentiment when he stated that,

> We can safely be as socially minded and as revolutionary as our spiritual forefathers, who "turned the world upside down" or right side up. Guidelines for this are furnished by the fundamental principles of holiness, including the wholeness of love, righteousness, and justice . . . Would not concern for people and social holiness both promote and aid evangelism?[65]

A laywoman from Illinois followed a similar line of thinking when she claimed,

> As Christians, we must take care that our testimony, our daily lives, are not marred by a misguided belief that any one race is inferior . . . This is a situation for Christians nationwide—of all denominations—to give serious attention to in prayer, lest a principle be undermined, a nation destroyed, or a soul lost for eternity because racism, or whatever other name is used, blinds us to our central goal in life—winning souls to Christ.[66]

Therefore, in many circles of the CN, even when one stood against racism, it was to promote the goal of evangelism. Even the statements by the General Assembly and Harper did not require or challenge the denomination to develop a systematic plan to work towards racial justice in society or in the church. Addressing civil rights or racial injustice never became a requirement by denominational leaders, pastors, districts, or church members. Instead, if congregations or ministers were going to support civil rights systematically, organizationally, or financially, they had to do so on their own merit and when left alone to do so, most Nazarene congregations chose to tackle racism, civil rights, or racial injustice at the individual level. Nazarene historians Floyd Cunningham, Stan Ingersol, Harold Raser, and David Whitelaw underscore this point when they note that, "Nazarenes distrusted social intervention. Legislation would accomplish nothing unless the heart was changed. Inward reform must precede social reform."[67]

This overarching position in the denomination, however, did not preclude some districts and African American congregations from taking systematic efforts to address racial injustice. As it was just mentioned, in

---

[65]E.E. Barrett, "Holiness is Wholeness," *The Herald of Holiness*, 29 November 1967, 3-4. Church of the Nazarene Archives, Lenexa, KS.

[66]Martha J. Sherman, "On Racism and Civil Rights," *The Herald of Holiness*, 4 November 1964, 18. Church of the Nazarene Archives, Lenexa, KS.

[67]Floyd Cunningham, Stan Ingersol, Harold E. Raser, and David F. Whitelaw, ed., *Our Watchword & Song: The Centennial History of the Church of the Nazarene* (Kansas City, MO: Beacon Hill Press, 2009), 373-374.

the 1960s, Nazarene churches were technically free to join civil rights movements or causes. Nothing in denominational records or histories suggests that congregations, districts, or pastors were circumscribed or prevented from publically or systematically attacking racial injustice. Like the majority of congregations and pastors that had the freedom to focus on "inward transformation," others could take a different route and some in fact, did. In 1964, for instance, the Los Angeles District called on its churches to be "committed to racial justice and love in all areas of our social life, so that we may help speed the day no citizen of this country...be denied any other freedom which is generally provided for citizens..."[68]

Aside from this, African American ministers like Charles Johnson of Meridian, MS and Joe Edwards of Oklahoma City, OK contributed to local civil rights movements. Johnson, the pastor of Meridian Fitkin Memorial CN, arrived in Meridian, MS to build up the small congregation and to increase the income, ministries, and membership of the church in the early 1960s. He worked towards this end, but in 1964 Johnson joined the Council of Federated Organizations (COFO), an umbrella organization comprised of numerous civil rights groups working independently in the state of Mississippi. During that year, COFO had organized Freedom Summer, a large voter and education project for African Americans. Through his work with COFO, Johnson came to befriend one of his parishioner's grandsons, James Chaney and Michael Schwerner, a Jewish civil rights worker from New York City. Both of these young men worked with Freedom Summer and Johnson housed them and even gave them counsel on certain situations when they were trying to register African Americans to vote. However, his friendship with them ended in the summer after Ku Klux Klan members murdered them in an area close to Philadelphia, MS.[69]

Despite this unfortunate event, Johnson continued his civil rights work by organizing a boycott to improve the wages of black women who worked as domestics. After helping them achieve higher pay, Johnson felt it was necessary to begin an organization that could improve the economic conditions of African Americans in the city. Thus, Johnson formed the Meridian Action Committee (MAC) in 1968. This committee helped organize boycotts against downtown Meridian restaurants that wouldn't serve blacks and it also helped secure clerk and managerial positions for African Americans at local stores and businesses.[70]

Aside from this, in the late 1960s, Johnson opened up a local branch of the Opportunities Industrialization Center (OIC), which taught life and job skills to young blacks seeking employment. In addition to this, in 1968,

---

[68]Ibid., 374.

[69]"Neshoba Slaying Trial Begins at Federal Court House Here," *The Meridian Star*, 09 October 1967 and "First Witnesses Heard in Neshoba Slaying Case," *The Meridian Star*, 10 October 1967.

[70]"Pioneers Remember the Struggle, *The Meridian Star*, 14 January 2007.

Mississippi Action for Progress, Inc., an organization that established a credit union and other economic programs to improve the financial situation of African Americans throughout Mississippi, hired Johnson to head the branch in Meridian and Lauderdale County.

Moreover, during this period, Johnson was elected to both city and county offices and led one of the most influential committees in the county. Because of such successes, Johnson was appointed to state committees on race relations and three times during President Lyndon B. Johnson's and President Jimmy Carter's administrations, Johnson was invited to the White House to attend banquets and to meet with other governmental committees.[71]

Around this same time, Edwards witnessed local racial and economic oppression faced by black sanitation workers in Oklahoma City. Hearing and listening to the situations that they faced compelled him to help lead a strike of 2,000 African Americans against municipal officials on August 16, 1969. Edwards, along with other African American pastors, civic leaders, and organizations like the NAACP, the Coalition of Civil Leadership, and the Southern Christian Leadership Conference, led the strike for 75 days. Their efforts helped the laborers receive a 40-hour workweek, a $50 to $55 pay increase, overtime wages, and better working conditions.[72]

However, when Edwards was arrested for marching on City Hall on October 31st, local white Nazarenes expressed their consternation and disappointment over Edwards' actions. Undaunted, Edwards defended his position in an interview with a student reporter from Bethany Nazarene College in Bethany, Ok. In it, he chastised the racism among Nazarenes in Oklahoma City and claimed that white Nazarenes had always treated blacks poorly in their churches. He went on to state that regardless of what his denominational colleagues thought about his actions, he believed that "Christ said to feed your enemies" and that the poor workers around his church would only believe in Christ if he and others in his congregation did the "right thing" by reading the Bible and applying its moral principles to their physical and spiritual needs.[73]

---

[71]Polly Abbleby, *"What Color is God's Skin?": Stories of Ethnic Leaders in America* (Kansas City: Beacon Hill Press, 1984), 28-42; Kathy Trapp, "Another Title for Charles Johnson—Black Consultant," *The Herald of Holiness*, 1 August 1983, 5-6. Church of the Nazarene Archives, Lenexa, KS and Helen Bass Williams, "Mississippi Action For Progress, Inc., February 16, 1968, Selection of Field Services Personnel." Sovereignty Commission Online, Mississippi Department of Department Archives and History,
http://mdah.state.ms.us/arrec/digital_archives/sovcom/imagelisting.php. (accessed 01 April 2011).

[72]"Sanitation Workers Win Strike," *The Crisis* 76, no. 10 (Dec. 1969): 409-411.

[73]John Eppler, "Nazarene minister defends role in city sanitation controversy," in *The Reveille Echo* XLI, no. 9 (13 November 1969): 1-2. Church of the Nazarene Archives, Lenexa, KS.

This response of white Nazarenes to Edwards' actions highlights what was mentioned earlier, namely that most in the denomination in the United States frowned upon social activism as a form of holy living. However, as it also shows, black ministers could decide if they wanted to participate in local or national civil rights activity without official denouncement from denominational leaders. Even if fellow Nazarenes criticized black ministers or churches, they could still engage in such actions if they chose to or if local conditions propelled them into civil rights activities.

Yet, as it pertains to African American Nazarenes in the South, most did not follow the example of Johnson and Edwards. Instead, Rogers and others on the GCD aligned themselves with the theological and congregational mission of most Nazarenes in the United States by primarily focusing on personal holiness evangelism. Like they had in the 1950s, Southern black Nazarenes, like many of their white, Afro-Caribbean, and Cape Verdean counterparts in the United States, believed that their primary goals centered on spreading "scriptural holiness," beginning new churches, and recruiting more pastors. By doing this, African Americans in the South continued their contribution to the overall thrust and mission of the denomination without becoming embroiled in social activism. Neither in district minutes, congregational histories, autobiographical sketches, district publications, nor in other denominational publications is their evidence to suggest that African Americans took such a posture for any other reason. The goal was to evangelize African Americans with the message of personal holiness and to improve the overall infrastructure of their churches, even if the society around them was shaking the foundations of racism throughout the South.

This does not mean, however, that leaders and laity on the GCD condemned those that participated in the struggle for civil rights—as most clearly seen in the leadership's silence on Johnson's and Edward's actions.[74] What it does suggest, is that southern African Americans in the South had worked hard to contribute to the denominational mission during a time of social unrest and for them to attack denominational racism or to urge churches to get involved with civil rights could have deterred them from strengthening the ecclesiastical infrastructure that they had labored so hard to build since the late 1950s.

---

[74]It is important to remember that neither Rogers nor any of the leaders on the GCD encouraged blacks to accept second-class citizenship. Moreover, when Johnson and Edwards became involved in the struggle for civil rights in Meridian and Oklahoma City, both remained active on district boards and were never publicly condemned by any one on the district for their actions.

Continued Participation by African Americans Outside the South

Like their contemporary African American counterparts in the South, this ministerial and congregational commitment to focus on church growth, domestic evangelism, international missions, and denominational teaching to local black communities continued to shape African American congregations and leaders outside the South during the late 1950s and 1960s.

For example, those like R.W. Cunningham, president of NBI through the late 1950s and 1960s, continued to teach and train African American ministers for Christian ministry in the CN with the hopes of evangelizing blacks with the message of personal Christian holiness and improving the black presence within the denomination.[75] He, along with his wife Anna Bowman and black ministers like Clarence Bowman, taught black students a wide variety of courses in the fields of theology, missiology, church history, evangelism, pastoral theology, psychology, church polity, homiletics, New Testament, Old Testament, English, world history, music, and speech in an effort to make sure that all students met requirements for ordination within the CN.[76]

In addition to this, Cunningham, helped to secure small scholarships for prospective black students. In 1965, he, along with other laity and black pastors throughout the South, raised $1,303 to help young black students attend NBI. Two years later, Cunningham collected $1,877.41 for student scholarships after visiting Prentiss Industrial Institute in Prentiss, MS and several other high schools and churches in Mississippi. Similarly, by the following year, Cunningham had helped to secure $2,500 of scholarship money for blacks students to attend NBI.[77]

Aside from these activities, Cunningham also managed the everyday operations of the student body, which never totaled more than 42.[78]

---

[75]Even though the school targeted black students, the official school catalog noted that it welcomed "any and all young people and the young in heart who will agree to abide by reasonable rules and regulations, and who are desirous of a thorough preparation for any special work in connection with the Kingdom of God, to study with us." For further reference see, R.W. Cunningham, "Nazarene Bible Institute School Catalog, 1959-60-61," 1961, 8. Church of the Nazarene Archives, Lenexa, KS.

[76]Ibid., 8-12.

[77]Gulf Central District Church of the Nazarene Thirteenth Annual Assembly Journal, 15-21.

[78]In fact, according to a report done by the Department of Home Missions in 1969, the final year of its operation, "a number" of the students who were enrolled at the school were local white pastors that were attempting "to finish some of their ministerial courses" needed for ordination requirements. For further reference, see

According to an early 1960s school brochure, the president and pastor made sure that students maintained a physically healthy lifestyle, had regular meals, provided activities and games for students to play, and encouraged students to care for the maintenance of the school building and dormitories. In fact as it pertained to the last responsibility, Cunningham noted that every student would give a certain amount of "gratis" work towards the maintenance of NBI. He noted that the labor included "preparation of meals, cleaning of building, yard work, washing dishes, etc."[79]

Most important of all his duties, however, was guarding the students' Christian virtue. According to Cunningham and other school leaders, "wholesome social and cultural development" was critical in such a situation where "a number of young people are brought together in intimate relationship." Thus, he designed a rule where students were required to plan a week in advance with faculty and parents so that students wouldn't be tempted to engage in behavior unbecoming of a student enrolled at NBI. Moreover, students were required to abstain from such practices as the consumption of alcohol, smoking tobacco, dancing, card playing, movie going, "hazing, or other boisterous conduct." On top of this, the president made sure that students avoided wearing "elaborate, ultrafashionable, or expensive clothing." This was especially pertinent to the handful of female students that attended the school in the early 1960s. In the section entitled, "Standards of Conduct," Cunningham specifically targeted females with this requirement when he noted that,

> A complete outfit of simple but serviceable clothing should be brought by each student. We wish especially to discourage the wearing of elaborate, ultrafashionable, or expensive clothing. Rubber heels will be required. Ladies' dress that border on immodesty will not be permitted. Dark suits are preferred for men in Christian service on Sunday or special occasions.[80]

Moral conservatism not only impacted campus life, but it also shaped the classroom as well. Many classes were heavily geared toward biblical exegesis, preaching, church history and evangelism. Other courses related to topics like social ethics or contemporary theology were absent from the curriculum. In fact, the only courses taught outside the realm of evangelism, homiletics, church polity, church history, speech, and biblical theology were psychology, sociology, biology, logic, and church administration.[81]

By maintaining such duties and teaching such courses Cunningham, Bowman, and other leaders of school focused on training black pastors to

---

R.W. Hurn, "Department of Home Missions Minutes: Bible Colleges," 14 January 1969, 1. Church of the Nazarene Archives, Lenexa, KS.
[79]Cunningham, "Nazarene Bible Institute Catalog 1959-60-61," 14.
[80]Ibid., 13-14.
[81]Ibid., 11-12.

evangelize and lead churches and not to address racism inside and outside the church. As a result, NBI's overarching focus remained on training black holiness pastors. In other words, Cunningham's and NBI's predominant mission was to find those of "sterling" character and "consecration to God" and train them for "an immediate avenue of service" to spread the personal holiness message among African Americans around the country.

One former student, JoeAnn Ballard, recalls how this focus on moral purity, black evangelism, and social conservatism shaped and impacted those who attended NBI in the mid 1960s. During her first year at the school (1962-1963), Ballard states that she immediately noticed how Bowman lived with "integrity and purpose." She also notes how "thorough he was in the classroom" and how "he would go over and over the material until he was certain that every person understood" the subject matter. Likewise, when recalling the virtues of Cunningham in the classroom, Ballard claims that Cunningham was a holy man that "taught with vigor and insisted that his students do detailed work."[82]

At the same time, Ballard notes that these instructors rarely discussed ecclesiastical or societal racism in the classroom. In fact, Ballard asserts that racial issues were rarely discussed because students were largely isolated from the problems of U.S. society. The school, as she recalls, did not have televisions and radios and large newspapers were not available on campus. Thus, according to Ballard, students were kept abreast of racial issues only when they went on home visits for the summer or on holidays.

In addition to this, Ballard maintains that racial segregation or ecclesiastical racism were not mentioned in the classroom even though students from Mississippi often had conversations amongst themselves "about the racial divide." In fact, Ballard claims that such issues were never brought to the fore of classroom discussion or analyzed theologically by a professor, whether informally or formally. She reiterates this when she notes that, "It (ecclesiastical racism) was not addressed at our level anyway. If it was addressed at a higher level, we were not privy to that...it was not a class discussion." In Ballard's estimation, groups of students had more freedom to discuss these things because they would not face the possible repercussions that black professors could have faced—specifically financial ones. She reiterates this point when she notes that,

> You (students at NBI) were kept out of the knowledge of things because I don't feel like, that professors wanted to discuss it and I don't think that they wanted to get into that because it could've dealt with the financial activities

---

[82]JoeAnn Ballard with Susan Autry Currier, *I Belong Here: A Biography of a Community* (Union City, TN: Master Design Ministries, 2005), 25-27.

at the school and just looking back and knowing what I know, I'm sure they were very careful to not offend anyone.[83]

Whether or not this threat was real or perceived does not take away from the fact that a focus on training African American pastors that could effectively evangelize and strengthen black churches without becoming embroiled in issues of ecclesiastical or societal racism was the overarching goal of NBI and its leaders.

Administrators and leaders like Cunningham not only took this stance in the classroom, but also in the church as well. For instance, Cunningham's church, Institute CN, continued to minister to blacks in and around Institute, WV without becoming embroiled in the Civil Rights Movement. Moreover, there is no evidence to suggest that they addressed denominational racism or tried to forge racial alliances with other black churches around the country to increase the collective black presence in the denomination. Neither did they take on an active civic presence in their local community. Instead they, like their counterparts in the South, continued to commit themselves to denominational evangelism and to increasing the numerical strength of their church through local Nazarene ministries like Sunday school, NYPS, and NWMS.

In 1962, for example, Cunningham reported having a total of 51 members that regularly attended Sunday morning worship. At the same time, Institute reported having more than double the amount of Sunday school members than their total church membership—163. Likewise, when the total church numbers dropped to 43 four years later, the church still had more than 140 children, youth, and adults that regularly attended Sunday school lessons and activities at the church. Furthermore, when congregational numbers rebounded to 49 three years later—the church still had more than 120 Sunday school members.[84]

In proportion to their church membership, Institute also had many NYPS and NWMS members. In 1966, the church had 51 NYPS members that contributed to the church's youth bible studies, outings, and other weekly and monthly activities. Likewise, in the same year, Institute still had a total of 51 NWMS members, which were also three more than the total number of church members.[85] Moreover, at the close of the decade, the church still

---

[83]JoAnn Ballard, phone interview with Brandon Winstead, Quincy, IL, April 06, 2009. Brandon Winstead's Private Collection, Kansas City, KS.

[84]Church of the Nazarene Research Center, "Membership Status and Attendance of Institute Church of the Nazarene—West Virginia District." http://app.nazarene.org/FindAChurch/viewReport.jsp?reportId=21196&sIDType=rpt&orgId=9569. (accessed 02 April 2011).

[85]The larger numbers of NYPS and NFMS members as opposed to total church membership was probably due to the fact that many of the black students at NBI, who were members of other churches, attended the church and could be included in

possessed numerous youth who participated in the youth ministries of the NYPS and the NWMS had 58 members that still contributed their time and money to local and international evangelism.[86]

Through these actions, Cunningham and his church seemed to reflect the commitment of other African Americans during the 1960s that utilized their Sunday schools and NWMS and NYPS chapters to "reach out" to local blacks in the community. Furthermore, like their peers in the South, Institute's congregational focus was not limited or forced upon them by white ecclesiastical leaders. Instead, as non-segregated participants on their geographical districts, they focused on black evangelism, worship, and discipleship. Moreover, nothing suggests that Cunningham or any other members of the Institute were concerned about becoming embroiled in civil rights or addressing other systemic issues facing African Americans throughout the country.[87] Thus, like their southern counterparts, the main focus was to strengthen their congregational ministries, contribute to their district ministry chapters, and evangelize those in the community with the personal holiness message of the denomination.

Besides Cunningham, Bowman, and Institute CN, other African American pastors and churches around the country continued similar efforts. Black Nazarenes in Oakland, CA enhanced district evangelization by leading and maintaining active chapters of Nazarene ministries and contributing to district leadership. For instance, in 1965, Felix Goldsby led Oakland Bethel's (the church mentioned in the previous chapter that was started in 1957 as a Sunday school mission by Clifford Johnson) Sunday school department, while Mark Barbosa and "Mrs." M.A. Watson led the NYPS and NWMS ministries for the church of less than 50 members. Moreover, people like Goldsby and "Mrs." F. Barbosa contributed to the decision-making power of the district by sitting on the Church Schools Committee and the Education Committee. Aside from this, as acting presidents of Oakland Bethel's NYPS and NWMS chapters, Barbosa and Watson were able to sit on the district's Youth Work Committee and World Missions Committee. By sitting on these committees, Barbosa and Watson were able to contribute to how the district would allocate its funds and resources to spread the message of the denomination around the world and amongst youth who lived in northern California.[88]

---

the church's numbers without having to officially join the church. See Ballard, phone interview with Brandon Winstead, Quincy, IL, April 06, 2009.

[86] Church of the Nazarene Research Center, "Membership Status and Attendance of Institute Church of the Nazarene." (accessed 02 April 2011).

[87] Ballard, phone interview with Brandon Winstead, Quincy, IL, April 06, 2009.

[88] Northern California District Church of the Nazarene, Sixtieth Annual Assembly Journal (May 1965), 16-17, 30-31, 37-39. Church of the Nazarene Archives, Lenexa, KS.

Likewise, in places like Saginaw, MI black Nazarenes at Saginaw Burk Memorial CN sought to evangelize the local African American community through Nazarene ministries. Founded in 1962 by several white and black pastors and laity, the church, along with its minister Booker T. Lee, worked to accomplish this task even though there were only a handful of members that were a part of the congregation. For instance, in 1964, the church possessed a Sunday school membership of 27. Over the course of the next five years, those numbers steadily increased. In fact, by the end of the decade, the black Saginaw congregation had a total of 40 Sunday school members, which was double their total church membership and a greater percentage when compared to church membership of the other white churches in Saginaw such as Saginaw First Church of the Nazarene, Saginaw New Life Church of the Nazarene and Saginaw Swan Valley Church of the Nazarene. All three of these congregations had equal or greater number of people attending Sunday school, but none of them doubled the percentage of their church membership in Sunday school attendance.[89]

Nonetheless, this does not mean that either the Saginaw church or the white churches were more passionate or effective when it came to evangelizing and catechizing persons in the Church of the Nazarene. However, what it does reveal is that the small congregation contributed, as a non-segregated member of the Michigan district, to district ministries while specifically evangelizing black men, women, children, and youth. Thus, they tried to evangelize those in their surrounding communities and fulfill one of the foci of the denomination in the 1960s, which was to "evangelize the lost" with the message of personal Christian holiness.

Around the same time, other small congregations in California, like San Diego Southeast CN, attempted to "reach the lost" by seeking to evangelize African Americans in their local community. Roger Bowman (the first

---

[89] In fact, in 1963, the church had a membership of 18 and by the end of the decade the church still had less than 20 church members. For further reference see, Rev. Lewis W. Gould, "1972 Black Church Information, Saginaw Burk Memorial Church of the Nazarene," August 15, 1972, 1. Church of the Nazarene Archives, Lenexa, KS; Church of the Nazarene Research Center, "Membership Status and Attendance of Saginaw Burk Memorial Church of the Nazarene—Michigan District." http://app.nazarene.org/FindAChurch/viewReport.jsp?reportId=21196&orgId=3650. (accessed 07 April 2011); Church of the Nazarene Research Center, "Membership Status and Attendance of Saginaw New Life Church of the Nazarene—Michigan District." http://app.nazarene.org/FindAChurch/viewReport.jsp?reportId=21196&orgId=3651. (accessed 12 April 2011] and Church of the Nazarene Research Center, "Membership Status and Attendance of Saginaw Swan Valley Church of the Nazarene—Michigan District." http://app.nazarene.org/FindAChurch/viewReport.jsp?reportId=21196&orgId=3654. (accessed 12 April 2011).

pastor of the congregation and the son of the above-mentioned educator Clarence Bowman) left the confines of West Virginia to pastor the small congregation (the church was founded in 1962). As the pastoral leader, Bowman led the church for four years until another black minister by the name of Rev. Elvis Brown became the next pastor. Under their leadership of both men, the congregation never achieved more than 21 members.[90] However, like their smaller counterparts in Oakland and Saginaw, their small size did not stop them from maintaining NYPS and NWMS chapters in their congregation in an attempt to reach out to black constituents in their community.

Furthermore, throughout the tenure of both pastors, the congregation—like other black churches throughout the North, South, and West—sought to evangelize and transform the spiritual lives of African American children, youth, and adults through Sunday school classes and evangelistic worship services. In fact, by the middle of the decade, the church reported having an average Sunday school attendance of 80,[91] while at the same time holding worship services that changed the spiritual lives of those in the congregation. One woman, by the name of Brenda Winrow, was the recipient of such a transformation. "Mrs." Edward Glaze reconstructed Winrow's and another woman's transformation in a 1970 report given to the Department of Home Missions. In it, she recalled that,

> A young mother, Mrs. Brenda Winrow, went to the altar to be prayed for and found Christ as her Savior. Today (she) still testifies to the Christ of the cross she found in the Nazarene Church. Another young mother still saved and sanctified found Christ as her Savior and won't turn back, she has an unsaved husband who knows that she is different and unsaved brothers and sisters that hate her religion and faith but she doesn't give up the precious Christ she has found.[92]

Nonetheless, these efforts and testimonies symbolize and reveal that the church in San Diego actively chose, according to available data, to focus on evangelization and strengthening congregational ministries while at the same time foregoing public participation in addressing ecclesiastical or societal racism. Moreover, like African American Nazarenes around the country, they did not attempt to establish connections with other black

---

[90]Dr. Nicolas A. Hull, "1970 Negro Church Information, Southeast San Diego Church of the Nazarene," July 22, 1970, 1. Church of the Nazarene Archives, Lenexa, KS.

[91]Church of the Nazarene Research Center, ", Membership Status and Attendance of Southeast Church of the Nazarene—Southern California District." http://app.nazarene.org/FindAChurch/viewReport.jsp?reportId=21196&orgId=6519. (accessed 07 June 2010).

[92]Mrs. Edward Glaze, "1970 Negro Church Information, Southeast San Diego Church of the Nazarene," August 17, 1970, 1. Church of the Nazarene Archives, Lenexa, KS.

Nazarenes in the United States. Instead of collective black action, the church in San Diego chose to focus on "saving" souls and contributing to district ministries.

Yet, this specific concern with black evangelization in the 1960s was not unique to African American congregations in the South, West Virginia, Michigan, or California. It also resembled the congregational approach of black churches in one of the Midwest's largest urban centers—Chicago. Rufus Sanders, for instance, pastored at Ingleside Church of the Nazarene on the south side of the city and helped to improve the congregation's membership numbers from 8 in 1960 to 38 in 1969. Even though his congregation remained small, Sanders and Ingleside symbolized their commitment to denominational evangelization, both at home and abroad, by maintaining active NWMS and NYPS chapters. In fact, by 1966, the church had 54 young people who were registered members of the NYPS and 26 who served as NWMS members. Around the same time, the church also had more Sunday school attendees than those who were members of the congregation.[93] In 1965, Ingleside had 65 black children, youth, and adults that were exposed to biblical lessons and the teachings of the denomination and even though that number decreased by 1969, the congregation still had 40 Sunday school members, which was still more than its total church membership.[94]

In similar fashion, Robert Lyman, a white minister, sought to evangelize African Americans on Chicago's west side. After getting permission from the District Superintendent, Lyman began a mission amongst a few African Americans and over time, the outpost slowly grew. Because of this, in 1963 the worshipping body, along with the district, raised enough funds to purchase a two story storefront building. After purchasing the structure, they remodeled it and began holding worship services and Sunday school classes. Within a few years, the "Van Buren Nazarene Mission" began to grow and by 1965, it was organized into Chicago Central Church of the Nazarene with 16 charter members.[95]

---

[93]Again, as previous decades, Sunday school membership was higher than church membership in most Nazarene congregations throughout the United States. Moreover, church membership still required one to adhere to strict moral and ethical requirements like those mentioned in previous chapters.

[94]Church of the Nazarene Research Center, "Membership Status and Attendance of Ingleside Church of the Nazarene—Chicago Central District." http://app.nazarene.org/FindAChurch/viewReport.jsp?reportId=21196&orgId=1172. (accessed 08 June 2010).

[95]Rev. Robert Layman, "1970 Negro Church Information, Central Church of the Nazarene," August 10, 1970, 1. Church of the Nazarene Archives, Lenexa, KS and Rev. Dr. Robert Layman to Raymond Hurn, 7 August 1972, transcript in the hand of Rev. Robert Lyman, Church of the Nazarene Archives, Lenexa, KS.

The church never expanded much beyond these numbers throughout the late 1960s, but those who attended the congregation sought to spread the message of perrsonal Christian holiness, particularly among "children and families." They held numerous Sunday school classes for children and maintained a NYPS. Aside from studying the Bible and holiness themes, the youth also participated in a youth choir that Lyman noted was, "one of the best young peoples choir in the city."[96]

In addition to this, Chicago Central attempted to meet some of the physical needs of those in their church and community. They distributed canned food, fresh vegetables, and hundreds of loaves of bread to those in the neighborhood. Along with this, those in the congregation ran a clothing distribution center where clothes were given and disseminated amongst families in need. Furthermore, at Christmas time, they gave community members Christmas baskets that contained wool caps, fruit candy, toys, and other gifts.[97]

These attempts at addressing some of the physical concerns of community and church members did not deter the congregation from its main goal of evangelizing blacks and getting "them into the blessed experience of sanctification."[98] Even in a city like Chicago, which, by the summer of 1966, had become the new setting of Martin Luther King's and the Southern Christian Leadership Conference's civil rights campaign,[99] black Nazarenes remained committed to holding Sunday schools, hosting outreach activities, promoting domestic and foreign missions, and indoctrinating youth and families in "the experience of sanctification." Thus, the primary focus was on expanding the evangelistic work among local African Americans instead of joining local and national civil rights issues that were impacting black Americans in Chicago and around the country.

In other places outside the South, at small congregations like Bible Way CN in St. Louis, MO, Kansas City Park Avenue CN in Kansas City, MO and Wichita North Ash CN in Wichita, KS, the ministerial focus resembled most other African American congregations around the country.[100] In short, they

---

[96]Rev. Dr. Robert Victor Layman to Rev. E.G. Benson, 30 January 1963, transcript in the hand of Dr. Robert Victor Lyman, Church of the Nazarene Archives, Lenexa, KS.

[97]Ibid.

[98]Ibid.

[99]For a fuller discussion on King's and the SCLC's impact on local black civil rights organizations, the municipal government, and black churches in Chicago during the summer of 1966, see Taylor Branch, *At Canaan's Edge: America in the King Years, 1965-1968* (New York: Simon & Schuster, 2006), 501-522.

[100]Each of these congregations never possessed more than 30 members. For further reference, see Allen Winbush, "1970 Negro Church Information, Bible Way Church of the Nazarene," July 31, 1970, 1. Church of the Nazarene Archives, Lenexa, KS; Ray Hance, "1970 Negro Church Information, Wichita Ash Church of the Nazarene," July 23, 1970, 1. Church of the Nazarene Archives, Lenexa, KS and

supported the work of the CN by holding NWMS ministries, Sunday school outreach classes, NYPS sessions, and worship services in African American communities.

"Why so Small?": A Brief Excursus on African American Congregational Growth During the Late 1950s and 1960s

Even though the above mentioned churches and those in the South that remained segregated at the district level continued to spread the message of personal holiness to those in their communities, most still did not have total church membership of over 60 members. This reality could lead one to ask, "Why did African American congregations never increase in size beyond very small numbers during this period, given the single-minded evangelistic agenda?" Although the question may never be fully answered, it is important to remember that the average Nazarene church the late 1950s and 1960s was relatively small. In fact, in 1958, average church membership throughout the United States totaled less than 70 members and by 1967, average congregational membership remained under 75.[101]

Such numbers were operative even though church leaders placed heavy emphasis on denominational evangelism. During the 1950s and 1960s, denominational heads used the slogan "Evangelism First" as a rallying cry to help encourage churches to give to local and foreign missions and to continue the growth the CN experienced after WWII. For instance, from 1946 to 1956, 1,177 new Nazarene churches were started in the United States. However, from 1957 to 1967, growth for the CN slowed as the denomination added far less new churches (428) than it had in the previous decade. The church experienced a slower amount of overall growth during this period than it had in late 1940s and 1950s and membership for most congregations remained relatively small. Thus, it would seem that black churches were like their white counterparts in that their congregations remained relatively small despite their focus on evangelism.

Because of this, it would seem that there was not a particular reason that limited congregational growth among African Americans as opposed to white churches. As denominational historians have noted, former Nazarene evangelistic methods like holding revivals and door to door evangelism fell on hard times during this period and churches found it increasingly difficult

---

Beverly Burgess, "1970 Negro Church Information, Kansas City Park Avenue Church of the Nazarene," February 18, 1971, 1. Church of the Nazarene Archives, Lenexa, KS.

[101]Dale E. Jones, "Average US Churches Sizes, 1908-2010," November 1, 2010. Research Services, Global Ministry Center, Lenexa, KS.

to attract new members.¹⁰² Furthermore, as increasing social changes transpired in the 1960s, moral and behavioral norms of the past came into question and many felt it a threat to the future of the denomination. Many Nazarene leaders and pastors like Glenn Griffith, Hardy Powers, Joseph Pitts, and William Tidwell reacted against this by continuing to preach against the use of tobacco, sexual promiscuity, movie watching, immodest dress, and a host of other individual "sins" that they believed threatened the lives of holiness believers and the faith of churches. As a result of this—combined with the increasing outdated models of evangelism—many in the church became overly concerned about the maintenance of individual morality, thus curbing some of the zeal and growth that had transpired in the immediate post-WWII years.¹⁰³

In addition to this, one may also ask why African American churches failed to grow exponentially when they had such large Sunday school numbers. Again, a particular answer may never be found, but it is helpful to remember that Sunday schools, for both African American and white congregations, continued to be an evangelistic tool. In particular, Sunday school continued to be utilized as an evangelistic instrument to help others outside the church achieve "salvation," with the hope that this would lead them to become church members. As *The 1964 Church of the Nazarene Manual* stated, Sunday school's primary mission was to "seek the salvation of the unsaved and the entire sanctification of believers."¹⁰⁴

However, becoming a member of a congregation required one to adhere to strict moral codes outlined in the *Manual*. Among other things, members were not to attend movies, smoke, dance, play cards, or work on the Sabbath. These restrictions, as they had since the late 1910s, often proved too much for many who attended Sunday school and as a result, many avoided church membership during the mid to late 1960s. In short, this pattern probably helped many churches achieve a higher rate of Sunday school membership as opposed to church membership.¹⁰⁵

Nevertheless, the reality of small congregational numbers and the factors that lead to seemingly miniscule growth does not discount the fact that African Americans—despite being subjected to different levels of

---

¹⁰²Cunningham, Ingersol, Raser, and Whitelaw, 386-387.

¹⁰³Ibid, 410-413.

¹⁰⁴John Riley, B. Edgar Johnson, Leslie Parrot, Wilson P. Lanpher, and W.T. Purkiser, ed., *Manual of the Church of the Nazarene, 1964* (Kansas City, MO: Nazarene Publishing House, 1964), 82.

¹⁰⁵Ibid., 45-48, 346 and Stan Ingersol, singersol@nazarene.org. "Sunday School Attendance for the Church of the Nazarene." Private e-mail message to Brandon Winstead. 10 October 2010. In 1966, for instance, average Sunday school attendance in a Nazarene church stood at 88, while church membership averaged 74. For further reference, see Dale E. Jones, "Average US Churches Sizes, 1908-2010," November 1, 2010. Research Services, Global Ministry Center, Lenexa, KS.

ecclesiastical segregation and jurisdictional patterns—continued to contribute to the personal holiness message and evangelistic mission of the denomination. From West Virginia to Michigan to Kansas to California to Illinois to Missouri to Alabama to Virginia to Mississippi, churches and their leaders evangelized African Americans in their local context, while at the same time contributing to international missions and traditional Nazarene ministries like NWMS, NYPS, and Sunday school.

By embracing such practices and patterns, African American churches attempted to expand the mission of the denomination by contributing to global and domestic missions. Not only that, but African American congregations in the South and North continued to evangelize blacks in their communities while at the same time paying district budgets, supporting Nazarene missions, and maintaining Sunday schools, NWMS chapters, and NYPS ministries.

As a consequence of these actions and approach, however, it must be remembered that most African American Nazarenes throughout the country did not focus on challenging societal or denominational racism or trying to create a stronger black body within the CN that could have created a wider voting base to challenge segregation in the South or denominational racism. Instead, on the segregated GCD and on other geographical districts throughout the North and West, African Americans remained Nazarene in every sense of the word. They focused on evangelizing blacks with the message of personal Christian holiness. As a result, African Americans were central players in helping to expand the presence of the denomination in the United States in the middle decades of the 20th century.

Chapter Five

The Participation Continues: West Indian and Cape Verdean Contributions to Denominational Evangelism, 1958-1969

The West Indian Churches: Personal Holiness Evangelism and Congregational Growth

In many ways, the commitment to domestic evangelism and the expansion of denominational ministries with a largely conservative slant not only shaped African American Nazarenes during the heyday of the 1960s, but it also impacted the West Indian congregations in New York. Like they had in the late 1940s and 1950s, the Afro-Caribbean churches and ministers pursued personal holiness evangelism, was a part of district leadership, and sustained Nazarene ministries as fully participating members of the New York District and not as segregated participants like African Americans in the South. How they did this and the manner in which they and other black immigrants continued to carry on and promote the banner of the denomination in large urban areas like New York City will now be explored.

Clarence Jacobs—a native of Guyana and former senior minister of the black congregation in Indianapolis, IN that took over the pastorate of Miller Memorial Church of the Nazarene in the summer of 1957 following the retirement of William Greene[1] —exemplified this commitment in the city of

---

[1] "Rev. Greene Dead; Pastored Miller Church," *New York Amsterdam News*, 29 August 1959 and Clarence Jacobs, "The Miller Memorial Church of the Nazarene:

New York by voting at District Assembly and sitting on the Sabbath Observance Committee a year after his arrival in Brooklyn. Like Jacobs, ministers like Levi Franklin at Beulah CN, James Jessamy at Bedford Zion, and W. Eugene Hazard at Wyandanch CN sat on district committees like the Nominations Committee, Education Committee, Orders and Relations Committee, and Sabbath Observance Committee.[2]

Aside from this participation, black laymen and women like Laurie Gill, Gilbert Stuart (the future minister of Bedford Zion), Lenta Eastmond, Leroy Skeete, Lawrence King, Edith Clarke, Rudolph Rochester, and Ernetta Rochester were sent as lay delegates to the District Assembly on behalf of Bedford Zion, Beulah, Miller Memorial, and Wyandanch, all churches in the boroughs of Brooklyn and Long Island. At the same time, Mabel Catlyne and Gertrude Forde continued to serve as consecrated deaconesses for the New York District. These women continued to help the district decide how it would minister to the poor and sick throughout metropolitan New York and they persisted in helping to provide pastoral assistance by visiting and praying for the sick, preaching, and giving care to women in the church who had recently given birth.[3]

Besides this, at the end of the 1950s, black laity contributed to district ministries by leading and sustaining local chapters of the NFMS, NYPS, and Sunday school. At Beulah, women and men like Lillian Franklin, Denzil Thorpe, and Albert Braithwaite served as presidents of the church's NFMS, Sunday school, and NYPS. Meanwhile at Miller Memorial, Bedford Zion, and Wyandanch, laypersons like Lillian Corbin, Mabel Catlyne, Ophelia Mayers, Dorothy Howell, Louise Davis, Johanna Houston, Keturah Pilgrim, Joseph Forde, and Amelia Edwards provided needed leadership for their congregations' NFMS, NYPS, and Sunday school chapters.

By contributing and leading these ministries, black ministers and lay leaders at these congregations enabled their churches to remain contributors to the numerical presence of the CN in and around New York City. For instance, in 1958, the district gained a total of 74 new members, which brought the combined membership of all the churches to 1,688. Before this, the highest net gain was 65, which was recorded in 1948.

Of those 74 that became new members, 17 were from the Wyandanch church, making it the church with the highest gain of membership throughout the course of the year. In fact, the Wyandanch outgained such

---

Dedication of our Church," (May 8, 1977), 3. Church of the Nazarene Archives, Lenexa, KS.

[2]*New York District Church of the Nazarene, Fifty-First Annual Assembly Journal* (July 1958): 22-23.

[3]Ibid., 16, 29 and Grace Braithwaite, personal interview with Brandon Winstead, Brooklyn, New York, September 17, 2009. Brandon Winstead's Personal Collection, Kansas City, KS.

prominent white churches on the district such as Valley Stream CN (16), Poughkeepsie CN (14), Springfield Gardens CN (9), East Rockaway CN (6), Freeport CN (6), and Massapequa Park CN (6).[4] In addition to this, in the same year, Beulah (81), Wyandanch (81), Bedford Zion (41), and Miller Memorial (55) had a total membership of 258.[5] To the casual observer, this may seem like a miniscule amount, but of the thirty plus congregations on the district most of them did not possess total memberships of over 100. In fact, white churches like Richmond Hill CN in Richmond Hill, NY and East Rockaway CN in East Rockaway, NY were at the top of the membership scale for the district. The former church had 100 members, while the latter had a total of 138 on its membership rolls. Most of the other white congregations, including those such as Danbury CN (23 members) in Danbury, CT Poughkeepsie CN (41) in Poughkeepsie, NY, Norwalk CN (41) in Norwalk, CT, Patchogue CN (49) in Patchogue, NY, Edison CN (21) in Edison, NJ, Butler CN (73) in Butler, NJ, Valley Stream CN (68) in Valley Stream, NY, and Springfield Gardens CN (52) in Springfield Gardens, NY had membership numbers that hovered between 20 to 80 members.[6] Thus, when one compares these numbers with those of the black congregations, it would seem that in terms of membership, the West Indian congregations were substantial contributors to the numerical growth and size of the district in the late 1950s.

Likewise, as the decade closed and turned to the 1960s, black Nazarenes on the New York District continued their contribution to the overall membership numbers of the district. When the District Assembly gathered in 1962, Wyandanch had 88 members, Beulah 88, and Bedford Zion 54. Miller Memorial led all the black churches with a total membership of 100,

---

[4]New York District Church of the Nazarene, Fifty-First Annual Assembly Journal, 33-34.

[5]Church of the Nazarene Research Center, "Membership Status and Attendance of Wyandanch—Metro New York District." http://app.nazarene.org/FindAChurch/viewReport.jsp?reportId=21196&orgId=4402. (accessed 20 April 2011); Church of the Nazarene Research Center, "Membership Status and Attendance of Bedford Zion—Metro New York District." http://app.nazarene.org/FindAChurch/viewReport.jsp?reportId=21196&orgId=4318. (accessed 21 April 2011); Church of the Nazarene Research Center, "Membership Status and Attendance of Brooklyn Beulah—Metro New York District." http://app.nazarene.org/FindAChurch/viewReport.jsp?reportId=21196&orgId=4320. (accessed 21 April 2011) and Church of the Nazarene Research Center, "Membership Status and Attendance of Brooklyn Community Worship Center—Metro New York District." From http://app.nazarene.org/FindAChurch/viewReport.jsp?reportId=21196&orgId=4331. (accessed 21 April 2011).

[6]New York District Church of the Nazarene, Fifty-First Annual Assembly Journal, statistical index. Church of the Nazarene Archives, Lenexa, KS.

which made it one of the largest congregations on the New York District. These numbers brought the total membership of the predominantly black Caribbean congregations to 330, which was an increase of 72 over four years.[7] When membership numbers were totaled four years later in 1966, the churches still recorded an increase in church membership. Bedford Zion had 58 members and Beulah recorded a total membership of 105. Wyandanch also had 88 members on their rolls, while Miller Memorial increased its church membership to 155, an increase of over 50 since 1962. In addition to this, the newly formed West Indian church in the Bronx (which is today called Bronx Bethany Church of the Nazarene) had a total of 21 members under the leadership of Rev. Seymour Cole, an Afro-Caribbean Nazarene who also worked at Yale University.[8]

When one compares these numbers of the 1960s to the white churches mentioned above, it becomes apparent that the West Indian churches resembled, if not exceeded, average church membership on the district. In 1962, for instance, Danbury CN had only 18 members, while Poughkeepsie possessed a total membership of 48. In the same year, East Rockaway had 134 members, Norwalk 45, Patchogue 49, Edison 41, Butler 76, Valley Stream 73, Springfield Gardens 35, and Richmond Hill had decreased to a total membership of 84. Four years later, East Rockaway had 135 members, while Danbury possessed 28 church members and Poughkeepsie had 45 persons on their membership rolls. In addition to this, Norwalk increased its membership to 74, Patchogue to 50, Edison to 68, and Butler to 81. At the same time, Valley Stream's membership decreased to 66, while Springfield's and Richmond Hill's total congregational membership declined to 18 and 79.[9]

As its was mentioned previously, these congregations did not make up all the churches on the district, but their congregational membership numbers represented the lower, middle, and high averages of those on the jurisdiction and in the denomination. In fact, at the start of the decade, most

---

[7]*New York District Church of the Nazarene, Fifty-Fifth Annual Assembly Journal* (July 1962), statistical index. Church of the Nazarene Archives, Lenexa, KS.

[8]*New York District Church of the Nazarene, Fifty-Ninth Annual Assembly Journal* (July 1966), statistical index. Church of the Nazarene Archives, Lenexa, KS. According to the church's website, Bronx Bethany CN was started in the early 1960s, after a small contingent of Afro-Caribbeans migrated to the United States and could not find a suitable place for worship. They were unsuccessful in their attempts to find a suitable place of worship so they decided to gather together in their homes for worship. They continued to worship and in 1964, 21 charter members formally joined the CN and called Rev. Cole to be their minister. For further information, see Bronx Bethany, "Our History," http://www.bronxbethany.net/. (accessed 21 April 2011).

[9]Ibid, statistical index and *New York District Church of the Nazarene, Fifty-Fifth Annual Assembly Journal*, statistical index.

Nazarenes in the United States attended and worshipped in congregations with fewer than fifty members and only 2 percent attended churches with more than three hundred members. Moreover, from the late 1950s to late 1960s, most Nazarene congregations averaged between 80 and 100 members and by the start of the 1970s, only 15% of Nazarenes worshiped in congregations larger than 300 members.[10]

Thus, when one includes these numbers with those from the New York District, it becomes apparent that most churches in the New York metropolitan area were average size Nazarene congregations. However, when one takes into account the congregational membership of black churches like Miller Memorial and Beulah, it would seem that these churches were large Nazarene congregations. Not only that, but this reinforces that the West Indian congregations in the early to late 1960s actively contributed to the New York District's overall membership numbers.

As they grew, the Afro-Caribbean churches in Brooklyn and Long Island carried on the evangelistic message of the CN in New York. As it was mentioned previously, denominational leaders continued to preach and teach about the importance of supporting foreign and domestic missions. At the 1960 General Assembly, for instance, the General Superintendents chose "Evangelism First" as the theme for the 1960-1964 quadrennium. Evangelists and ministers like C. Hastings Smith, Paul Martin, Albert Lown, Mary Cooper, C. Helen Mooshian, Nettie Miller, Lelia Dell Miller and Estelle Crutcher, along with intellectuals and professors such as Mel-Thomas Rothwell, Reubel Welch, James McGraw, W.T. Purkiser, Richard Taylor, Mendell Taylor, and William Greathouse carried out this theme by speaking at churches, revivals, and camp meetings. In short, these ministers, evangelists, and academics preached sermons and delivered addresses stressing that Nazarenes should evangelize those who had not received salvation.[11]

Similarly, at the local level, New York District leaders and laypersons promoted this theme by stressing the local church's responsibility to evangelize those in their communities. In the district newsletter entitled, *The Ink-Links*, parishoners and pastors were urged to attend annual camp meetings with the hope that their presence would help to evangelize the

---

[10] Floyd Cunningham, Stan Ingersol, Harold E. Raser, and David P. Whitelaw, ed., *Our Watchword & Song: The Centennial History of the Church of the Nazarene* (Kansas City, MO: Beacon Hill Press, 2009), 433 and Kenneth E. Crow, "The Life Cycle of Nazarene Churches,"
http://www.nazarene.org/files/docs/The%20Life%20Cycle%20of%20Nazarene%20Churches.pdf. (accessed 22 April 2011).

[11] Cunningham, Ingersol, Raser, and Whitelaw, *Our Watchword & Song: The Centennial History of the Church of the Nazarene*, 381-385.

"non-saved" and increase the spiritual fervor of congregants. In June 1961, pastors were "expected to attend Camp Meeting with the same regularity that they would like their members to attend a revival in the local church." Not only that, but they, along with their parishioners, were encouraged to attend and pray that there would be a "high evangelistic tide to rise to Camp." In the same newsletter, other entries stressing the evangelistic responsibility of New York Nazarenes were written. Some of the titles included, "Have You Paid Your Home Mission Pledge?" and "Laymen Lead Home Mission Challenge."[12]

In addition to this, the district's Church Schools Committee stressed that churches should work to improve their membership numbers over the course of the summer. To do this, they noted that churches needed to hold vibrant Sunday schools during the summer months and make the necessary preparations to have a successful Vacation Bible School. Moreover, the department of the NYPS encouraged churches on the district to reach out to young people and increase its membership. In particular, the NYPS wanted each church to "Stop the Summer Slump With an Attendance Goal Jump" of 10%. If churches could increase their membership by this percentage amount, then they would receive a Certificate of Commendation at the upcoming District Assembly.[13]

Likewise, the NFMS stated that churches and local chapters of the NFMS needed to give to local and international missions. In particular, they stressed that women and men should give to radio ministries in Mexico, South America, and Spain so that "thousands would hear the Word of God." For them, radio was a medium that could help "send the Gospel to those who otherwise would never hear the name of Jesus. Thus, they argued that if those on the district were concerned about spreading the personal holiness message, then they should support the mission "One Hundred Percent." Aside from this, the committee urged NFMS chapters to continue giving their pledges to finish construction on a "water system project" in Trinidad, support missionary endeavors in Panama, and improve new outreach ministries on the district.[14]

The stress on evangelism continued four years later. In a February edition of *The Ink-Links,* the District Superintendent Rev. Jack H. White expressed his appreciation for the district's commitment to local and international evangelism when he noted that the district was faithful in its giving to foreign missions and for helping to support the evangelistic outreach of local churches. Moreover, both the Church Schools Department and the NYPS challenged churches to expand their outreach to children and

---

[12]*The Ink-Links of the New York District Church of the Nazarene* 23, no. 8 (June 1961), 1-3. Brandon Winstead's Private Collection, Kansas City, KS.
[13]Ibid., 2-3.
[14]Ibid., 4.

youth by reading evangelistic books, attending conferences and retreats and by stressing the importance of faithful attendance to weekly meetings. Similarly, the Nazarene World Missionary Society (hereafter referred to as NWMS) (formerly called the NFMS) continued its primary mission of supporting local and international missions. District president "Mrs." Roland Stanford and Mary Spencer encouraged members to financially support missionaries around the globe. They also encouraged local chapter members to attend missionary conventions so that they could be inspired to evangelize those in their local communities and feel personally connected to those who were attempting to evangelize other nations.[15]

In a later issue of *The Ink Links*, the Church Schools Committee revealed how the district remained committed to evangelization through its Sunday school ministries. In addition to posting the average Sunday school attendance of all the churches on the district, it also praised churches like Brightwaters CN and Miller Memorial for increasing their membership rolls. The chairman of the committee, Rev. Robert J. Cerrato, praised Brightwaters for increasing its average Sunday school attendance by 23 since the end of 1966 and Miller Memorial for having a 20% increase in Sunday school during the same period of time. Because of these gains, Brightwaters had a total of 82 that attended Sunday school, while Miller Memorial had an average attendance of 237, which made it the fifth largest Sunday school on the district.[16]

On the last page of the same issue, the NWMS also stressed that white and black Nazarenes needed to continue their support of domestic and foreign missions. Spencer and Stanford noted that if NWMS members wanted to "evangelize in the power of the Spirit," then they needed to pray for and give monetary funds to mission work in New Guinea, Uruguay, and Guatemala. Moreover, as believers in "personal holiness evangelism," they argued that local NWMS chapters needed to read missionary books so that they could nurture their passion for home missions. Spencer and Stanford believed that the latter endeavor was particular arduous and that men and women needed to realize the difficulty of establishing Nazarene congregations in the New York area. They emphasized this point when they noted that,

> You may think its glamorous to be a representative for World Missions in the Islands where the white cottages look out on the pink sandy beaches on the edge of the blue ocean, but on the contrary, it is a very difficult thing to

---

[15]*The Ink-Links of the New York District Church of the Nazarene* 27, no. 2 (February 1965), 1-4. Brandon Winstead's Private Collection, Kansas City, KS.

[16]*The Ink-Links of the New York District Church of the Nazarene* (February 1967), 1-2. Brandon Winstead's Private Collection, Kansas City, KS.

establish the Church of the Nazarene in a country where the "Established" church has been there for decades and looks on newcomers as intruders.[17]

Since it was "difficult" to evangelize and start Nazarene congregations, Stanford and Spencer went on to note that NWMS members and churches needed to not only read and give money, but to pray as well. If domestic evangelism was going to take place and new churches were going to be established, then NWMS adherents needed to pray. If they didn't, then Stanford and Spencer noted that the church would not "prevail" in its evangelistic endeavors.[18]

This evangelistic thrust that Afro-Caribbeans heard during this period was also advocated by the words and messages of black ministers as well. For instance, J. Gilbertson Stuart, an Afro-Bajan who pastored Bedford Zion after James Jessamy in 1963, often preached about the importance of receiving salvation and personal holiness and the responsibility of Christians to carry out the same message to those in their communities. He preached this message partly because of his own personal experiences and theological background. Stuart was originally a member of the Pilgrim Holiness Church. Stuart joined the body after hearing a Pilgrim Holiness preacher on February 10, 1937 in Bridgetown, Barbados. During the sermon, the minister stated that God had come to both "save" and "sanctify" those who were in attendance. Stuart was convicted and then experienced the "fullness of salvation." After having this experience, Stuart felt that he should preach the same message to those who would listen. Thus, when he immigrated to the New York City in 1954 and later joined the CN around 1960, he found a denomination that aligned with his religious upbringing and a faith community that encouraged him to preach the message of salvation and personal holiness to Afro-Caribbeans in and around the borough of Brooklyn.[19]

After he settled in with the CN, Stuart began preaching and teaching about personal holiness to his congregants. On July 15, 1962, for instance, Stuart used the biblical example of Daniel to show how God could "save" the person who put their trust in God. As he noted, Daniel had devoted himself to a consistent life of prayer that allowed him to commune with God daily. Stuart claimed that Daniel's consistent prayer life is what sustained him throughout his lifelong trials and tribulations. When royal authorities and Babylonian "politicians" persecuted Daniel, it was his "steadfastly" prayers to God that saved him and kept him from harm. Not only that, but because of his prayers, Daniel was kept blameless and holy before God. Stuart

---

[17]Ibid., 4.

[18]Ibid., 4.

[19]J. Gilbertson Stuart of Brooklyn, New York, personal interview with Brandon Winstead, September 18, 2009, Brooklyn, New York. Brandon Winstead's Private Collection, Kansas City, KS.

underscored this point when he noted that it was Daniel's commitment to prayer and God that kept him righteous before the ancient Babylonian King Nebuchadnezzar. He stated that if Daniel had not prayed and served God "blamelessly," then he would have defiled himself by eating and drinking the food and wine of the King's Court. Likewise, Stuart claimed that it was Daniel's commitment to prayer, personal holiness, and belief in the power of God that delivered him from being devoured by a lion when he was thrown into the Lion's Den for not placating the royal desires of King Darius.

In Stuart's estimation, if one wanted to experience the fullness of salvation and personal holiness, then they needed to follow Daniel's example and devote themselves continually to prayer. By persistently praying, Stuart argued that God would "deliver thee" from sin and strengthen one to "fully" follow God like Daniel did thousands of years in the past. If not, then full salvation would merely be an idea, something that could not be grasped.[20]

Likewise, when Stuart delivered another sermon in June of 1966, he argued that if one wanted to experience salvation and personal holiness then they needed to confess their lack of dependence in God so that they could be filled with Christian "enthusiasm." As he noted,

> God must be sought as the only source of spiritual revival. We cannot remedy evils by any form of personal effect, if those are made apart from dependence on God...we have our faith; but we have not the same fearless confidence in what we say we believe. We have a little love, but it has lost its warmth. We pray still, but our prayers are forced and formal, not the simple, happy outpouring of a full heart... We have our part in Christian service, but there is no enthusiasm in it...

In order to achieve "enthusiasm," Stuart argued that believers in his congregation needed to seek and pray for the presence of God in their lives. He noted that seeking for the empowering presence of the Spirit was the key to long-lasting salvation in the Christian's life and the only source that could revive the soul, remedy "evil," and grant the believer a "full heart" for Christian service. Not only that, but he argued that seeking for this presence could bring about a revival that restored souls and the community and empowered believers for evangelism. Stuart emphasized this when he exclaimed at the conclusion of his sermon that,

> Revival in our church! Revival in our day! Revival now! Revival in my heart! Revival that transforms hearts and lives! Revival that unites families! Revival that has a mighty impact on the community! Revival that restores meaning to lives! Revival that restores joy to souls! Revival that impels us out into the

[20] J. Gilbertson Stuart, Sermon: Daniel 6:10, written at Bedford Zion Church of the Nazarene, Brooklyn, [07 May 1967]. Brandon Winstead's Private Collection, Kansas City, KS.

street to tell the good news! This must be the cry from our pulpits and from our pews. This is church programming at its highest level and the progress by which we will be used by Christ to build the church.[21]

Like Stuart, other black ministers on the district such as Clarence Jacobs from Miller Memorial, stressed the importance of how Christian scriptures could empower the church to evangelize and address the existential concerns of "man." In particular, Jacobs felt that the power of "God's Word" could speak to the realities and situations brought about by "the tremendous shakings, which these days are visiting upon us." Jacobs believed this because he felt that the scriptures revealed how God spoke a "Word" to the people of Israel when they were in need. As he asserted,

> God had a "Word" for men at Mount Sinai, and He spoke it in the Law. God had a "Word" for men in the dark days of the Captivity, when His people were languishing in Babylon and He spoke it ... through the prophet Haggai. Just when Jerusalem was in shambles, and Solomon's Temple was in ruins, and the future of Israel seemed most hopeless, came the Word of the Lord like a trumpet, announcing that He would shake things into life and hope and a grand new destiny would take shape among the ashes of their plight.[22]

Similarly to Jacobs, when Cole and other West Indians formed the West Indian congregation in Long Island in 1964, they stated that their main purpose was to spread the message of personal holiness to those in the city of New York. In a small article for *The Ink-Links of the New York District*, Cole reiterated this point. In it, he stated that the main purpose of the church was to "conserve the work, strengthen the cause, and make us all stronger to bring the message of the Cross to the millions of this City." Cole and others went on to note that the newly formed congregation would use their musical talents, Christian zeal, youthful energy, and personal and ecclesiastical relationships on the district so that others in the city of New York could experience the fullness of this "message" and have a "blessed fellowship" with those who followed in the footsteps of holiness.[23]

Thus, for Jacobs, Stuart, Cole, and others, the message of personal holiness was meant to speak to the spiritual realities of those in their communities. Similarly to white denominational and district leaders and

---

[21]J. Gilbertson Stuart, Sermon: The Church of Christ Constantly Needs Reviving: Psalm 85:6, written at Bedford Zion Church of the Nazarene, Brooklyn [22 June 1966]. Brandon Winstead's Private Collection, Kansas City, KS.

[22]Clarence Jacobs, "The Miller Memorial Church of the Nazarene Celebrates Its 50th Anniversary of the Church" (November 22, 1964), 1-2. Brandon Winstead's Private Collection, Kansas City, KS.

[23]*The Ink-Links of the New York District* 26, no.5 (March 1964), 1. Brandon Winstead's Private Collection, Kansas City, KS and *The Ink-Links of the New York District* 26, no. 8 (June 1964), 1. Brandon Winstead's Private Collection, Kansas City, KS..

like their work and beliefs in previous decades, West Indians in New York continued to feel that churches should be empowered to live a life of holiness and evangelize those in their neighborhoods with the "living word." Because of this, Miller Memorial and other Afro-Caribeann churches continued to take concrete steps to evangelize and "reach" those in their neighborhoods.

One of the ways they attempted to do this was through Sunday schools, which continued to be sizeable in large part because of the same reasons mentioned previously. In 1958, for example, two years after the Homes Missions and Church Extension committee called on churches to "make a special effort" to expand their "Sunday school ministries," the total Sunday school enrollment for the Afro-Caribbean churches was 409. This number was greater than the combined sum church membership of all the congregations, which stood at 305 at year's end.[24] In fact, every congregation had a higher Sunday school membership than they did church membership.

Likewise, by the next year, Sunday school numbers still remained strong among black churches when one places them in comparison to the white churches on the New York District. Beulah had 155 members, Bedford Zion 90, Miller Memorial 135, and Wyandanch had 150 and of the twenty-nine churches on the district, only East Rockaway (250), Freeport (150), Valley Stream (155), Patchogue (140), and Dover (170) had more Sunday school members than Beulah, Miller Memorial and Wyandanch. Moreover, even though Bedford Zion had less than one hundred Sunday school members, there were thirteen other churches on the district that had lower membership totals than the Bed-Stuy congregation.[25]

In the early 1960s, these numbers remained higher than the churches' membership numbers even when the emphasis on Sunday schools declined among Brooklyn and New York churches. According to Robert Wuthnow, in Brooklyn in particular, the old Sunday school parades that used to line the streets in the 1930s and 40s had subsided and become a relic of the past. In 1946, he noted that there were some 90,000 children and parents gathered on the roads and streets of Brooklyn to celebrate the Sunday schools in the borough. However, by the late 1950s, Wuthnow maintains that black and

---

[24]The Ink-Links of the New York District Church of the Nazarene (June 1961), 2 and New York District Church of the Nazarene, Fifty-Ninth Annual Assembly Journal, statistical index.
[25]The Ink Links of the New York District Church of the Nazarene (October 1962), 25, no. 1. Brandon Winstead's Private Collection, Kansas City, KS. For a statistical comparison see Appendix III, which is located on page 235.

white churches had all but abandoned the religious spectacle, thus making it a "relic of the past."[26]

Of course, Wuthnow's assessment comes in the context of a broader argument about the secularization of religion that took place in urban areas during the late 1950s through the 1960s, but it nonetheless highlights how black Nazarene churches remained committed to Sunday school ministries when the general religious environment in Brooklyn no longer placed a public premium on celebrating youth participation in Sunday schools. Moreover, even though this particular religious emphasis largely disappeared from Brooklyn's social environment, the West Indian churches continued their emphasis on using Sunday schools to evangelize youth and adults throughout the 1960s. In September of 1963, for instance, Miller Memorial still had 90 Sunday school members, while Beulah had 104, Bedford Zion 40, and Wyandanch had 80. By 1964, these churches still had large Sunday school numbers. Bedford Zion had 42 members and Beulah, Miller Memorial, and Wyandanch had a total of 306 and only six other churches on the district had higher membership numbers than Beulah—Brightwaters (105), Butler (112), Dover (131), East Rockaway (167), Edison (97), and Patterson (112). Likewise, when numbers were tallied at the end of 1966, each black congregation, along with other white churches on the district increased their numbers dramatically. Beulah had 179 enrolled in Sunday school, while Miller Memorial had 237. Furthermore, Wyandanch increased its membership to 196 and Bedford Zion had a total membership of 70. Because of this growth in Sunday school members, the total number of members on the district added up to 4,952 by the start of 1967.[27]

Until 1969, numbers like this remained steady at the West Indian congregations—even at places like Springfield Gardens CN, which became predominantly Afro-Caribbean around September 1968 after Rev. Louis Gardenline, a West Indian minister, assumed the pastorate of the church and Bronx Bethany CN, which was founded by West Indian immigrants in the northernmost borough of New York in 1964.[28] For instance, in 1969, black Nazarene churches in New York still had large Sunday school membership numbers in comparison to their total church membership. Miller Memorial had a total membership of 180 and 145 who regularly attended Sunday school. Beulah was the second largest with 142 church

---

[26]Robert Wuthnow, The Restructuring of American Religion (Princeton, N.J.: Princeton University Press, 1990), 3-4.

[27]The Ink-Links of the New York District Church of the Nazarene (February 1967), 2.

[28]Rev. Louis Gardenline, "1972 Black Church Information: Springfield Gardens Church of the Nazarene, New York, 13 October 1972," 1. Church of the Nazarene Archives, Lenexa, KS.

members and 107 Sunday school members. In addition to this, Wyandanch had almost the same amount of church and Sunday school members. On a typical Sunday they had 85 black Nazarenes in worship and 82 that attended Sunday school. Moreover, churches like Bedford Zion, Bronx Bethany, and Springfield Gardens had a total of 86 Sunday school members and 134 church members.[29] Thus, at the end of 1969, the total Sunday school membership of all six black churches stood at 455.[30]

By outlining these numbers, it seems that black Nazarene churches in New York were committed to using Sunday school ministries as an avenue to evangelize those in their communities. Sunday school, as a concrete expression of the evangelistic desires of black and white leaders was not a mere reflection of the broader religious culture like it had been in previous decades (recall again the Sunday school parades that Miller Memorial and Beulah participated in during the 1930s and 40s). Instead, it was an evangelistic tool that could "save" black souls.

This evangelistic thrust also persisted among the West Indian churches in other district ministries like the NYPS. For instance, at Miller Memorial, individuals such as Ludwick Jones, Beryl Brown, Beryl Forrest, Irene Maloney, Nina Jacobs, Ronald Brown, Eloise Jackson, Kenrick Belgraves, Elaine Welch, Irene Elder, Euneta DePeiza, James Davis, Clarence Jacobs Jr., Mark Buchanan, Velmer Woods, George Clarke, Jackie Dais, Carmen Brown, Lorraine Grimes, Wilber Jones, Oswald Jones, Jackie Lewis, Grace Maynard, Adrienne Cos, Bertha Mae Lewis, Israel Allen, and Donald Meyers attempted to evangelize youth through their NYPS.[31] Moreover, at Bedford Zion, Amy Howell led the NYPS, while Albert Braithwaite, and Gwendolyn Ifill were the

---

[29]Church of the Nazarene Research Center, "Membership Status and Attendance of Wyandanch—Metro New York District." (accessed 23 April 2011); Church of the Nazarene Research Center, "Membership Status and Attendance of Bedford Zion—Metro New York District." (accessed 06 March 2010); Church of the Nazarene Research Center, "Membership Status and Attendance of Brooklyn Beulah—Metro New York District." (accessed 23 April 2011); Church of the Nazarene Research Center, "Membership Status and Attendance of Brooklyn Community Worship Center—Metro New York District." (accessed 23 April 2011); Church of the Nazarene Research Center, "Membership Status and Attendance of Springfield Gardens—Metro New York District."
http://app.nazarene.org/FindAChurch/viewReport.jsp?reportId=21196&sIDType=rpt&orgId=438906. (accessed 23 April 2011) and Church of the Nazarene, "Membership Status and Attendance of Bronx Bethany—Metro New York District." http://app.nazarene.org/FindAChurch/viewReport.jsp?reportId=21196&sIDType=rpt&orgId=4316. (accessed 23 April 2011).

[30]For a statistical outline of Sunday school membership of the West Indian congregations from 1959-1969, see Appendix III on page 236.

[31]Rev. Clarence Jacobs, "The Miller Memorial Church of the Nazarene: 50th Anniversary of the Church" (November 15-22, 1964), 6. Brandon Winstead's Private Collection, Kansas City, KS.

organizing heads of the NYPS at Beulah and Wyandanch.³² Aside from this, West Indian churches encouraged evangelism and discipleship among youth by encouraging them to attend district youth rallies and retreats and by holding regular mid-week Bible studies.³³

As the churches supported NYPS ministries and encouraged such actions, NYPS membership numbers increased. In 1964, the NYPS numbers of Miller Memorial, Bedford Zion, Beulah, Wyandanch stood at 57, 20, 52, and 22. Four years later, every church increased its membership. Miller Memorial increased to 79, while Bedford Zion, Beulah, and Wyandanch pushed their membership totals to 22, 78, and 33. At the same time, the newly formed churches like the Bronx church and the Springfield Gardens congregation both had NYPS members.³⁴

In an effort to bolster their support of evangelization, Afro-Caribbeans maintained local NFMS (later NWMS) chapters. As it was mentioned previously, district leaders stressed the importance of NFMS members contributing to home and domestic missions. In their estimation, local NFMS chapters provided necessary monetary and human capital to "reach the lost" both at home and abroad. Black men and women in Brooklyn understood this denominational emphasis and like they had in previous decades, they continued to send voting delegates to district NFMS conventions and support missionary efforts around the world.

Towards the beginning of the 1960s, women at the black Brooklyn churches such as Lillian Corbin, Dorothy Howell, and Mabel Catlyne (the long time consecrated deaconess from Bedford Zion), Louise Davis, and Ophelia Mayers submitted district reports that detailed their financial support of world missions.³⁵ In 1962, black men and women at Bedford

---

³²*The Ink-Links of the New York District Church of the Nazarene* 26, no. 4, 3.

³³Ibid., 3; *The Ink-Links of the New York District Church of the Nazarene* 27, no. 2, 3 and *The Ink-Links of the New York District Church of the Nazarene* (February 1967), 3.

³⁴Church of the Nazarene Research Center, "Membership Status and Attendance of Wyandanch—Metro New York District." (accessed 23 April 2011); Church of the Nazarene Research Center, "Membership Status and Attendance of Bedford Zion—Metro New York District." (accessed 23 April 2011); Church of the Nazarene Research Center, "Membership Status and Attendance of Brooklyn Beulah—Metro New York District." (accessed 23 April 2011); Church of the Nazarene Research Center, "Membership Status and Attendance of Brooklyn Community Worship Center—Metro New York District." (accessed 23 April 2011); Church of the Nazarene Research Center, "Membership Status and Attendance of Springfield Gardens—Metro New York District." (accessed 23 April 2011) and Church of the Nazarene, "Membership Status and Attendance of Bronx Bethany—Metro New York District." (accessed 23 April 2011).

³⁵*New York District Church of the Nazarene, Fifty-First Annual Assembly Journal*, 74.

Zion reported giving $170.00 to world evangelism, while Miller Memorial gave $461.00, Beulah $732.00, and Wyandanch $209.00. For the modern observer, these numbers may seem small, but they paralleled the financial giving of most white churches on the district. At congregations like Danbury, the church paid $439.00 to world missions, while churches such as Flushing gave $876.00 and Patchogue $304.00. Of course, wealthier congregations like Richmond Hill and Poughkeepsie gave over a thousand dollars to world missions. However, most of the congregations paralleled the pattern of giving reflected in both the black Brooklyn churches and the white churches at Danbury, Flushing, and Patchogue. And, the pattern was similar by the close of the decade. In 1969, Bedford Zion gave $645.00 and Miller Memorial donated $1,216.00 to spread the mission and message of the denomination both at home and abroad. Likewise, Beulah's NWMS distributed $1003.00 to missions and Wyandanch gave $515.00, which was double the amount that they gave seven years prior. In addition to these contributions, by the end of 1969, the newly formed congregations in the Bronx and Long Island gave a total of $625.00, even though these congregations had less than a combined membership of 50.[36]

Of course, local NWMS chapters continued to give to missionary efforts of the district because black men and women (those who usually dominated the roles of NWMS societies) continued to join its ranks. In 1962, Miller Memorial, Bedford Zion, Beulah, and Wyandanch had a total of 238 members on the district NWMS rolls. Seven years later, that number increased to 256, a considerable amount when most large white churches on the district such as Richmond Hill had East Rockaway had no more than 170 NWMS members between the two congregations. Moreover, even though the new congregation in the Bronx and Springfield Gardens did not have as many NWMS members as the more established black churches, they still had a combined total of 43 NWMS members by the end of 1969.[37]

---

[36]For a statistical outline of NWMS membership and monetary giving in 1962 and 1969 of the black congregations, see Appendix IV on page 237.

[37]Church of the Nazarene Research Center, "Membership Status and Attendance of Wyandanch—Metro New York District." (accessed 23 April 2011); Church of the Nazarene Research Center, "Membership Status and Attendance of Bedford Zion—Metro New York District." (accessed 23 April 2011); Church of the Nazarene Research Center, "Membership Status and Attendance of Brooklyn Beulah—Metro New York District." (accessed 23 April 2011); Church of the Nazarene Research Center, "Membership Status and Attendance of Brooklyn Community Worship Center—Metro New York District." (accessed 23 April 2011); Church of the Nazarene Research Center, "Membership Status and Attendance of Springfield Gardens—Metro New York District."
http://app.nazarene.org/FindAChurch/viewReport.jsp?reportId=21196&sIDType=rpt&orgId=438906. (accessed 23 April 2011) and Church of the Nazarene, "Membership Status and Attendance of Bronx Bethany—Metro New York District."

In sum, what all this suggests is that the Afro-Caribbean churches continued to actively contribute to the New York District by contributing to denominational missions while at the same time evangelizing blacks in their local communities. By doing this, they helped to increase the presence of the CN in the northeast section of the United States in a time when great political, economic, and social issues were being addressed by black Americans in their local communities.

For instance, during this time, African-American ministers and churches protested the dearth of economic opportunity for Hispanic and black residents of Bedford-Stuyvesant. Black pastors and organizations such as the Ministers' Committee for Job Opportunities for Brooklyn conducted a protest campaign at the construct site of the Downstate Medical Center in the summer of 1963. They demanded that ¼ of all the construction jobs at the hospital be granted to Puerto Ricans and blacks. Also, Milton Galamison, the pastor of Siloam Presbyterian Church and leader of the Brooklyn chapter of the Congress of Racial Equality (hereafter referred to as CORE), launched a campaign to improve the educational infrastructure of black schools in Brooklyn. Furthermore, Galamison and other black ministers that were a part of CORE, launched "Operation Cleansweep" in September of 1962 to improve sanitary conditions in Bedford-Stuyvesant. Moreover, the same organization helped apartment tenants file complaints with the city's

---

(accessed 23 April 2011). Church of the Nazarene Resource Center, "Membership Status and Attendance of Real Life—Metro New York District."
http://app.nazarene.org/FindAChurch/viewReport.jsp?reportId=21196&orgId=43
35. (accessed 23 April 2011); Church of the Nazarene Resource Center, "Membership Status and Attendance of Poughkeepsie Vassar Road—Metro New York District."
http://app.nazarene.org/FindAChurch/viewReport.jsp?reportId=21196&orgId=43
81. (accessed 23 April 2011); Church of the Nazarene Resource Center, "Membership Status and Attendance of Queens Flushing First—Metro New York District."
http://app.nazarene.org/FindAChurch/viewReport.jsp?reportId=21196&orgId=43
43. (accessed 23 April 2011); Church of the Nazarene Resource Center, "Membership Status and Attendance of Patchogue—Metro New York District."
http://app.nazarene.org/FindAChurch/viewReport.jsp?reportId=21196&orgId=43
78. (accessed 23 April 2011); Church of the Nazarene Resource Center, "Membership Status and Attendance of Queens Richmond Hill—Metro New York District."
http://app.nazarene.org/FindAChurch/viewReport.jsp?reportId=21196&orgId=43
84. (accessed 23 April 2011) and Church of the Nazarene Resource Center, "Membership Status and Attendance of East Rockaway—Metro New York District."
http://app.nazarene.org/FindAChurch/viewReport.jsp?reportId=21196&orgId=43
38. (accessed 23 April 2011).

Building Department and encouraged them to hold rent strikes in an effort to improve their living conditions.[38]

As these actions took place, however, West Indian Nazarene ministers remained relatively absent from participating and the only times they were mentioned in the public domain is when they held ceremonies like wedding services for a middle-class West Indian couples. For instance, in *The New York Amsterdam* in 1968, it was stated that Clarence Jacobs married "Miss Esther Rice" and "Alton G. Cumberbach." The former, it was noted, was a daughter of a West Indian woman named "Mrs. Ann Rice" and the latter was the son of Mr. and Mrs. Walter Cumberbach. After noting their familial lineage, the article went on to state that the bride was majoring in "commercial and liberal art" at New York City Community College, while the groom was a graduate of Howard University and a graduate student at the college's School of Pharmacy.[39]

Aside from this, Jacobs and Miller Memorial also hosted funeral and family reunion services for non-Nazarene ministers in the greater New York area and for influential Afro-Caribbeans. In 1959 Jacobs and the congregation held a funeral for Rev. Samuel Pilgrim of Bible Truth Church of God in Manhattan. At the funeral, a "Bishop Leon Bynoe" eulogized at the services, while Jacobs presided over the ceremony. Eight years later, Miller Memorial held a memorial service for a family reunion of an "old well-known" West Indian family by the last name of Wiles. As the *New York Amsterdam News* noted, senator William Thompson was in attendance, along with judges Franklin Morton and Thomas Russell Jones. The paper also stated that three doctors and another "Assemblyman" by the name of Samuel Wright celebrated by eating dinner with the family.[40]

Furthermore, when churches like Miller Memorial were mentioned publicly it was done with the hopes of extending the church's evangelistic presence in the community. For example, in 1965, Jacobs brought in black holiness singers from different parts of the country and published when the performers would be in town with the hopes that those outside of the church would attend and accept the message of salvation and individual holiness.[41]

---

[38]Clarence Taylor, *The Black Churches of Brooklyn* (New York: Columbia University Press, 1993), 139-155. Of course, other social and political actions taken by black ministers, such as Galamison's citywide school boycotts in the mid-1960s, William Jones' leadership in "Operation Breadbasket," and Gardner C. Taylor's involvement in President Lyndon Johnson's "War on Poverty." For further reference see, Ibid., 156-163.

[39]"Esther Rice Marries," *New York Amsterdam News,* 07 September 1968.

[40]"Rites Held for Rev. Pilgrim," *New York Amsterdam News*, 24 January 1959 and "Wiles Family Reunion," *New York Amsterdam News*, 16 December 1967.

[41]"In Brooklyn, News of Churches," *New York Amsterdam News*, 21 August 1965.

Besides these actions, Afro-Caribbean churches Miller Memorial were publicly mentioned for their outreach to black youth in Bedford-Stuyvesant. As it was noted previously, Miller Memorial and other black Brooklyn churches sought to improve the moral and religious lives of youth by strengthening their Sunday schools and their local chapters of the NYPS and by regularly holding youth Bible studies. In addition to this, Jacobs held youth rallies for teenagers in the community in an effort "to get the youngsters off the streets." These rallies allowed black youth the opportunity to develop their talents in music or the arts by giving them the space to perform songs or other artistic acts. Furthermore at these gatherings, youth held debates, Bible quizzes, and listened to special speakers that talked about the benefits of leading a Christian life. Lastly, Jacobs occasionally used these rallies to show popular Hollywood films to emphasize "a definite and beneficial message" to the youth who gathered at Miller Memorial.[42]

In addition to Miller Memorial, Beulah maintained an active presence among black youth by continuing to work with interdenominational youth organizations. Grace Braithwaite, a long-time member of Beulah, led one of these organizations called The Interfaith Summer Schools, a black interdenominational program that was privately funded by African American and West Indian churches in Brooklyn with the expressed intent to keep youth out of trouble during the summer months by providing youth programs and biblical studies. She emphasizes this point when she notes that,

> I realize afterwards, the thrust was, from the point of view of the pastors, we've got to give our young people something because in the summers was mostly when they get into difficulties and they wanted to have things for youth to do, something for children to do, so we had these programs during the summer.[43]

Furthermore, Braithwaite, along with other women from Beulah and congregations, started and formed a group called "The Christian Workshop," which was formed after a Billy Graham crusade in 1957. The aim of this organization was to evangelize the youth of Brooklyn through Vacation Bible Schools. Armed with religious passion, an evangelistic fervor to "save" souls, and zeal to improve the moral and religious lives of local black youth, Braithwaite, along with other black and white Christian women, held these schools at various locations around the city. Because it was a part of an inter-denominational body, the schools were held at different churches and locations throughout the summer and extended

---

[42]"Church Size Doubles Under Rev. Jacobs," *New York Amsterdam News*, 07 Nov. 1964.

[43]Grace Braithwaite, personal interview with Brandon Winstead, Brooklyn, New York, September 17, 2009. Brandon Winstead's Private Collection, Kansas City, KS.

anywhere from one week to three weeks, depending on the availability of workers, resources, and its success among youth in the neighborhood. In Braithwaite's estimation, because of this approach, the group was able to evangelize 100 to 150 local youth each time they held a school.[44]

Again, it is important to remember that these "outreach" activities were largely driven by the churches' evangelistic desire to "save" or "reach" young and old West Indians. Broader political, racial, social, and economic issues that weighed heavily on African American communities in Brooklyn, New York, and around the country were not addressed by black Nazarene churches in New York. In fact, according to one former pastor, he and his congregation largely ignored civil rights issues. In the words of Rev. Gilbertson Stuart—the minister of Bedford Zion during the mid to late 1960s—he was a "strict churchman" that was not "involved in the Civil Rights Movement." Even though he met and had a relationship with Gardner C. Taylor, a politically active pastor, and preached at his church—Concord Baptist Church—on more than one occasion during the height of the Civil Rights Movement, Stuart felt that his main duty was to preach the Gospel so that others might hear and accept the message of Christian salvation and personal holiness.[45]

Likewise, Braithwaite remembers that the Civil Rights Movement was not "a foremost thing" for her and other West Indian Nazarenes. She states that on the whole, "it was not a primary thing" for the Caribbean churches and that her "awareness" about actions taking place around the country "was not church related but more personal."[46] Likewise, in an interview with Ludwick Jones, a long-time member of Miller Memorial, he notes that no one at Miller Memorial was publicly involved in the local Civil Rights Movement in the late 1960s and that his experience of gaining knowledge about local and national civil rights came "in the classroom" and not in his local congregation. In his estimation, some congregants were concerned about certain civil rights concerns, but few, if any, were engaged in local civil rights action. Jones underscores this point, when he states that,

> I believe that, that the older people were probably concerned about it (civil rights concerns), but it didn't show in any kind of activism, or any kind of uh, of well you know, we are not going to support that or this or go to this store or anything or we are going to attend this rally that is called by these so-called activists . . . They just went about business, you know, um, that, you know, they had to do. They went to work and did what they had to do

---

[44]Ibid.

[45]J. Gilbertson Stuart of Brooklyn, New York, personal interview with Brandon Winstead, September 18, 2009, Brooklyn, New York. Brandon Winstead's Private Collection, Kansas City, KS.

[46]Grace Braithwaite, personal interview with Brandon Winstead, Brooklyn, New York, September 17, 2009. Brandon Winstead's Private Collection, Kansas City, KS.

. . . . They weren't involved in any stretch of the imagination, um, with this activism.⁴⁷

Jones also states that the conversation surrounding civil rights never surfaced inside the walls of the church. He stresses this point when he claims "that we really ever had a discussion about it in the church."⁴⁸

Again, what these examples and evidence suggests is that the West Indian Nazarene churches in and around New York City were primarily concerned, like black and white Nazarenes throughout the country, with evangelizing those in their community, building up their NYPS, planning Vacation Bible Schools for area youth, and contributing to local and international missions through the NWMS. As it was mentioned in the previous chapter, other Nazarenes during this time did not call on the denomination to systematically address ecclesiastical or societal racism during the turbulent decades of the 1960s even though they were free to do so without official denominational repercussion. Similarly, like their white and African American counterparts throughout the country, West Indians were free to use their collective resources to attack racism or to address issues pertinent to those in the African Diaspora. However, they chose not to take up such a course of action. Instead, they followed a similar path as African American and white Nazarenes by primarily focusing their leadership and congregational resources on evangelism and growing the overall infrastructure of their churches in the city of New York and the New York District.

Furthermore, even though individuals and groups in churches like Miller Memorial and Beulah continued to minister to some of the religious and moral needs of those in their communities and although they reached out to the youth in their neighborhoods in creative ways, they did not feel compelled to form alliances or partnerships with other black churches in and around Brooklyn. Instead, the overall goal was to extend the evangelistic message of the CN to black adherents and to support the expansion of the denomination around the globe. Thus, West Indian Nazarenes, like so many other Nazarenes sought to "reach out" to those in their communities with the message of Christian salvation and personal holiness while at the same time publicly avoiding systemic social, racial, political, economic, or educational issues around the country.

---

⁴⁷Ludwick Jones, personal interview with Brandon Winstead, Brooklyn, New York, September 18, 2009. Brandon Winstead's Private Collection, Kansas City, KS.

⁴⁸In Jones estimation, the position taken by black Nazarene churches like Miller Memorial reflected the general stance of West Indians towards the Civil Rights Movement. Most West Indian churches, he asserts, rarely tried to "rebuke" racism in an active way by starting or joining civil rights organization. For further reference see Ibid.

Of course, this is not a definitive answer for why West Indians took such a position, but there is no written evidence in district minutes, congregational histories, local newspapers, or other secondary resources that explicitly state why Afro-Caribbean Nazarenes took an apolitical position during a period of deep national social change along racial lines. The most thorough response seems to reside in what has been outlined so far—namely that West Indian Nazarenes in New York, like most Nazarenes around the country, did not seek to address systemic injustices in their communities, but to evangelize those in their community with the message of personal holiness and to support Nazarene missions around the globe. By doing this, West Indians, like their African American counterparts, continued to actively participate in the denomination's ecclesiastical governance and evangelistic mission throughout the late 1950s and 1960s.

Expanding the Black Immigrant Presence: Cape Verdean Nazarene Evangelization

During this same period, the Cape Verdean Nazarenes in New Bedford—as participants and under the governance of the New England district—continued their participation in the CN by contributing to evangelistic ministries outside the church, by strengthening their Sunday school, NYPS, and NFMS chapters, and by evangelizing and ministering to others through local ministry initiatives. For instance, at the beginning of the decade Manuel Chavier, the senior minister of the Portuguese CN, began a weekly evangelistic radio program, which was broadcast over the airwaves of a local radio station called WBSM. In the estimation of New Bedford's mayor, John A. Markey, Chavier's radio broadcast was instrumental for thousands in the "Greater New Bedford area" because it brought numerous "people relief from despair and discouragement."[49]

Chavier extended his church's evangelistic influence by serving as a chaplain for the Capeway Seafood Company throughout the 1960s. In this capacity, Chavier regularly preached to dock workers during their lunch or break periods on Wednesday afternoons with the hope that they would receive Christian salvation. In addition to this, Chavier thought it would be beneficial to use his speaking and leadership gifts to help lead other Christian organizations outside of his denomination. In the 1960s, for instance, he served as President of both the Baptists Young People's Association and Portuguese Cape Verdean Christian Association. Moreover, as a prominent evangelical minister in his community, Chavier was also

---

[49]Mayor John A. Markey, "Resolution to Rev. Manuel Chavier," October 7, 1973. Church of the Nazarene Archives, Lenexa, KS.

elected to serve as the President of the Evangelical Ministers Fellowship of New England.[50]

Aside from his local evangelical involvement, Chavier held an active presence among civic organizations that sought to enhance the legal, economic, and social lives of adults and youth in New Bedford. In particular, Chavier took on leadership in such civic organizations as the Legal Aid Society of New Bedford, the Concentrated Employment Program, The Kiwanas Club, The Red Cross, and the local chapter of the Boy's Club of New Bedford.[51]

By engaging in such actions and participating in such diverse religious and civic organizations, Chavier left an indelible impact on some of his Cape Verdean contemporaries, both inside and outside his church community. This was exemplified in an article written in *The Cape Verdean* in July of 1969. The author of the article noted that Chavier received the annual Cape Verdean achievement award because he served the community

> as a student an assiduous scholar, as a husband a model of nuptial constancy, benevolence and devotion, as a soldier, a courageous defender, as a teacher, a diligent and dedicated educator, as a reverend, an inspirational and devout minister, as a civic leader, a conscientious and resourceful guide, and as an American of Cape Verdean heritage, an inspiration to our youth.

With these descriptions in mind, the author went on to note the main purpose for why Chavier received the annual award when they noted that,

> To such a dedicated person, on who is loved by so many, one who leaves a charismatic effect everywhere he goes, one who loves so many; to Rev. Manuel Chavier, we would like to show our love and appreciation. So with a proud feeling and great esteem, I would like to present the achievement award...at New Bedford, Massachusetts June 29, 1969.[52]

Nonetheless, aside from Chavier's activities, church members continued to reach out to the Cape Verdean community, much like they had in early to mid 1950s. For example, the church taught youth how to develop home making skills such as sewing clothes. Moreover, they held a weekly outreach group meeting for children and youth in an effort to teach area youth biblical principles and the denomination's teaching on holiness. Reaching out to youth and families outside their congregation extended to their annual Mother-Daughter Banquet and Father-Son Banquet as well.

---

[50]"1969 Achievement Award: Rev. Manuel Chavier," *The Cape Verdean*, July 1969, 15. Church of the Nazarene Archives, Lenexa, KS.

[51]Unknown author, "History of the Portuguese Nazarene Church," Church of the Nazarene Archives, Lenexa, KS and Unknown Author, "Pastor Chavier Serves One Church Fifty Years," in *Grow: A Journal of Church Growth, Evangelism, and Discipleship*, Fall 1999, 5. Church of the Nazarene Archives, Lenexa, KS.

[52]1969 Achievement Award: Rev. Manuel Chavier," 15.

These yearly gatherings were held for members and non-members of the Portuguese CN. The main goal was to celebrate the familial bonds that existed both inside and outside the local church body. As such, the church provided a space where local Cape Verdeans could celebrate and acknowledge the relationships that sustained their familial structures.[53]

Reaching out in such ways extended the presence of Portuguese CN in the local Cape Verdean community and revealed their concern for communicating the message of holiness outside its walls, but, neither Rev. Chavier nor the congregation developed a comprehensive plan to address the broader systemic issues that were affecting various groups from the African Diaspora in the United States during the 1960s. Instead, like the West Indian churches in New York City and African Americans around the country, their primarily purpose was to evangelize those in their communities and to improve aspects of their educational, moral, and religious lives. Moreover, they, like their African American and Afro-Caribbean counterparts, attended to some of their local ethnic concerns in a way that did not connect their struggles with other black groups around the country or in a manner that did not distract them from their overarching goal of reaching Cape Verdeans with the message of personal holiness.

For instance, the Cape Verdean congregation, like African Americans and West Indians, chose to evangelize youth and adults, both locally and internationally, through the NFMS and NYPS. In 1963, Amelia Rebeiro, who was the president of the Portuguese CN's NFMS, had 74 members in a church that possessed a total of 81 members. Four years later, the church expanded its membership to 121, while Ribeiro helped to expand the membership of the NWMS (the name of the organization changed from NFMS to NWMS in the years between 1963 and 1967) to 112. As a healthy and contributing chapter of the New England District's main missionary body, the conglomerate of mainly women not only participated in the ministries of the NWMS by reading missionary books, listening to missionary speakers, and attending district and national NWMS gatherings, but they also contributed monies to the missionary organization. At the beginning of the 1960s, they distributed $271.00 to international missions. By 1963, that number had increased to $276.00, a steady but significant increase over the course of two years. Four years later, the monies given to foreign missions by Portuguese CN increased to well over a thousand dollars to $1,350. In that same year, the local NWMS chapter also helped to raise money to support local missions as well. In fact, in 1967, Riberio and the rest of the NWMS contributed to the total amount of $343.00 raised for missions, which was an increase of $255.00 since 1963.[54]

---

[53]Ibid.,15.

[54]Church of the Nazarene, "Membership Status and Attendance of New Bedford International Church of the Nazarene—New England District."

Like their West Indian counterparts in New York, these numbers, when compared to predominantly white congregations on the New England District, reveal how the Cape Verdean congregation substantially committed to the district's ministerial and financial commitment to foreign missions. In 1963, for example, Burlington CN in Burlington, Vermont, an average size CN on the northeastern district, only had 39 church members and 26 people who were members of the congregation's NWMS. Moreover, larger churches such as Beverly CN in Beverly, MA had 100 church members and 82 members of the NWMS in 1963. Four years later, they decreased to 56 NWMS members and 99 total church members.[55]

In that same year, other white congregations like Haverhill CN in Haverhill, MA had 89 church members and 70 NWMS adherents, while Providence CN in Providence, RI had 112 enlisted on the membership rolls of the congregation and 98 NWMS members. Moreover, in terms of giving to world missions, the above-mentioned churches were very similar to the Portuguese CN. In fact, Providence CN gave $1,269.00 in the same year, while Burlington CN gave $752.00, Beverly CN $1,769.00, and Haverhill CN $1,455.00.[56]

Again, when one briefly compares the congregational size of the Portuguese CN along with its NWMS membership numbers and financial giving with other white churches on the district, it highlights how the Cape Verdean congregation more than proportionately contributed to foreign missions. By utilizing its financial resources, its numerical strength (by 1969, the Portuguese CN had 140 church members, making it one of the few churches on a district of over fifty churches that had more than a hundred

http://app.nazarene.org/FindAChurch/viewReport.jsp?reportId=21196&sIDType=rpt&orgId=4316. (accessed 26 April 2011).

[55]See Appendix V on page 237 for a statistical outline of some of the information provided above regarding the comparisons between the Cape Verdean and white churches.

[56]Church of the Nazarene, "Membership Status and Attendance of Haverhill Church of the Nazarene—New England District."
http://app.nazarene.org/FindAChurch/viewReport.jsp?reportId=21196&sIDType=rpt&orgId=4316. (accessed 25 April 2011); Church of the Nazarene, "Membership Status and Attendance of Providence Church of the Nazarene—New England District."
http://app.nazarene.org/FindAChurch/viewReport.jsp?reportId=21196&orgId=8236. (accessed 25 April 2011); Church of the Nazarene, "Membership Status and Attendance of Beverly Living Hope Church of the Nazarene—New England District."
http://app.nazarene.org/FindAChurch/viewReport.jsp?reportId=21196&sIDType=rpt&orgId=8177. (accessed 25 April 2011); Church of the Nazarene, "Membership Status and Attendance of Burlington-Williston Church of the Nazarene—New England District,"
http://app.nazarene.org/FindAChurch/viewReport.jsp?reportId=21196&sIDType=rpt&orgId=8181. (accessed 25 April 2011).

church members) and concern for outreach, lay members and leaders like Chavier and Ribeiro situated the church as an important contributor to home and foreign missions on the New England district.[57]

The church's dedication to personal holiness evangelism, like other black churches around the country, also extended to the support of traditional Nazarene ministries like NYPS. During the mid to late 1960s, the Portuguese CN regularly had over 75 NYPS members who attended weekly Bible school, summer youth camps, and district conventions. By maintaining such numbers, the church regularly taught biblical principles, their understanding of salvation, and the denomination's teaching on Personal holiness to numerous youth.

Moreover, because of their commitment to evangelism and due to the active presence of the congregation in the local Cape Verdean community, the church was able to steadily grow its Sunday school ministry during the 1960s. In 1960, for instance, the Portuguese CN had 87 children, youth, and adults who consistently attended Sunday school. However, within three years that number increased to 135 and even though it took another five years until the congregation had over 150 people that attended Sunday school, it stood as a numerically large ministry on the New England District. In fact, when one compares the Cape Verdean church's numbers to other larger white congregations on the district like Beverly CN (116) Cambridge CN in Cambridge, MA (104), Brockton CN in Brockton, MA (160), and Malden CN in Malden, MA (160), it appears that the congregation was one of leading Sunday school ministries on the district.[58]

Aside from this, Chavier and other black Portuguese contributed to denominational evangelism by becoming district ministry leaders and by participating as voting members at district assemblies. For example, in 1963, Cape Verdeans like David Rebeiro deliberated on youth affairs

---

[57] *New England District Church of the Nazarene, Sixtieth Annual Assembly Journal* (June 1967): statistical index. Church of the Nazarene Archives, Lenexa, KS.

[58] Church of the Nazarene, "Membership Status and Attendance of New Bedford International Church of the Nazarene—New England District." (accessed 15 May 2010); Church of the Nazarene, "Membership Status and Attendance of Beverly Church of the Nazarene—New England District." (accessed 27 April 2011); Church of the Nazarene, "Membership Status and Attendance of Cambridge Church of the Nazarene—New England District." http://app.nazarene.org/FindAChurch/viewReport.jsp?reportId=21196&sIDType=rpt&orgId=8182. (accessed 27 April 2011); Church of the Nazarene, "Membership Status and Attendance of Brockton Church of the Nazarene—New England District." http://app.nazarene.org/FindAChurch/viewReport.jsp?reportId=21196&orgId=8180. (accessed 27 April 2011) and Church of the Nazarene, "Membership Status and Attendance of Malden Church of the Nazarene—New England District." http://app.nazarene.org/FindAChurch/viewReport.jsp?reportId=21196&orgId=8215. (accessed 27 April 2011).

alongside white officers at the District Assembly. Also, Adelina Baptiste, the Sunday school superintendent of the Portuguese CN, helped the ecclesiastical body make decisions regarding the district's approach to Sunday school ministries. In addition to this, in the same year, Rebeiro (the same Rebeiro mentioned previously) helped the district's NWMS decide how it would contribute finances to missionaries around the globe.

Likewise, four years later, the Portuguese CN sent their NYPS, Sunday school, and Sunday school presidents to the District Assembly to deliberate on ecclesiastical matters that affected the direction and goal of each district auxiliary. Moreover, the newly formed Cape Verdean church called New Bedford Third CN also sent representatives to District Assembly to help legislate on ecclesiastical matters. Persons like Gamaliel Ferreira (the Sunday school superintendent), Rafael Azevedo (the NYPS president), and Sara Ferreira (the NWMS president) helped to decide, alongside white laity and leaders, how these three ministries would continue to use their collective resources to evangelize and disciple those both outside and inside their respective congregations.[59]

District participation also extended to black ministers like Rev. Chavier. In 1967, Chavier sat on district committees like the Court of Appeals Committee, which oversaw and ruled on ministerial and lay grievances against their local churches or district leadership. Moreover, he sat on the Orders and Relations Committee, which screened men and women for ordination and was a part of a panel of thirteen people that made final decisions on how the district was going to evangelize and catechize persons through Sunday school and other educational ministries of the New England District. Aside from this, in 1964 and 1968, Chavier was selected to be one of the district's representatives to General Assembly, which was held in Portland, OR in the previous year and in Kansas City, MO in the latter. At this gathering, Chavier deliberated alongside other delegates and denominational leaders on important denominational matters for the CN, such as ministerial education, ecclesiastical polity, doctrine, and ethics, and the distribution of funds for global and national missions.[60]

Like Chavier, laity in the Portuguese CN who didn't lead church or district ministries were asked to contribute to decision-making processes of the district in the 1960s. In 1963, lay members of the congregation such as Norman Noreiga went to Wollaston CN in Wollaston Park, MA to vote on ecclesiastical matters such as the renewal of minister's license, the granting

---

[59]New England District Church of the Nazarene, Fifty-Sixth Annual Assembly Journal (June 1963): 16-17, 30-35. Church of the Nazarene Archives, Lenexa, KS and New England District Church of the Nazarene, Sixtieth Annual Assembly Journal, 20-22.

[60]"1969 Achievement Award: Rev. Manuel Chavier," 15 and New England District Church of the Nazarene, Sixtieth Annual Assembly Journal, 8-9.

of licensure for evangelists, the acceptance of church reports, the appointment of the District Advisory Board, and on who would be sent on behalf of the district as voting delegates to the General Assembly.[61] In similar fashion, when district churches gathered in 1967, the Portuguese CN once again sent lay delegates to vote on the same matters and to make sure that the congregation continued to utilize its decision-making power on the New England District.[62]

In sum, these participatory actions on the district and commitment to denominational ministries on the local and district levels reveal that throughout the 1960s, Cape Verdeans in New Bedford were dedicated to spreading the evangelistic mission of the denomination and expanding the overall institutional structure of their churches. In particular, they, like their black counterparts throughout the rest of the United States, were preoccupied with reaching people in their local communities and throughout the world with the message of personal holiness. Through Chavier's actions and through the church's work in the NWMS, NYPS, and Sunday school, the Portuguese CN brought the evangelistic message of the denomination to numerous Cape Verdean immigrants. By doing this, they endeavored to evangelize Cape Verdeans in their local community and carry out the overarching emphasis of the denomination during the 1960s, which was "Evangelism First."[63]

Cape Verdean immigrants, like other blacks throughout the United States, heard the sermons and admonitions based on this theme at the district level from denominational leaders and white ministers. At the 1963 District Assembly, for instance, lay delegates and other leaders from the Portuguese CN heard General Superintendents like G.B. Williamson exhort the assembly of churches to be filled with "the power of the Spirit" so that they could "win men" to the Gospel. If they did not, Williamson argued, then churches would lose their sense of mission and slowly fade away. He emphasized this when he stated that, "whenever the church loses its great urgency to give the gospel to all the world, the church has begun its decline."

The following day, a minister by the name of Robert Glasgow exhorted the gathered body to realize the importance of domestic missions and pointed out that if local churches were going to fulfill its "missionary task" then they needed to have "a spirit and burden of prayer...for the work of God." In an effort to support this point, at the following service Williamson stressed the contemporary church's responsibility to continually share the

---

[61]New England District Church of the Nazarene, Fifty-Sixth Annual Assembly Journal, 45-52.
[62]New England District Church of the Nazarene, Sixtieth Annual Assembly Journal, 10-14.
[63]Cunningham, Ingersol, Raser, and Whitelaw, 385.

message of Christ around the world and specifically in their communities and neighborhoods. He noted that this practice fulfilled the will of God for the church and was also a continuation of ancient Christianity's "program" for growth. Williamson highlighted this assertion when he claimed,

> It is evidently the will of God that the Church shall never become localized. It shall always have an outreach. It is part of our Christian philosophy that we grow by sharing, and we increase where we are by sending. We might as well apply this to home missions as well as foreign. This apparently was what the Christians adopted as their program at Antioch.[64]

When the district gathered four years later in the summer of 1967, similar theological and evangelistic admonitions were given to white and Cape Verdean churches that were in attendance. Ecclesiastical leaders spoke on the importance of evangelization and they challenged churches to harness their fiscal and leadership resources in an effort to "reach" the "lost." In addition to this, NWMS leaders challenged NWMS members to persevere in their commitment to raise money for global and domestic missions. Specifically, Irene Spruce, the NWMS president, stated that,

> "Total Commitment"—our theme for this year—challenges us, not only as we think of the commitment that we have made to Him in the past, but as we renew our commitment to Christ for the year just ahead. Let our banner be: "All for Jesus." Let us "war a good warfare" against the hoards of Satan and press the battle for precious souls everywhere in earth's harvest so white.[65]

Again, it is important to remember that as Cape Verdeans heard such messages and as they worked in the NWMS, NYPS, Sunday school, and other outreach ministries in the community, they, like African Americans and West Indians, sought to actively participate in the denominational mission in the late 1950s and 1960s. Moreover, as one of the larger churches on the district by the late 1960s, the Portuguese CN played an important role in helping the CN expand its presence in the state of Massachusetts. As such, they were not only vital agents in helping to reach black immigrants in the city of New Bedford, but they were also active agents in spreading the overall mission of the denomination on the New England District. Unlike their African American peers and like their West Indian counterparts, they did so on an integrated basis and not as segregated participants. As such, they were included in every aspect of district life and thus were able to grow and expand their congregational ministries while at the same time

---

[64]*New England District Church of the Nazarene, Fifty-Sixth Annual Assembly Journal*, 47-49. Some of the ancient practices of the Antioch church can be found in the biblical book of Acts, chapters eleven and thirteen.

[65]New England District Church of the Nazarene, Sixtieth Annual Assembly Journal, 40-50, 77.

contributing to the overall direction and mission of the CN on the New England District.

Cape Verdean Evangelization Amidst Social Change

Despite these efforts and contributions, Cape Verdean Nazarenes remained focus on evangelization even though there existed a growing black consciousness in New Bedford. As Marilyn Salter has noted, systemic racism against Cape Verdeans existed during the modern Civil Rights Era in and around New Bedford. She notes that Cape Verdeans, like African Americans, were often unable to purchase homes in predominantly white neighborhoods in New Bedford and in other areas of the Cape Cod region. Moreover, Salter claims that ever since the early days of their immigration in the late 1890s, Cape Verdeans occupied the lowest strata of the economy because they worked in the cranberry bogs, on the loading docks, and in the factories and households of wealthy whites. In addition to racial discrimination in the arenas of housing and employment, Cape Verdeans often had to hold religious services apart from whites and they constantly subjected to racial epithets from whites. For instance, on several occasions in the 1950s and 1960s, Cape Verdeans were derided in New Bedford as poor "Negroes," which, in Portuguese, conveyed the same meaning as the same insulting connation as the word "nigger."[66]

Thus, the binary U.S. racial distinctions of "black" and "white" often shaped the lives of Cape Verdeans in and around New Bedford in negative ways and many of the older Cape Verdeans tried to overcome this by disassociating themselves from the local African American population. Salter maintains that Cape Verdeans understood that if they wanted to overcome the discrimination that African Americans faced on a daily basis, they needed to remain aloof from racially identifying with black Americans. She emphasizes this point, when she notes that, "Most of the immigrants (Cape Verdeans) felt much more in common with the other Portuguese than they did with African Americans. Although clearly an Afro-Portuguese people, they had learned, over four hundred years of Portuguese rule, to identify with the colonizer..."[67]

Despite this trend, as the turbulent decades of the 1960s rolled on, Cape Verdeans, and especially children and youth of first generation immigrants, began to struggle with the notion of distancing themselves from "black" concerns. During the 1960s, the island of Cape Verde was involved in a

---

[66]Marilyn Salter, *Between Race and Ethnicity: Cape Verdean American Immigrants, 1860-1965* (Urbana, IL: The University of Illinois Press, 1993), 100-125, 141-149.
[67]Ibid., 150-151.

struggle for independence from the country of Portugal and many older black Cape Verdeans had to rethink, for the first time, of what it would mean for their home island to break its long-standing ties with Portugal and change to a more African-identified cultural, social, and political ideology. Moreover, in New Bedford, many younger Cape Verdeans were developing sympathies for the Civil Rights Movement and the burgeoning Black Power Movement of the late 1960s. Because of this, Salter claims that they "were beginning to identify themselves with the African American struggle not only in political thought but also in cultural expression through the wearing of colorful dashikis and Afros or by self-identifying themselves as black."

The emergence of this black identification amidst younger Cape Verdeans in the 1960s can be exemplified by a retelling of one man's experience in the South End of New Bedford, a historically Cape Verdean neighborhood. In his estimation, his increasing identification as "black" emerged as he had more conversations with Duncan Dottin, an African American sociologist, who lived in the historic African American neighborhood on the West End. His experience is worth retelling at length:

> By the time of the "searing" sixties, I had started to change. By that time I had bumped into Duncan Dottin, a sociologist from Cambridge, an Afro-American who lives in the West End. He was fascinated. Here he is talking to me and I'm calling him a "nigger" and here I am telling him I'm white. One thing I've got to give Duncan credit for, Duncan has never, never held this against me. He knew my background. But God bless the man. He knew my potential . . .
>
> I'll never forget the time when he said something about Langston Hughes and I said to him, "Who's Langston Hughes?" He wanted to hit me. I began to recognize one thing, while I was not a "nigger" and I was Cape Verdean, they didn't accept Cape Verdeans and the more and more I looked around—you know the minute you hit School Street [Cape Verdean neighborhood in New Bedford] you know where you are . . . You know they're not white. And if you're not a white, man, in this country you've got to be black and when I say black—it is in the context of the oppression, the subjugation. So, who am I kidding?[68]

Unlike this personal example, other young Cape Verdeans did not come to self-identify as black after having prolonged discussions about the meaning of blackness in America society. Instead, some, such as children and youth, chose to identify as "black" because of the increasing polarization of racial categorization that took place in some of New Bedford's public arenas. For instance, according to Lucille Ramos, a one time mother and adoptive-mother of over twenty Cape-Verdean children, many youth were forced to take a "stand" of whether they would be "black" or "white." She underlies this point when she notes that,

---

[68]Interview with Joaquim A. Custodio, 28 July 1988, quoted in Ibid., 170.

In the sixties we had lots of problems here locally with the labels "Black" and "White." You see, up till then the kids identified themselves as Cape Verdean. But at that point they had to take a stand, especially in high school. You were either Black or you were White, there was no in-between. So you had to decide then, "Am I a Black or am I a White?" And nobody wanted to hear whether you were a Cape Verdean or not. It was just Black or White. The kids had a difficult time then because they had to make that decision.[69]

Nevertheless, even though this increasing identification with blackness emerged in the Cape Verdean community of New Bedford, there is no evidence that this self-identification with blackness shaped the racial understanding of the two Cape Verdean Nazarene churches by the late 1960s. Neither in district minutes, documents from denominational archives, or in correspondence letters between white leaders and local church leadership is there evidence to suggest that Cape Verdean Nazarenes took on a more "black" identity.[70]

Moreover, as it was mentioned previously, the increasing issues surrounding systemic racism in New Bedford and throughout American society seemed to fall outside the purview of the Cape Verdean churches in New England. Instead, all evidence suggests that they remained focused on evangelizing and reaching out to the local Cape Verdean community—even though Rev. Chavier participated and contributed to non-Cape Verdean Christian and civic organizations throughout the 1960s. Not only that, but they continued to dedicate themselves to expanding the denominational message of personal holiness among Cape Verdeans in the city of New Bedford and thus were able to become one of the largest churches on the New England District.

In sum, their primary focus remained on increasing their ministerial presence in New Bedford, creating outreach ministries to local youth and Cape Verdean families, and contributing to district leadership. By taking such a position, they embodied a religious presence in the CN and in New Bedford's black Portuguese community that was premised on evangelism and spreading the message of "scriptural holiness." As such, they remained, like their black counterparts around the country, primary agents in helping to further the work of the Church of the Nazarene to all who would hear and accept its message.

---

[69]Lucille Ramos, "Black, White or Portuguese? A Cape Verdean Dilemma," in *Spinner: People and Culture in Southeastern Massachusetts*, vol. 1 (New Bedford, MA: Spinner Publications, 1981), 34-37, quoted in Ibid., 71.

[70]"Church Dedication Photo of the New Cape Verdean Church of the Nazarene in New Bedford," circa 1949. Church of the Nazarene Archives, Lenexa, KS.

Conclusion

The brightest hope of this work has been to point out a simply fact, namely that because of their commitment to the holiness experience and message of the denomination, persons of African descent—despite their different ethnic particularities, geographical locations, historical backgrounds, and racial experiences in the CN—participated in ecclesiastical governance, local congregational development, and the evangelistic thrust of the CN from 1914 to 1969. Since the founding date of the first Afro-Caribbean congregation in Brooklyn, New York, until the disbanding of the Gulf Central District, blacks sustained Nazarene ministries, contributed to denominational leadership, supported international missions, created outreach ministries, and at times, addressed social and racial issues in their communities.

Even as the denomination and its leaders failed to develop a national plan to evangelize blacks in the early years of the CN, Afro-Caribbeans and African Americans in New York and Kansas ministered and carried out the mission and vision of the denomination among different black communities. They embraced the personal holiness and evangelistic theology in the process and sought to shape the life of their respective jurisdictions. At the same time, certain West Indian ministers like William Greene and Levi Franklin sought to reach out to their communities by participating in interdenominational worship services, attending Black nationalist gatherings, and helping to address certain social issues in the Bedford-Stuyvesant neighborhood of Brooklyn during the 1930s to mid 1940s. Likewise, as the denomination decided to evangelize and segregate African Americans throughout the country under a national segregated jurisdiction in 1944 and then beneath a southern segregated district in 1953, African Americans throughout the country continued to participate in district life, evangelize blacks, train African American pastors, contribute to foreign missions, and sustain Nazarene missions. At times, especially during the latter years of the GCD, certain African American ministers doubled their ministerial duties by becoming involved in civil rights campaigns in Mississippi and in Oklahoma City.

Likewise, Cape Verdeans in New Bedford also participated in denominational life and evangelized those in their communities as non-segregated members of their respective districts. They voted alongside white delegates at district assemblies and NWMS conventions, legislated on matters related to youth discipleship and evangelism, helped to decide who would be ordained or licensed as ministers, participated in district worship services, shaped the direction and goals of district ministries, and promoted the advancement and growth of Sunday schools. Furthermore, Cape Verdeans and Rev. Chavier sought to "reach out" to the Cape Verdean by joining civic organizations, evangelical associations, and beginning other creative outreach ministries to children, youth, and families in the local community and throughout New England.

In Brooklyn, the Afro-Caribbean churches carried on similar activities by contributing to district leadership, possessing active Sunday schools, NWMS chapters, NYPS ministries, ministering to the poor through the work of deaconesses, and voting on ecclesiastical matters every year at the New York District Assembly. Also, during the late 1940s, ministers like Levi Franklin remained involved in ministerial associations and civic organizations that addressed certain racial, economic, and social issues of blacks in Brooklyn and others in the African Diaspora. Moreover, in the 1950s to the late 1960s, certain laity ministered in interdenominational bodies in an effort to evangelize black youth and children, while others in congregations like Miller Memorial, addressed some of the economic needs of Afro-Caribbean immigrants.

Thus, the elementary fact remains. That certainty being that black Nazarenes, in various times and locations and under different ecclesiastical realities, remained committed to spreading the mission and message of the denomination. Their commitment came at a cost however by choosing to largely overlook concerns related to social, economic, political, and racial issues that impacted blacks and African Americans around the country. Even during the heightened period of racial and urban unrest that surfaced in the South and in various northern cities like New York and Chicago during the late 1950s and 1960s, the majority of black Nazarenes remained committed to personal holiness evangelism and shaping others in the doctrinal, theological, and ecclesiastical tradition of the CN. Except for the few instances of Charles Johnson in Meridian, MS, Joe Edwards in Oklahoma City, and Levi Franklin in Brooklyn, most black Nazarenes throughout the United States chose not to become involved in local or national civil rights issues. As a result, their ability to have a greater impact on their respective communities did not come to fruition.

Yet, it is precisely in this ministerial matrix that we see how theological belief played a vital role in the history of black Nazarene life from 1914 to 1969. Beginning with the black immigrants who joined the CN in the early 20th century to the African American women and men on the GCD, black Nazarenes understood themselves to be bearers of the holiness message of the CN. This understanding was actualized throughout the 20th century as African Americans, West Indians, and Cape Verdeans listened to holiness and evangelistic sermons of white denominational leaders, began Sunday school, NYPS, and NWMS ministries, gave to foreign missions, and helped their respective districts make the necessary decisions to bring more constituents into the fold of Nazarene life.

It was actualized further in the late 1950s and 1960s as Afro-Caribbean and African American ministers and laity delivered sermons, composed articles, and taught about the importance of evangelizing blacks with the message of personal holiness. Warren Rogers and Gilbertson Stuart, for instance, often wrote and preached about the churches' responsibility to evangelize and indoctrinate blacks with the "fullness of salvation." At the same time, female leaders on the GCD's NWMS spoke and wrote about, in *The Gulf Central Informer* and at District Assemblies, the importance of African Americans preaching "on the plight of the lost world" and spreading the message of holiness among southern blacks and others around the globe.

Not only did this adherence to the theology of the CN reveal the important role that theological belief played in the lives of black Nazarenes during this period, but it also highlights how theology contributed to the diversity of religious belief among black Americans that participated in predominantly white holiness and Pentecostal denominations in the early to mid-20th century. For example, black women and men in the CN believed in the doctrine of personal holiness and the importance of evangelistic ministries so that others could be "saved," while black churches in the Church of God (Anderson, IN) were drawn to the theological beliefs of holiness and unity. Moreover, in the Church of God (Cleveland, TN), blacks held to the belief that sanctification happened after receiving evidence of "speaking in tongues."[1] Therefore, even in predominantly white holiness and Pentecostal bodies, the theological commitments of black Nazarenes highlight that there is no monolithic interpretation of black religious thought in predominantly white holiness and Pentecostal bodies during the 20th century.

Aside from this, by revealing the various ways in which black women remained committed to the personal holiness message and experience of the CN from 1914 to 1969, this work shows how gender, ecclesiastical, and black ethnic realities in the CN shaped black Nazarene women in different ways than those who participated in other predominantly African American denominations. It should be remembered that black Nazarene women were not circumscribed to the "gendered spaces" that women in some other predominantly African American denominations faced. Unlike women in

---

[1] James Earl Massey, African Americans and the Church of God (Anderson, IN): Aspects of a Social History (Anderson, IN: Anderson University Press, 2005) and David Michel, Telling the Story: Black Pentecostals in the Church of God (Cleveland, TN: Pathway Press, 2000).

National Baptist Convention and the Church of God in Christ, black Nazarene did not have to officially create a "gendered space" such as the WC and WD to live out or fulfill their ministerial callings because they were not barred from pastoring churches and contributing to their congregational and denominational leadership alongside their male peers.

Instead, denominational policies and polity allowed women, regardless of color, educational background, or class standing, to further the evangelistic and personal holiness mission of the CN by preaching, becoming ordained elders, leading Sunday schools and churches, joining NWMS chapters, and legislating on matters at District Assemblies. Thus, unlike other African American women, black Nazarene women were not prohibited along gender lines from fulfilling their ministerial callings alongside their male counterparts and achieving the highest positions of congregational and district leadership.

Yet, in the midst of this reality, ethnic differences shaped African American and black immigrant women in different ways—even though all black women in the CN remained committed to the personal holiness message and evangelistic mission of the denomination. Beginning in 1944, for instance, African American women (and men) ministered under national segregation until the denomination set up a regional segregated jurisdiction in the South in 1953. During these transitions, however, black immigrant women contributed to the ministries of their congregations and the denomination alongside white men and women on racially integrated jurisdictions. As a result, as already noted, African American women were often placed in a secondary racial status within the denomination, while black immigrant women were not.

Thus, this differentiation along ethnic lines, combined with the gender openness of the denomination, created a multifaceted reality of black Nazarene female participation that was unique when compared to certain black bodies such as black Baptists and the COGIC. As a result of this uniqueness, one is challenged to consider whether or not such dynamics impacted or shaped female participation in black denominations in the United States or in other countries where they had congregations in the early to mid 20th century (i.e. in the Caribbean and West Africa).[2] Moreover, one is challenged to consider whether or not such gender, ecclesiastical, and ethnic realities shaped the various ways black females contributed to

---

[2] Bettye Collier-Thomas, Jesus, Jobs, and Justice: African American Women and Religion (New York: Knopf Doubleday Publishing Group, 2010), 188-256; William J. Walls, The African Methodist Episcopal Zion Church: Reality of the Black Church (Charlotte, NC: A.M.E. Zion Publishing Group, 1974), 237-250 and Othal Hawthorne Lakey, The History of the CME Church (Memphis: The CME Publishing House, 1996), 573-578.

predominantly white Pentecostal and holiness bodies like the CN in the early to mid 20th century.³

Finally, the example of how blacks remained committed to the teachings of the CN reveal that without analyzing denominational life as recorded in district minutes, denominational periodicals, and other denominational records, one could not understand the complexities of how theological commitment and ecclesiastical realities shaped certain black Christians in the mid 20th century. The scholarly temptation is to avoid such denominational research, especially of black holiness groups, because they usually avoided attacking systemic racism in the 20th century.⁴ Yet, if one succumbs to that temptation and avoids the tedious work of investigating the denominational life of blacks who worshipped in holiness bodies or in other socially "conservative" denominations, then one is left without knowing how the complexities of denominational life, theological belief, or congregational polity shaped different expressions of black religion in the United States, especially during the middle decades of the 1900s.

Furthermore, if scholars do not take the time to explore how blacks participated in white denominational life, then we may have an incomplete picture of why certain blacks decided to forsake black denominations or become involved in social activism during the mid 20th century. Not only that, without denominational analyses we may never see how blacks in different white denominations continued to labor amidst various racial and ecclesiastical realities to not only shape and sustain their congregations, but to also help expand and strengthen the theological, ministerial, and ecclesiastical goals of their respective denominations. In the end, we could be left without knowing how African Americans and other black groups contributed to the multifaceted reality of American Protestantism during the 20th century.

---

³Evelyn Brooks Higginbotham, "The Black Church: A Gender Perspective," in African-American Religion: Interpretative Essays in History and Culture, ed., Timothy E. Fulop and Albert J. Raboteau (New York: Routledge Press, 1997), 202-225.

⁴Gayraud Wilmore, Black Religion and Black Radicalism: An Interpretation of the Religious History of Afro-American People, 2nd ed. (Maryknoll, NY: Orbis Books, 1991), ix-x, 135-166 and Henry H. Mitchell, Black Church Beginnings: The Long-Hidden Realities of the First Years (Grand Rapids, MI: William B. Eerdmans Publishing Company, 2004), 140.

Epilogue

After the end of the 1960s and the closing of the GCD and NBI (i.e. Nazarene Training College), black Nazarenes continued to participate in local congregational development, ecclesiastical governance, and the evangelistic mission of the denomination. By 1971, African American congregations, missions, and Sunday schools were still operating on integrated districts in California, Kansas, Missouri, Oklahoma, Texas, Louisiana, Mississippi, Alabama, Mississippi, Tennessee, Georgia, Florida, Ohio, Michigan, Indiana, Illinois, West Virginia, Virginia, Delaware, Maryland, New Jersey, Massachusetts, and Pennsylvania. Many of those from the South and in places like Michigan, Illinois, and California such as Chattanooga Alton Park CN, Meridian Fitkin Memorial CN, Richmond Woodville CN, Oklahoma City Providence CN, New Orleans Bethel CN, San Antonio Morning Glory CN, Goulds First CN, Saginaw Burk Memorial CN, Institute CN, Chicago Ingleside CN, and Oakland Bethel CN, still supported Nazarene missions and had Sunday school ministries, NYPS chapters, NWMS branches.[1] Likewise, the Cape Verdean and West Indian congregations in New York and Massachusetts continued their decades of participation on their local districts. Like their African American counterparts around the country,

---

[1] Unknown Author, "Negro Churches in the United States," in *The Herald of Holiness* (May 26, 1971), 20-21. Church of the Nazarene Archives, Lenexa, KS; James M. Patton, "1972 Black Church Information: Fresno Emmanuel Church of the Nazarene," (July 1972): 1. Church of the Nazarene Archives, Lenexa, KS; Rev. Mrs. Essie M. Surratt, "1970 Negro Church Information: Detroit Faith Church of the Nazarene," (August 1970): 1. Church of the Nazarene Archives, Lenexa, KS; Rev. Lewis W. Gould, "1972 Black Church Information: Saginaw Burk Memorial Church of the Nazarene," (August 1972): 1. Church of the Nazarene Archives, Lenexa, KS; Cora Dials, "1972 Black Church Information: Faith Church of the Nazarene," (September 1972): 1. Church of the Nazarene Archives, Lenexa, KS; Rev. Roland Chopfield, "1972 Black Church Information: Woodville Church of the Nazarene," (August 1972): 1. Church of the Nazarene Archives, Lenexa, KS; Rev. Robert Layman, "1972 Black Church Information: Chicago Central Church of the Nazarene," (August 1972): 1. Church of the Nazarene Archives, Lenexa, KS and Rev. Clinton Schultz, "1972 Black Church Information: Bethel Church of the Nazarene," (August 1972): 1. Church of the Nazarene Archives, Lenexa, KS.

these churches continued to evangelize others in their communities, maintain Nazarene ministries, and shape how the CN would evangelize blacks and African Americans after the age of ecclesiastical segregation had officially ended in the CN.[2]

In addition to this, black and Afro-Caribbean ministers worked together to help black churches and the denomination better strategize how the CN would address "Negro" evangelization. In the fall of 1968, the denomination formed the Negro Advisory Committee (hereafter referred to as NAC), which was comprised of twelve African American and Afro-Caribbean ministers and laity.[3] The main purpose of the committee, as outlined by the Department of Home Missions executive secretary, Raymond Hurn, was to help the denomination "find answers for more effective evangelism among the Negro population." As those who aided with this purpose, black ministers like Jacobs, Roland Chopfield, Roger Bowman, Warren Rogers, and R.W. Cunningham, decided in January of 1971 to establish a summer ministerial program for black and African American pastors around the country. Under the plan, 60 black ministers were invited to attend "summer refresher courses" at Nazarene colleges closest to their churches (in 1971 there were six Nazarene colleges, which were located in Nampa, ID, San Diego, CA, Bethany, OK, Nashville, TN, Olathe, KS, Mt. Vernon, OH, and Quincy, MA) to receive theological training and the necessary skills to develop Sunday school teachers, "musicians, youth workers, etc." If one agreed to attend, their expenses were paid, including travel, board, room, and tuition.[4]

In addition to this, the committee counseled African American churches and pastors in an effort to help them "understand the problems related to the total integration of all Negro churches" (i.e. the African American churches that were governed by the GCD and integrated onto local jurisdictions in 1969).[5] Moreover, the NAC worked alongside other "minority groups" in the CN "to give attention to the broader aspects of ministering to minorities." By doing this, the NAC helped denominational leaders make decisions about how to address racial concerns and evangelize other communities of color in the United States.[6]

[2]Unknown Author, "Negro Churches in the United States" and Rev. Louis Gardenhire, "1972 Negro Church Information: Springfield Gardens Church of the Nazarene." (October 1972): 1. Church of the Nazarene Archives, Lenexa, KS.
[3]Raymond Hurn, "Black Ministers Train" in *The Herald of Holiness* (May 26, 1971), 19. Church of the Nazarene Archives, Lenexa, KS.
[4]Ibid., 19 and Raymond Hurn, "Negro Advisory Committee: Department of Home Missions' Minutes" (January 1971): 4. Church of the Nazarene Archives, Lenexa, KS.
[5]Hurn, "Negro Advisory Committee: Department of Home Missions' Minutes," 4.
[6]Ibid., 4; Hurn, "Black Ministers Train" and Raymond Hurn, "Bonds of Brotherhood" in *The Herald of Holiness* (February 16, 1972), 21. Church of the Nazarene Archives, Lenexa, KS.

As the NAC worked to improve race relations and black and "minority" evangelization, calls for "racial brotherhood" and interracial fellowship were echoed in bodies like the NAC and in local churches after the General Assembly voted to disband the GCD. For example, African American congregations like Richmond Woodville advocated for "interracial fellowship within the bond of a sanctified spirit" so that the CN could unify blacks and whites in the "will of God."[7] Moreover, *The Herald of Holiness* described how black leaders were helping to establish interracial networks to improve black evangelization. It retold how Warren Rogers worked with blacks and whites to establish interracial evangelistic services and NWMS rallies among the "50,000 black people in the Sacramento area" and how he held an "outreach Bible class" in the county sheriff's department each Thursday at noon in the winter of 1971-1972.[8] Around the same time, another article outlined how Rogers and other whites held evangelistic services for black youth in the urban core of Philadelphia.[9]

In short, after the closing of the GCD, the racial environment had changed once again in the CN. On the one hand, the denomination tried to shed the vestiges of any form of ecclesiastical segregation by integrating southern churches to geographical districts, encouraging black students to attend Nazarene colleges and the Nazarene Bible College in Colorado Springs, Colorado, working to raise awareness about black and "minority" concerns within the denomination, and by encouraging racial fellowship among all Nazarenes.

At the same time, the denomination, like other white Protestant bodies in the United States, established a black ministerial caucus to give more decision making power to blacks regarding racial issues and black evangelization within the CN. As the main black ministerial body in the CN, the NAC brought together different black ministers and laypersons to address specific racial problems in CN and to influence how the denomination would evangelize blacks and other persons of color around the country. By doing this, the denomination promoted interracial cooperation *and* black solidarity as various black congregations and pastors carried on their long tradition of contributing to the evangelistic and personal holiness mission of the denomination.

---

[7]Unknown Author, "Richmond (VA.) Woodville Church Expands Facilities," in *The Herald of Holiness* (February 17, 1972), no pagination. Church of the Nazarene Archives, Lenexa, KS.

[8]Unknown Author, "Sacramento District Builds a Bridge of Fellowship," in *The Herald of Holiness* (February 16, 1972). Church of the Nazarene Archives, Lenexa, KS.

[9]Darrell E. Luther, "Partnership with a Miracle," in *The Herald of Holiness* (November 19, 1969), 13-14. Church of the Nazarene Archives, Lenexa, KS.

Yet, in the midst of these changes in the structures of ecclesiastical governance and in the racial realities of the CN, blacks continued to embrace the personal holiness message and experience of the denomination. This pattern, constituted one of the main characteristics of black Nazarene life since the early 20th century and still to this day, blacks carry out the message and experience of the denomination in their local communities and throughout the world.

Appendix 1:

PREDOMINANTLY BLACK NAZARENE CHURCHES, 1914-1969

Church Name	Location	Founding Date[1]	Ethnic Composition
Grace CN	Pasadena, CA	1909	African American and White
Miller Memorial Church of the Nazarene	Brooklyn, NY	1914	West Indian
Hutchinson, Second CN	Hutchinson, KS	1916	African American
Plainville, Second CN	Plainville, KS	1920	African American
Brooklyn Beulah CN	Brooklyn, NY	1924	West Indian
Free Gospel CN[2]	Brooklyn, NY	1929	West Indian
East New York CN	Brooklyn, NY	Circa 1939/1940	West Indian
Institute CN	Institute, WV	1942	African American
Oakland Bethel CN	Oakland, CA	1944	African American
New Orleans Bethel CN	New Orleans, LA	1946	African American
Aliceville CN	Aliceville, AL	Circa 1947	African American
Columbus St. Mark CN	Columbus, MS	Circa 1947	African American
Indianapolis First Colored CN	Indianapolis, IN	Circa 1947	African American
Mashulaville CN	Mashulaville, MS	Circa 1947	African American

[1]This chart only gives the founding dates of congregations and not their total life span since some congregations did not exist throughout the entire time period or only existed as an organized church for a few years.

[2]This church was later renamed Bedford Zion CN.

Fitkin Memorial CN	Meridian, MS	Circa 1947	African American
Okolona CN	Okolona, MS	Circa 1947	African American
West Point CN	West Point, MS	Circa 1947	African American
Wyandanch CN	Long Island, NY	1948	West Indian
Portuguese CN	New Bedford, MA	1949	Cape Verdean
Brookhaven CN	Brookhaven, MS	Circa 1951	African American
Chicago Friendly CN	Chicago, IL	Circa 1951	African American
Detroit Jubilee CN	Detroit, CN	Circa 1951	African American
Marshall Memorial CN	Los Angeles, LA	Circa 1951	African American
Oklahoma City Alice Street CN[3]	Oklahoma City, OK	Circa 1951	African American
San Antonio West CN	San Antonio, TX	Circa 1951	African American
Archer Heights CN	Colliers, WV	1953	African American
Shawmut Bethel CN	Lanett, AL	1954	African American
Memphis Friendship CN	Memphis, TN	1954	African American
Faith CN	Calvert, AL	1956	African American
Mt. Zion CN	Richmond, VA	1956	
Woodville CN	Chattanooga, TN	1956	African American
Alton Park CN	Richmond, VA	Circa 1957	African American
Concord Emmanuel CN	Concord, NC	Circa 1957	African American
Miami Overcoming CN[4]	Miami, FL	Circa 1957	African American
Nashville	Nashville, TN	Circa 1957	

[3]The church was later called the Providence Church of the Nazarene.

[4]The church was later renamed as Miami St. John the Baptist CN.

Appendix I

Community CN			
San Antonio Morning Glory CN	San Antonio, TX	1957	African American
Bible Way CN	Saint Louis, MO	1958	African American
Detroit-Faith CN	Detroit, MI	1958	African American
Gorman Memorial CN	Orlando, FL	1958	African American
St. John CN	Miami, FL	1958	African American
Columbus First CN	Columbus, TX	1959	African American
Shiloh CN	Winnsboro, LA	1959	African American
Goulds First CN	Goulds, FL	1961	African American
Ingleside CN	Chicago, IL	Circa 1960	African American
Lawton Grace CN	Lawton, OK	Circa 1961	African American
Orlando Praise Temple CN	Orlando, FL	Circa 1961	African American
Kansas City North Park CN	Kansas City, MO	Circa 1961	African American
Saginaw Burk Memorial CN	Saginaw, MI	1962	African American
Southeast San Diego CN	San Diego, CA	1962	African American
Memphis New Prospect CN	Memphis, TN	Circa 1962	African American
Taft CN	Taft, FL	1963	African American
Bronx Bethany CN	Bronx, NY	1964	West Indian
Emmanuel CN	Fresno, CA	1964	African American
Chicago Central CN	Chicago, IL	1965	African American
East St. Louis CN	East St. Louis, IL	1965	African American
Dover CN	Dover, DE	1966	African American

Rogers Chapel CN	Nashville, TN	1966	African American
Wichita North Ash CN	Wichita, KS	1966	African American
New Bedford Third CN	New Bedford, MA	Circa 1966/1967	Cape Verdean
Prentiss J.E. Johnson Memorial CN	Prentiss, MS	1967	African American
Gainesville Bethel CN	Gainesville, GA	1968	African American
Springfield Gardens CN[5]	Queens, NY	1968	West Indian

[5]This date reflects when the church switched from a predominantly white congregation to a black congregation and not its founding date.

Appendix II:

A MEMBERSHIP SAMPLING OF BLACK AND WHITE NAZARENE CHURCHES ON THE NEW YORK DISTRICT, 1958-1966

Church Name	Church Membership: 1958	Church Membership 1962	Church Membership 1966
Bedford Zion CN (Black)	41	54	58
Brooklyn Beulah CN (Black)	81	88	105
Miller Memorial CN (Black)	55	100	155
Wyandanch CN (Black)	81	88	88
Bronx Bethany CN (Black)	N/A	N/A	21
Butler CN (White)	73	76	81
Danbury CN (White)	23	15	28
East Rockaway CN (White)	138	134	135
Edison CN (White)	21	41	68
Norwalk CN (White)	41	45	74
Patchogue CN (White)	49	49	50
Poughkeepsie CN (White)	41	48	45
Richmond Hill CN (White)	100	84	79
Springfields Garden CN (White)	52	35	18
Valley Stream CN (White)	68	73	66

Appendix III:

SUNDAY SCHOOL MEMBERSHIP AMONG BLACK NAZARENE CHURCHS ON THE NEW YORK DISTIRCT, 1959-1969

Church Name:	Sunday School Membership, 1959	Sunday School Membership, 1963	Sunday School Membership, 1964	Sunday School Membership, 1966	Sunday School Membership, 1969
Bedford Zion CN	90	40	42	70	33
Brooklyn Beulah CN	155	104	93	179	107
Bronx Bethany CN	N/A	N/A	N/A	21	15
Miller Memorial CN	135	90	90	237	180
Springfield Gardens CN	N/A	N/A	N/A	N/A	38
Wyandanch CN	150	80	81	196	82

Appendix IV:

MEMBERSHIP AND MONETARY GIVING OF BLACK NWMS CHAPTERS ON THE NEW YORK DISTRICT, 1962, 1969

Church Name	NWMS Monetary Contributions in 1962	NWMS Membership, 1962	NWMS Monetary Contributions in 1969	NWMS Membership, 1969
Bedford Zion CN	$170.00	31	$645.00	35
Beulah CN	$732.00	77	$1,003.00	92
Bronx Bethany CN	N/A	N/A	$280.00	17
Miller Memorial CN	$461.00	61	$1,216.00	60
Springfield Gardens CN	N/A	N/A	$345.00	26
Wyandanch CN	$209.00	69	$515.00	69

Appendix V:

A SAMPLING OF CONGREGATIONAL AND NWMS MEMBERSHIP AND MONETARY CONTRIBUTIONS TO MISSIONS OF BLACK AND WHITE NAZARENE CHURCHES ON THE NEW ENGLAND DISTRICT, 1963 AND 1967

Church Name	Church Membership, 1963—1967	NWMS Membership, 1963—1967	Monetary Contributions to Missions, 1967
Portuguese CN (Black)	81—121	74—112	$1,350.00
Burlington CN (White)	39—42	26—10	$752.00
Beverly CN (White)	100—95	82—56	$1,769.00
Haverhill CN (White)	84—89	52—70	$1,455.00
Providence CN (White)	116—112	67—98	$1,269.00

Bibliography

Archival Sources
Brandon Winstead's Private Collection, Kansas City, KS

Ballard, JoAnn. Interview by Brandon Winstead (Quincy, IL, April 2009).
Braithwaite, E. Albert. "50th Anniversary Booklet: The Beulah Church of the Nazarene." Unpublished Paper, 1974.
Braithwaite, Grace. Interview by Brandon Winstead (Brooklyn, NY, September 2009).
Gillett, Dr. Elmer. Interview by Brandon Winstead (Brooklyn, NY, September 2009).
Ingersol, Stan. E-mail message to Brandon Winstead, October 10, 2010.
Jacobs, Clarence. "The Miller Memorial Church of the Nazarene Celebrates Its 50th Anniversary of the Church." 22 November 1964, 1-6.
Jones, Ludwick. Interview by Brandon Winstead (Brooklyn, NY, September 2009).
Stuart, J. Gilbertson. Interview by Brandon Winstead (Brooklyn, NY, September 2009).
____. Sermon: Daniel 6:10, written at Bedford Zion Church of the Nazarene, Brooklyn [07 May 1967].
____. Sermon: The Church of Christ Constantly Needs Reviving: Psalm 85:6, written at Bedford Zion Church of the Nazarene, Brooklyn [22 June 1966].
The Ink-Links of the New York District Church of the Nazarene (June 1961, October 1962, September 1963, November 1963, February 1964, March 1964, April 1964, June 1964, February 1965, February 1967).

Brooklyn Federation of Churches Papers, Brooklyn Historical Society, Brooklyn, NY.

Brooklyn Federation of Churches. *Brooklyn Protestantism, 1930-1945: A Study of the Social Changes and Church Trends made by the Committee for Cooperative Field Research for the Brooklyn Church and Mission Federation and Cooperating Denominations*. Brooklyn, NY: Brooklyn Federation of Churches, 1946. Box 5, Folder 1.

____. *The 1932 Year Book.* Brooklyn, NY: Brooklyn Federation of Churches, 1933. Box 10, Folder 1.

Federal Writers' Project Papers, Schomburg Center for Research in Black Culture, New York Public Library, Harlem Branch, New York, N.Y.

Bryan, Louis B. "Concord Baptist Church Sunday-School." June 1937, 1-2. Reel 2, Folder B.

Milton A. Galamison Papers, Schomburg Center for Research in Black Culture, New York Public Library, Harlem Branch, New York, N.Y.

Galamison, Milton. Sermon: The Social Significance of the Crucifixion, Exodus 6:1-13, written at Siloam Presbyterian Church, Brooklyn [23 March 1949]. Box 2, Folder 7.

Galamison, Milton. Sermon: The Tie That Binds, written at Siloam Presbyterian Church, Brooklyn [05 June 1955]. Box 3, Folder 17.

"The New York Bible Society: 141st Anniversary Celebration and Universal Bible Sunday Observance at First African Methodist Episcopal Zion Church, December 3, 1950." Box 94, Folder 14.

"The New York Bible Society: 142nd Anniversary Celebration at the Concord Baptist Church, December 2, 1951." Box 94, Folder 14.

Newspapers and Magazine Articles

"About Religion and Education in our City of Churches." *New York Amsterdam News* (New York City). 04 January 1947.

"Abyssinian Church Holds Services in New Community Edifice." *New York Amsterdam News* (New York City). 28 February 1923.

"Beulah Church of the Nazarene." *New York Amsterdam News* (New York City). 31 March 1945.

"Brooklyn Church Bulletin." *New York Amsterdam News* (New York City). 30 September 1944.

"Brooklynites At Richard's House." *New York Amsterdam News* (New York City). 23 August 1952.

"Brooklynites Cheer Ethiopia's Envoy." *New York Amsterdam News* (New York City). 22 February 1936.

"Church Group Offers Prayers for Minister." *New York Amsterdam News* (New York City). 13 August 1938.

"Church Honors Levi Franklin." *New York Amsterdam News* (New York City). 11 February 1950.

"Church Size Doubles Under Jacobs." *New York Amsterdam News* (New York City). 07 November 1964.

"Cite Record of Poll Winners." *New York Amsterdam News* (New York City). 08 January 1949.

"Cops Itch to Mop Up Brooklyn: La Guardia Moves to Prevent Terrorism Against Negro Citizens." *New York Amsterdam News* (New York City). 20 November 1943.

"Dr. Eldridge Gets Special Activities GOP Position." *New York Amsterdam News* (New York City). 30 September 1944.

"Eat Brown Bomber Bread and Rolls at Every Meal." *New York Amsterdam News* (New York City). 05 January 1943.

"Escaping Brooklyn." *New York Amsterdam News* (New York City). 18 March 1944.

"Esther Rice Marries." *New York Amsterdam News* (New York City). 07 September 1968.

"Feted." *New York Amsterdam News* (New York City). 04 February 1950.

"First Witnesses Heard in Neshoba Slaying Case (Meridian, MS). 10 October 1967.

"Hundreds Help Boro Celebration." *New York Amsterdam News* (New York City). 12 June 1937.

"In Brooklyn, News of Churches." *New York Amsterdam News* (New York City). 21 August 1965.

"Inter-Ministerial Alliance Sends Protest Against Smuts." *New York Amsterdam News* (New York City). 28 December 1946.

"Metropolitan Community Center." *Chicago Defender* (Chicago). 04 December 1920.

"Miller Memorial Church Closing 30th Anniversary." *New York Amsterdam News* (New York City). 22 February 1936.

"Mt. Olivet Baptist Church." *New York Amsterdam News* (New York City). 31 October 1928.

"Nazarene Pastors Return." *The Brooklyn Daily Eagle* (Brooklyn). 16 May 1921.

"Negro Freedom Rally Duck Alien 'Isms' in Program." *New York Amsterdam News* (New York City). 19 April 1947.

"Negro Ministers Protest Lynchings." *The Brooklyn Daily Eagle* (Brooklyn). 14 June 1947.

"Neshoba Slaying Trail Begins at Federal Court House Here. *The Meridian Star* (Meridian, MS). 09 October 1967.

"New Bethel Church Dedicated in Detroit." *New York Amsterdam News* (New York City). 10 June 1925.

"New Playground Opened at Monroe-Ralph Avenue Site." *New York Amsterdam News* (New York City). 27 January 1945.

"New Setup Seen in Bedford Area." *New York Amsterdam News* (New York City). 12 February 1944.

"Olivet in the Limelight." *Chicago Defender* (Chicago). 20 November 1920.

"Parents Group Enlists Aid of Public in 'Curb Crime' Effort." *New York Amsterdam News* (New York City). 14 November 1942.

"Pioneers Remember the Struggle." *The Meridian Star* (Meridian, MS). 14 January 2007.

"Rev. Greene Dead; Pastored Miller Church." *New York Amsterdam News* (New York City). 29 August 1959.

"Rev. S. Eldridge Installed As President of Alliance." *New York Amsterdam News* (New York City). 11 March 1944.

"Rites Held for Rev. Pilgrim." *New York Amsterdam News* (New York City). 24 January 1959.

"Sanitation Workers Win Strike." *The Crisis* (Baltimore, MD) 76, No. 10 (December 1969): 409-411.

"School Conditions Assailed." *New York Amsterdam News* (New York City). 3 February 1945.
"Seek Efficient Bedford Teachers: Local Group Begins Drive to Help Area." *New York Amsterdam News* (New York City). 24 March 1945.
"Sunday School Kiddies' Parade, Again Made Splendid Showing Among Great Throng of Marchers." *New York Amsterdam News* (New York City). 11 June 1930.
"To Celebrate Emancipation January First." *New York Amsterdam News* (New York City). 30 December 1944.
"Unity in Business Urged Upon Harlem." *New York Amsterdam News* (New York City). 11 December 1929.
"What to Do With Delinquent Girls Discussed at Federation Meeting." *New York Amsterdam News* (New York City). 09 May 1928.
"Wiles Family Reunion." *New York Amsterdam News* (New York City). 16 December 1967.

Church of the Nazarene Archives, Lenexa, KS

General Assembly Manuals and District Assembly Journals

Colored District Church of the Nazarene Journals (1947-1948).
Gulf Central District Church of the Nazarene Journals (1953-1969).
Indianapolis District Church of the Nazarene Journals (1955).
Kansas District Church of the Nazarene Journals (1915-1939).
New England District Church of the Nazarene Journals (1908, 1949, 1951-1952, 1956-1957, 1963, 1967).
New York District Church of the Nazarene Journals (1909-1969).
Northern California District Church of the Nazarene Journal (1954, 1965).
Southern California District Church of the Nazarene Journals (1909-1915).
The General Assembly Journals of the Church of the Nazarene (1919, 1940, 1944, 1948,).

Periodicals, Articles, Letters, and Other Denominational Documents

"1969 Achievement Award, Rev. Manuel Chavier." *The Cape Verdean* (New Bedford, MA). July 1969.
Barrett, E.E. "Holiness is Wholeness." *The Herald of Holiness,* 29 November 1967, 3-4.
Board of General Superintendents. "Policy Covering the Setup and Organization for Colored Work as Authorized by the General Assembly." September 1954, 1.
Bowes, Alvin P. "Annual Meeting of the Board of Trustees of Nazarene Bible Institute." 07 January 1954, 1-3.
_____. "Annual Meeting of the Board of Trustees of Nazarene Bible Institute." 11 January 1955, 1-4.
Burgess, Beverly. "1970 Negro Church Information, Kansas City Park Avenue Church of the Nazarene." 18 February 1971, 1.
Chambers, H.M. "Our Church and the American Negro." *The Herald of Holiness*, 09 August 1922, 9.
Chambers, Leon to Dr. R.W. Hurn, 25 July 1972. Transcript in the hand of Leon Chambers.

Cunningham, R.W. "Nazarene Bible Institute Catalog, 1959-60-61." 1961, 1-18.
Chopfield, Roland. "1972 Black Church Information: Woodville Church of the Nazarene." August 1972, 1.
_____. "N.Y.P.S. Meet in Orlando, Fla." *The Gulf Central Informer* 7, No 3 (June 1965): 1-2.
Department of Home Missions and Evangelism. "Colored Work: Annual Report to the Board of General Superintendents and Members of the General Board." January 1950, 1-2.
Dials, Cora. "1972 Black Church Information: Faith Church of the Nazarene." September 1972, 1.
Gardenline, Rev. Louis. "1972 Black Church Information: Springfield Gardens Church of the Nazarene." 13 October 1962, 1.
Glaze, Mrs. Edward. "1970 Negro Church Information, Southeast San Diego Church of the Nazarene." 17 August 1970, 1.
Goodman, William. "My Duty to My Neighbor." *The Herald of Holiness*, 24 February 1965, 9.
Gould, Rev. Lewis W. "1972 Black Church Information: Saginaw Burk Memorial Church of the Nazarene." August 1972, 1.
Edwards, Joe. "When People Pray." *The Herald of Holiness*, 12 February 1958, 6.
Eppler, John. "Nazarene Minister Defends Role in City Sanitation Controversy." *The Reveille Echo* XLI, No. 9 (13 November 1969): 1-2.
Harper, A.F. "Toward Christian Understanding." *The Herald of Holiness*, 3 February 1965, 5.
Hale, E.E. "Report of the President, Nazarene Bible Institute." 13 January 1953, 1.
Hance, Ray. "1970 Negro Church Information, Wichita Ash Church of the Nazarene."23 July 1970, 1.
Haynes, B.F. "A Problem to be Met." *The Herald of Holiness*, 26 September 1917, 2.
Hull, Dr. Nicolas A. "1970 Negro Church Information, Southeast San Diego Church of the Nazarene." 22 June 1970, 1.
Hurn, R.W. "Department of Home Missions Minutes: Bible Colleges, 14 January1969, 1.
_____. "Black Ministers Train." *The Herald of Holiness,* 26 May 1971. 19.
_____. "Bonds of Brotherhood." *The Herald of Holiness*, 16 February 1972, 21.
_____. "Negro Advisory Committee: Department of Home Missions' Minutes." January 1971, 1-4.
Ingersol, Stan. "Merging Holiness Bodies: Documentary Sources on the History of Ten Nazarene Parent Bodies." April 2007, 1-4.
Jackson, Mrs. Arthur. "N.W.M.S." *The Gulf Central Informer* 8, No.1 (June 1966): 1-3.
_____. "N.W.M.S." *The Gulf Central Informer* 10, No. 4 (February 1968): 1-4.
_____. "N.W.M.S.: Be a Star Society." *The Gulf Central Informer* 10, No. 1 (June 1969): 1-4.
Jacobs, Clarence. "The Miller Memorial Church of the Nazarene: Dedication ofOur Church." 08 May 1977.
Jones, C. Warren. "Home Missionary Passion." *The Herald of Holiness*, 04 December 1937, 10.
Kirkland, Rev. R.J. "The Negro Problem." *The Herald of Holiness*, 07 May 1919, 6.

Layman, Rev. Dr. Robert. "1970 Negro Church Information, Central Church of theNazarene." 10 August 1970, 1.
_____. "1972 Black Church Information: Chicago Central Church of the Nazarene." August 1972, 1.
_____to Raymond Hurn, 07 August 1972. Transcript in the hand of Rev. Dr. Robert Layman.
_____. to Rev. E.G. Benson, 30 January 1963. Transcript in the hand of Rev. Dr. Robert Layman.
Ludwig, S.T.. "Minutes of the Board of Trustees Meeting, Nazarene Bible Institute." 11 January 1949, 1-3.
_____. "Report of the Present Status of the Colored Work." September 1947, 1.
_____. "Report of Individual Churches." 1948, 1-8.
_____. "Third Annual Board Meeting of the Trustees of Nazarene Bible Institute." 09 January 1951, 1-3.
Luther, Darrell E. "Partnership with a Miracle." *The Herald of Holiness*, 19 November 1969, 13-14.
Mann, Mrs. Edward to Dr. R. W. Hurn, 10 October 1972. Transcript in the hand of Mrs. Edward Mann.
Markey, Mayor John A. "Resolution to Rev. Manuel Chavier." 07 October 1973.
Patton, James M. "1972 Black Church Information: Immanuel Church of the Nazarene." July 1972, 1.
Purkiser, W.T. "The Church Speaks on Current Issues." *The Herald of Holiness*, 05 August 1964, 12.
Rogers, Warren. "Florida Churches Transfer to Florida District." *The Gulf Central Informer* 8, No.1 (July 1966): 1-2.
_____ to R.W. Hurn, 09 September 1972. Transcript in the hand of Warren Rogers.
_____. "Nazarene Training College." *The Gulf Central Informer* 10, No. 6 (May 1968): 1-4
_____. "Nazarene Training College Tour." *The Gulf Central Informer* 10, No.3 (August 1967): 1-2.
_____. "The District Superintendent's Notes." *The Gulf Central Informer* 7, No. 2 (June 1965): 1-2.
_____. "The District Superintendent's Notes." *The Gulf Central Informer* 8, No. 1 (July 1966): 1-2.
_____. "What the General Budget Means to Our Negro Work." *The Herald of Holiness*, 18 March 1959, 11.
Rowe, Rev. G. Howard, to Dr. R. W. Hurn, 29 November 1972. Transcript in the hand of Rev. G. Howard Rowe.
Schultz, Rev. Clinton. "1972 Black Church Information: Bethel Church of the Nazarene." August 1972, 1.
Scott, Mrs. John. "Pro: Civil Rights." *The Herald of Holiness*, 07 April 1965, 18.
Sherman, Martha J. "On Racism and Civil Rights." *The Herald of Holiness*, 04 November 1964, 18.
Smee, Roy F. "Missionary Societies Pray for U.S. Chinese and Negro Work." *The Herald of Holiness*, 20 August 1958, 16-17.
Stowe, General Superintendent. "The Gulf Central District—Hail and Farewell." *The Herald of Holiness*, 11 June 1969, 2.
Surratt, Rev. Mrs. Essie M. "1970 Negro Church Information: Detroit Faith Church of the Nazarene." August 1970, 1.

Trapp, Kathy. "Another Title for Charles Johnson—Black Consultant." *The Herald of Holiness*, 01 August 1983, 5-6.

Unknown Author. "Beulah Church of the Nazarene: 1972 Black Church Information." 11 October 1972.

_____. "Church Dedication Photo of the New Cape Verdean Church of the Nazarene in New Bedford." Circa 1949.

_____. "Creeds Make Split in Church: Grace Nazarene Withdraws From General Body of Organization." Undated, 1.

_____. "In Memoriam, Rev. John Dias, 1873-1964, Cape Verde Islands." *The Other Sheep*, 06 March 1965, 11.

_____. "Nazarene Roots, The Ties That Bind: Part 1." *The Herald of Holiness*, 15 October 1988, 11.

_____. "Negro Churches in the United States." *The Herald of Holiness*, 26 May 1971, 20-21.

_____. "Pastor Chavier Serves One Church Fifty Years." *Grow: A Journal of Church Growth, Evangelism, and Discipleship* (Fall 1999): 5.

_____. "Recorded History of the Portuguese Nazarene Church." Unknown Date.

_____. "Report of Individual Colored Churches, Indianapolis, Indiana. 1948, 6.

_____. "Richmond (VA.) Woodville Church Expands Facilities. *The Herald of Holiness*, 17 February 1972, no pagination.

_____. "Sacramento District Builds a Bridge of Fellowship. *The Herald of Holiness*, 16 February 1972, no pagination.

Williamson, G.B. "Meritocracy." *The Herald of Holiness*, 22 July 1964, No pagination.

Winbush, Allen. "1970 Negro Church Information, Bible Way Church of the Nazarene." 31 July 1970, 1.

Official Website Sources:

Almeida, Ray, "The Church and the People of Cape Verde." http://www.sec.state.ma.us/mhc/mhcpdf/townreports/Cape/hrw.pdf. [accessed 01 March 2011].

Bronx Bethany, "Our History." http://www.bronxbethany.net/. [accessed 04 March 2010].

Church of the Nazarene Research Center, "Membership Status and Attendance of Bedford Zion—Metro New York District." http://app.nazarene.org/FindAChurch/viewReport.jsp?reportId=21196&orgId=4318. [accessed 02 March 2010 and 06 March 2010].

Church of the Nazarene, "Membership Status and Attendance of Beverly Living Hope Church of the Nazarene—New England District." http://app.nazarene.org/FindAChurch/viewReport.jsp?reportId=21196&sIDType=rpt&orgId=8177. [accessed 15 May 2010].

Church of the Nazarene, "Membership Status and Attendance of Brockton Church of the Nazarene—New England District." http://app.nazarene.org/FindAChurch/viewReport.jsp?reportId=21196&orgId=8180. [accessed 17 May 2010].

Church of the Nazarene Research Center, "Membership Status and Attendance of Brooklyn Beulah Church of the Nazarene—New York District."

http://app.nazarene.org/FindAChurch/viewReport.jsp?reportId=21196&sIDType=rpt&orgId=4320. [accessed 02 March 2010, 06 March 2010, and 04 August 2010].

Church of the Nazarene, "Membership Status and Attendance of Bronx Bethany—Metro New York District." http://app.nazarene.org/FindAChurch/viewReport.jsp?reportId=21196&sIDType=rpt&orgId=4316. [accessed 06 March 2010].

Church of the Nazarene, "Membership Status and Attendance of Burlington-illiston Church of the Nazarene—New England District," http://app.nazarene.org/FindAChurch/viewReport.jsp?reportId=21196&sIDType=rpt&orgId=8181. [accessed 15 May 2010].

Church of the Nazarene, "Membership Status and Attendance of Cambridge Church of the Nazarene—New England District." http://app.nazarene.org/FindAChurch/viewReport.jsp?reportId=21196&sIDType=rpt&orgId=8182. [accessed 17 May 2010].

Church of the Nazarene Research Center, "Membership Status and Attendance of Community Worship Center—New York District." http://app.nazarene.org/FindAChurch/viewReport.jsp?reportId=21196&orgId=4331. [accessed 02 March 2010, 06 March 2010, and 04 August 2010].

Church of the Nazarene Resource Center, "Membership Status and Attendance of East Rockaway—Metro New York District." http://app.nazarene.org/FindAChurch/viewReport.jsp?reportId=21196&orgId=4338. [accessed 06 March 2010].

Church of the Nazarene Research Center, "Membership Status and Attendance of Emporia Church of the Nazarene—Kansas District." http://app.nazarene.org/FindAChurch/viewReport.jsp?reportId=21196&orgId=2935. [accessed 01 November 2010].

Church of the Nazarene Resource Center, "Membership Status and Attendance of Framingham Church of the Nazarene—New England District." http://app.nazarene.org/FindAChurch/viewReport.jsp?reportId=21196&orgId=8199. [accessed 02 March 2010].

Church of the Nazarene Research Center, "Membership Status and Attendance of Free Gospel Church of the Nazarene—New York District." http://app.nazarene.org/FindAChurch/viewReport.jsp?reportId=21196&orgId=4318. [accessed 04 August 2010].

Church of the Nazarene, "Membership Status and Attendance of Haverhill Church of the Nazarene—New England District." http://app.nazarene.org/FindAChurch/viewReport.jsp?reportId=21196&sIDType=rpt&orgId=4316. [accessed 15 May 2010].

Church of the Nazarene Research Center, "Membership Status and Attendance of Hays Church of the Nazarene—Kansas District." http://app.nazarene.org/FindAChurch/viewReport.jsp?reportId=21196&sIDType=rpt&orgId=2963. [accessed 01 November 2010].

Church of the Nazarene Research Center, "Membership Status and Attendance of Ingleside Church of the Nazarene—Chicago Central District." http://app.nazarene.org/FindAChurch/viewReport.jsp?reportId=21196&orgId=1172. [accessed 08 June 2010].

Church of the Nazarene Research Center, "Membership Status and Attendance of Institute—West Virginia South District."

http://app.nazarene.org/FindAChurch/viewReport.jsp?reportId=107639&sIDType=rpt&orgId=9569. [accessed 01 February 2010 and 05 June 2010].

Church of the Nazarene Research Center, "Membership Status and Attendance of Junction City Church of the Nazarene—Kansas District." http://app.nazarene.org/FindAChurch/viewReport.jsp?reportId=21196&orgId=2953. [accessed 01 November 2010].

Church of the Nazarene Resource Center, "Membership Status and Attendance of Lowell First Church of the Nazarene—New England District." http://app.nazarene.org/FindAChurch/viewReport.jsp?reportId=21196&orgId=8212. [accessed 02 March 2010].

Church of the Nazarene, "Membership Status and Attendance of Malden Church of the Nazarene—New England District." http://app.nazarene.org/FindAChurch/viewReport.jsp?reportId=21196&orgId=8215. [accessed 17 May 2010].

Church of the Nazarene Research Center, "Membership Status and Attendance of Manhattan Church of the Nazarene—Kansas District." http://app.nazarene.org/FindAChurch/viewReport.jsp?reportId=21196&orgId=2944. [accessed 01 November 2010].

Church of the Nazarene Resource Center, "Membership Status and Attendance of Nashua Church of the Nazarene—New England District." http://app.nazarene.org/FindAChurch/viewReport.jsp?reportId=21196&orgId=8222. [accessed 02 March 2010].

Church of the Nazarene, "Membership Status and Attendance of New Bedford International Church of the Nazarene—New England District." http://app.nazarene.org/FindAChurch/viewReport.jsp?reportId=21196&sIDType=rpt&orgId=4316. [accessed 15 May 2010].

Church of the Nazarene Resource Center, "Membership Status and Attendance of Newport Church of the Nazarene—New England District." http://app.nazarene.org/FindAChurch/viewReport.jsp?reportId=21196&orgId=8229. [accessed 02 March 2010].

Church of the Nazarene Resource Center, "Membership Status and Attendance of Patchogue—Metro New York District." http://app.nazarene.org/FindAChurch/viewReport.jsp?reportId=21196&orgId=4378. [accessed 06 March 2010].

Church of the Nazarene, "Membership Status and Attendance of Providence Church of the Nazarene—New England District." http://app.nazarene.org/FindAChurch/viewReport.jsp?reportId=21196&orgId=8236. [accessed 15 May 2010].

Church of the Nazarene Resource Center, "Membership Status and Attendance of Queens Flushing First—Metro New York District." http://app.nazarene.org/FindAChurch/viewReport.jsp?reportId=21196&orgId=4343. [accessed 06 March 2010].

Church of the Nazarene Resource Center, "Membership Status and Attendance of Queens Richmond Hill—Metro New York District." http://app.nazarene.org/FindAChurch/viewReport.jsp?reportId=21196&orgId=4384. [accessed 06 March 2010].

Church of the Nazarene Resource Center, "Membership Status and Attendance of Real Life—Metro New York District."

http://app.nazarene.org/FindAChurch/viewReport.jsp?reportId=21196&orgId=4335. [accessed 06 March 2010].

Church of the Nazarene Research Center, "Membership Status and Attendance of Saginaw Burk Memorial Church of the Nazarene—Michigan District." http://app.nazarene.org/FindAChurch/viewReport.jsp?reportId=21196&orgId=3650. [accessed 07 June 2010].

Church of the Nazarene Research Center, "Membership Status and Attendance of Saginaw New Life Church of the Nazarene—Michigan District." http://app.nazarene.org/FindAChurch/viewReport.jsp?reportId=21196&orgId=3651. [accessed 07 June 2010].

Church of the Nazarene Research Center, "Membership Status and Attendance of Saginaw Swan Valley Church of the Nazarene—Michigan District." http://app.nazarene.org/FindAChurch/viewReport.jsp?reportId=21196&orgId=3654. [accessed 07 June 2010].

Church of the Nazarene Research Center, ", Membership Status and Attendance of Southeast Church of the Nazarene—Southern California District." http://app.nazarene.org/FindAChurch/viewReport.jsp?reportId=21196&orgId=6519. [accessed 07 June 2010].

Church of the Nazarene Research Center, "Membership Status and Attendance of Springfield Gardens—Metro New York District." http://app.nazarene.org/FindAChurch/viewReport.jsp?reportId=21196&sIDType=rpt&orgId=438906. [accessed 06 March 2010].

Church of the Nazarene Research Center, "Membership Status and Attendance of Wyandanch—Metro New York District." http://app.nazarene.org/FindAChurch/viewReport.jsp?reportId=21196&orgId=4402. [accessed 02 March 2010 and 06 March 2010].

Church of the Nazarene Resource Center, "Membership Status and Attendance of Yarmouth Church of the Nazarene—New England District." http://app.nazarene.org/FindAChurch/viewReport.jsp?reportId=21196&orgId=8229. [accessed 02 March 2010].

Crow, Kenneth. "The Life Cycle of Nazarene Churches." http://www.nazarene.org/files/docs/The%20Life%20Cycle%20of%20Nazarene%20Churches.pdf. [accessed 02 March 2010].

Helen Bass Williams, "Mississippi Action For Progress, Inc., February 16, 1968, Selection of Field Services Personnel." Sovereignty Commission Online, Mississippi Department of Department Archives and History, http://mdah.state.ms.us/arrec/digital_archives/sovcom/imagelisting.php. [accessed 06 June 2010].

Kenneth E. Crow, "The Life Cycle of Nazarene Churches." http://www.nazarene.org/files/docs/The%20Life%20Cycle%20of%20Nazarene%20Churches.pdf. [accessed 02 March 2010].

Lynton, Tony. "Historical Sketch of the Barbados District." The Wesleyan Holiness Church in the Caribbean: The Source Information for the Official Website. http://vikratistos.com/bdh.html. [accessed November 13, 2009].

Massachusetts Historical Commission, "MHC Reconnaissance Survey Town Report, Harwich: Report Date: 1984, Associated Regional Report: Cape Cod and the Islands." http://www.sec.state.ma.us/mhc/mhcpdf/townreports/Cape/hrw.pdf. [accessed 01 March 2011].

Official Website of Bronx Bethany Church of the Nazarene, "Our History." http://www.bronxbethany.net/. [accessed 04 March 2010].

Official Website of Mission Support USA/Canada of the Church of the Nazarene, "Black Churches of the Nazarene: Canada and USA, (1999-2009)." http://www.missionstrategy.org/missionstrategy/Portals/0/pdf/mmpdf/Black.pdf. [accessed 03 December 2010].

Official Website of Mission Support USA/Canada of the Church of the Nazarene, "Predominantly Black Churches." http://www.missionstrategy.org/missionstrategy/portals/0/pdf/bmpdf/blackchurches.pdf. [accessed 03 December 2010].

Official Website of the Mission Support USA/Canada of the Church of the Nazarene, "Predominantly Black Churches, Over 100 in Average A.M. Attendance (2009)." http://www.missionstrategy.org/missionstrategy/Ministries/BlackMinistries/stats/tabid/169/Default.aspx. [accessed 03 December 2010].

Official Website of Mission Support USA/Canada of the Church of the Nazarene, "Black Churches and Pastors Directory." http://www.missionstrategy.org/missionstrategy/ChurchesandPastorsDirectory/tabid/118/Default.aspx. [accessed 04 December 2010].

Webmaster, "Our Church, Our History: The History of the Christian Mission, "Welches Christian Mission." http://welchescm.com/ourchurch_history.html. [accessed 13 March 2011].

Printed Secondary Sources:

Ahlstrom, Sydney. *A Religious History of the American People*. New Haven, CT: Yale University Press, 1972.

Appleby, Polly. *"What Color is God's Skin?": Stories of Ethnic Leaders in America*. Kansas City, MO: Beacon Hill Press, 1984.

Baer, Hans A. and Merrill Singer. "Religious Diversification during the Era of Advanced Industrial Capitalism." In *African American Religious Thought: An Anthology*, edited by Cornel West and Eddie S. Glaude Jr., 495-533 Louisville: Westminster John Knox Press, 2003.

Ballard, JoeAnn. With Susan Autry Currier. *I Belong Here: A Biography of Community*. Union City, TN: Master Design Ministries, 2005.

Bassett, Paul and William Greathouse, eds. *Exploring Christian Holiness: The Historical Development*. Vol. 2. Kansas City: Beacon Hill Press, 1985.

Best, Wallace. *Passionately Human, No Less Divine: Religion and Culture in Black Chicago, 1915-1952*. Princeton, NJ: Princeton University Press, 2008.

Blantz, Thomas E. "Father Haas and the Minneapolis Truckers' Strike of 1934." *Minnesota History* 42, No. 1 (Spring 1970): 5-15.

Bowman, Roger. *Color Us Christian: The Story of the Church of the Nazarene Among American Blacks*. Kansas City: Beacon Hill Press, 1975.

Branch, Taylor. *At Canaan's Edge: America in the King Years, 1965-1968*. New York: Simon & Schuster, 2006.

_____. *Parting the Waters: America in the King Years, 1954-1963*. New York: Simon & Schuster, Inc., 1989.

Butler, Anthea D. *Women in the Church of God in Christ: Making a Sanctified World*. Chapel Hill, NC: The University of North Carolina Press, 2008.

Brooklyn Federation of Churches. *Brooklyn Daily Almanac: A Book of Information, General of the World, and Special of New York City and Long Island, 1921*. New York. Allied Publishers, 1921.

Carter, Henderson. *Moulding Communities, Touching Lives: A History of the Church of the Nazarene in Barbados, 1926-2008*. Kingston, Jamaica: Ian Randle Publishers, 2008.

Cayton, Horace R. and St. Clair Drake. *Black Metropolis: A Study of Negro Life in a Northern City*. New York: Harcourt Brace and Company, 1945.

Childs, John Brown. *The Political Black Minister: A Study in Afro-American Politics and Religion*. Boston: G.K. Hall & Co., 1980.

Church of the Nazarene, *1964 Manual of the Church of the Nazarene*. Kansas City, MO: Nazarene Publishing House, 1964.

Collier-Thomas, Bettye. *Jesus, Jobs, and Justice: African American Women and Religion*. New York: Knopf Doubleday Publishing Group, 2010.

Cone, James H. *Martin & Malcolm & America: A Dream or a Nightmare*. Maryknoll, NY: Orbis Books, 1991.

Crawford, Vicki L., Jacqueline Anne Rouse, and Barbara Woods. *Women in the Civil Rights Movement: Trailblazers & Torchbearers, 1941-1965*. Bloomington, IN: Indiana University Press, 1990.

Culver, Dwight. *Negro Segregation in the Methodist Church*. New Haven, CT: Yale University Press, 1953.

Cunningham, Floyd, Stan Ingersol, Harold E. Raser, and David P. Whitelaw, eds. *Our Watchword & Song: The Centennial History of the Church of the Nazarene*. Kansas City: Beacon Hill Press, 2009.

Daniels, David. "The Cultural Renewal of Slave Religion: Charles Price Jones and the Emergence of the Holiness Movement in Mississippi." Ph.D. diss., Union Theological Seminary, 1992.

Dieter, Melvin. *The Holiness Revival of the Nineteenth Century*. Metuchen, NJ: The Scarecrow Press, 1980.

Dayton, Donald. *Discovering an Evangelical Heritage*. USA: Hendrickson Publishers, 2000.

Duiker, William J. and Jackson J. Spielvogel, eds. *World History: Comprehensive Volume*, 2nd ed. Belmont, CA: Wadsworth Publishing Company, 1998.

Eubanks, Annie. *Pilgrim Missions in the Caribbean Area: Adult Missionary Society Programs and Field Studies*. Indianapolis: Pilgrim Holiness Church, 1962.

Gilkes, Cheryl Townsend. "Together and in Harness: Women's Traditions in the Sanctified Church." In *African American Religious Thought: An Anthology*, edited by Cornel West and Eddie S. Glaude, Jr, 629-650. Louisville: Westminster John Knox Press, 2003.

Graham, J.H. *Black United Methodists: Retrospect and Prospect*. New York: Vantage Press, 1979.

Finke, Roger and Rodney Stark, eds. *The Churching of America, 1776-1990: Winners and Losers in our Religious Economy*. New Brunswick, NJ: Rutgers University Press, 1992.

Finney, Charles Grandison. "Memoirs." In *American Religions: A Documentary History*, edited by R. Marie Griffith, 189-196. New York: Oxford University Press, 2008.

Franklin, John Hope. *From Slavery to Freedom: A History of African Americans*, 7th ed. New York: McGraw Hill, Inc., 1994.

Halter, Marilyn. *Cape Verdean American Immigrants, 1860-1965*. Champaign, IL: The University of Illinois Press, 1993.
Hamilton, Charles V. *The Black Preacher in America*. New York: William Morrow & Company, Inc., 1972.
Hardesty, Nancy. "Holiness Movements." In *Encyclopedia of Women and Religion in North America* 1, edited by Rosemary Skinner Keller and Rosemary Radford Reuther, 424-430. Bloomington, IN: Indiana University Press, 2006.
Harrell, David Edwin Jr. *White Sects and Black Men in the Recent South*. Nashville: Vanderbilt University Press, 1971.
Harris, Michael W. *The Rise of Gospel Blues: The Music of Thomas Dorsey in the Urban Church*. New York: Oxford University Press, 1992.
Henry, Keith S. "The Black Political Tradition in New York: A Conjunction of Political Cultures." *Journal of Black Studies*, 7, No. 4 (June 1977): 455-484.
Higginbotham, Evelyn Brooks. *Righteous Discontent: The Women's Movement in the Black Baptist Church, 1880-1920*. Cambridge, MA: Harvard University Press, 1993.
_____. "The Black Church: A Gender Perspective." In *African-American Religion: Interpretative Essays in History and Culture*, edited by Timothy E. Fulop and Albert J. Raboteau, 201-226. New York: Routledge Press, 1997.
Honey, Michael K. *Going Down Jericho Road: The Memphis Strike, Martin Luther King's Las Campaign*. New York: W.W. Norton & Company, 2007.
Hudson, Winthrop and John Corrigan, eds. *Religion in America*, 6th ed. Upper Saddle River, NJ: Prentice Hall, 1999.
Ingersol, Stan. *Nazarene Roots: Pastors, Prophets, Revivalists, & Reformers*. Kansas City: Beacon Hill Press, 2009.
_____ and Wes Tracy. *What is a Nazarene: Understanding Our Place in the Religious Community*. Kansas City: Beacon Hill Press, 1998.
King Jr., Martin Luther King. *Stride Toward Freedom: The Montgomery Story*. SanFrancisco: Harper Collins, 1958. Reprint, Eugene, OR: Wipf & Stock Publishers, 2001.
James, Winston. "Explaining Afro-Caribbean Social Mobility in the United States: Beyond the Sowell Thesis." *Comparative Studies in Society and History*, 44, No. 2 (April 2002): 218-262.
Jones, Charles Edwin. *Black Holiness: A Guide to the Study of Black Participation in Wesleyan Perfectionist and Glossolalic Pentecostal Movements*. Lanham, MD: The Scarecrow Press, 1987.
_____. *Perfectionist Persuasion: The Holiness Movement and Methodism, 1867-1936*. Lanham, MD: The Scarecrow Press, Inc., 2002.
Jones, Dale. "Average US Nazarene Church Sizes, 1908-2010: Unpublished Statistical Graph." Lenexa, KS: Research Services of the Church of the Nazarene Global Research Center, 2010.
Jones, Lawrence. "The Black Churches: A New Agenda." In *African American Religious History: A Documentary History*, 2nd ed. edited by Milton C. Sernett, 580-588. Durham, NC: Duke University Press, 1999.
Lakey, Othal Hawthorne. *The History of the CME Church*. Memphis: The CME Publishing House, 1996.
Launius, Roger D. "A Black Woman in a White Man's Church: Amy E. Robbins and the Reorganization." In *This Far by Faith: Readings in African-American Women's*

Religious Biography, edited by Judith Weisenfeld and Richard Newman, 158-176. New York: Routledge Press, 1996.

Lincoln, C. Eric and Lawrence H. Mamiya. *The Black Church in the African American Experience*. Durham, NC: Duke University Press, 1990.

Marsden, George M. *Understanding Fundamentalism and Evangelicalism*. Grand Rapids, MI: William B. Eerdmans Publishing Company, 1991.

Massey, James Earl. *African Americans and the Church of God (Anderson, IN): Aspects of a Social History*. Anderson, IN: Anderson University Press, 2000.

———. "Race Relations and the American Holiness Movement." *The Wesleyan Theological Journal* 31, No.1 (Spring 1996): 40-50.

Maye, Warren L. *Soldiers of Uncommon Valor: The History of Salvationists of African Descent in the United States*. West Nyack, NY: Others Press, 2008.

McKinley, William. *Marching to Glory: The History of the Salvation Army in the United States, 1880-1992*, 2nd ed. Grand Rapids, MI: William B. Eerdmans Publishing Company, 1995.

Michel, David. *Telling the Story: Black Pentecostals in the Church of God*. Cleveland, TN: Pathway Press, 2000.

Mitchell, Henry H. *Black Church Beginnings: The Long-Hidden Realities of the First Years*. Grand Rapids, MI: William B. Eerdmans Publishing Company, 2004.

Mitchell, Stacy, "Union in the North Woods: The Timber Strikes of 1937." *Minnesota History* 56, No. 5 (Spring 1999): 262-277.

Murray, Peter C. *Methodists and the Crucible of Race, 1930-1975*. Columbia, MO. The University of Missouri Press, 2004.

Murray, Pauli. *Pauli Murray: The Autobiography of a Black Activist, Feminist, Lawyer, Priest, and Poet*. Knoxville, TN: The University of Tennessee Press, 1989.

Noll, Mark A., Nathan Hatch, George M. Marsden, David F. Wells, and John D. Woodbridge, eds. *Eerdman's Handbook to Christianity in America*. Grand Rapids, MI: William B. Eerdmans Publishing Company, 1983.

———. *The Work We Have to Do: A History of Protestants in America*. New York: Oxford University Press, 2002.

Palmer, Phoebe. "The Way of Holiness, with notes by the way: being a narrative of religious experience resulting from a determination to be a Bible Christian." In *A Documentary History of Religion in America to 1877*, 3rd ed., edited by Edwin Gaustad and Mark. A. Noll, 415-416. Grand Rapids, MI: William B. Eerdmans Publishing Company, 2003.

Parker, J. Fred. *Mission to the World: A History of Missions in the Church of the Nazarene Through 1985*. Kansas City, MO: Nazarene Publishing House, 1988.

Parker, Jason. ""Capital of the Caribbean": The African American-West Indian "Harlem Nexus" and the Transnational Drive for Black Freedom, 1940-1948." *The Journal of African American History* 89, No. 2 (Spring 2004): 98-117.

Purkiser, W.T. *Called Unto Holiness: The Second Twenty-Five Years, 1933-1958*. Vol. 2. Kansas City: Beacon Hill Press, 1983.

Quirke, Carol. "Reframing Chicago's Memorial Day Massacre, May 30, 1937." *American Quarterly* 60, No. 1 (March 2008): 128-157.

Raboteau, Albert. *Canaan Land: A Religious History of African Americans*. New York: Oxford University Press, 2001.

———. *A Fire in the Bones: Reflections on African-American Religious History*. Boston: Beacon Press, 1995.

Ramos, Lucille. "Black, White or Portuguese? A Cape Verdean Dilemma." In *Spinner: People and Culture in Southeastern Massachusetts*, Vol. 1. New Bedford, MA: Spinner Publications, 1981, 34-37. Quoted in Marilyn Salter, Marilyn Salter, *Between Race and Ethnicity: Cape Verdean American Immigrants, 1860-1965*, 71. Urbana, IL: The University of Illinois Press, 1993.

Riley, John, B. Edgar Johnson, Leslie Parrott, Wilson P. Lanpher, and W.T. Purkiser, eds. *Manual Church of the Nazarene, 1964*. Kansas City, MO: Nazarene Publishing House, 1964.

Ross, Rosetta E. *Witnessing & Testifying: Black Women, Religion, and Civil Rights*. Minneapolis: Fortress Press, 2003.

Sanders, Cheryl. *Saints in Exile: The Holiness-Pentecostal Experience in African American Religion and Culture*. New York: Oxford University Press, 1996.

Sofchalk, Donald G. "The Chicago Memorial Day Incident: An Episode of Mass Action." *Labor History* 6 (Winter 1965): 3-43.

Simpson, George Eaton. "Black Pentecostalism in the United States." *Phlyon* 35, No. 2 (2nd Qtr. 1976): 203-211.

Sernett, Milton C. *Bound for the Promised Land: African American Religion and the Great Migration*. Durham, NC: Duke University Press, 1997.

Smith, Herbert Morrisohn. "Elder Lucy Smith." In *African American Religious History: A Documentary Witness*, 2nd ed. edited by Milton C. Sernett, 487-498. Durham, NC: Duke University Press, 1999.

Smith, Timothy L. *Called Unto Holiness: The Story of the Nazarenes, The Formative Years*. Kansas City: Beacon Hill Press, 1962.

_____. *Revivalism and Social Reform in the Mid-Nineteenth Century*. Nashville: Abingdon Press, 1957.

Stanley, Susie. *Holy Boldness: Women Preachers' Autobiographies and the Sanctified Self*. Knoxville, TN: University of Tennessee Press, 2002.

Taylor, Clarence. *The Black Churches of Brooklyn*. New York: Columbia University Press, 1994.

Taylor, Mendall. *Fifty Years of Mission: World Outreach Through Home Missions*. Vol. 3. Kansas City: Beacon Hill Press, 1958.

The Kansas City District Church of the Nazarene Trinidad and Tobago. *History of the Church of the Nazarene Trinidad and Tobago*. Barataria, Trinidad: Christian Printers, 2008.

Thomas, James S. *Methodism's Racial Dilemma: The Story of the Central Jurisdiction*. Nashville: Abingdon Press, 1992.

Turner, W. Burghardt and Joyce Moore Turner, eds. *Richard P. Moore: Caribbean Militant in Harlem: Collected Writings, 1920-1972*. Bloomington, IN: Indiana University Press, 1992.

Walls, William J. *The African Methodist Episcopal Zion Church*. Charlotte: A.M.E. Zion Publishing House, 1974.

Warburton, T. Rennie. "Holiness Religion: An Anomaly of Sectarian Typologies." *The Journal for the Scientific Study of Religion* 8, No. 1 (Spring 1969): 130-139.

Wesley, John. *Plain Account of Christian Perfection*. London: Wesley Conference Office, 1872. Reprint, Kansas City, MO: Beacon Hill Publishing Company, 1966.

Wilmore, Gayraud S. *Black Religion and Black Radicalism: An Interpretation of the Religious History of Afro-American People*, 2nd ed. Maryknoll: Orbis Books, 1991.

Woodson, Carter G. "Insurance Business Among Negroes." *The Journal of Negro History* 14, No. 2 (April 1929): 202-226.

Wuthnow, Robert. *The Restructuring American Religion*. Princeton, NJ: Princeton University Press, 1990.

Zinn, Howard. *A People's History of the United States: 1492-Present*. New York: HarperCollins Publishers, 2003.

www.ingramcontent.com/pod-product-compliance
Lightning Source LLC
Chambersburg PA
CBHW020649300426
44112CB00007B/303